North Sea Passage Pilot

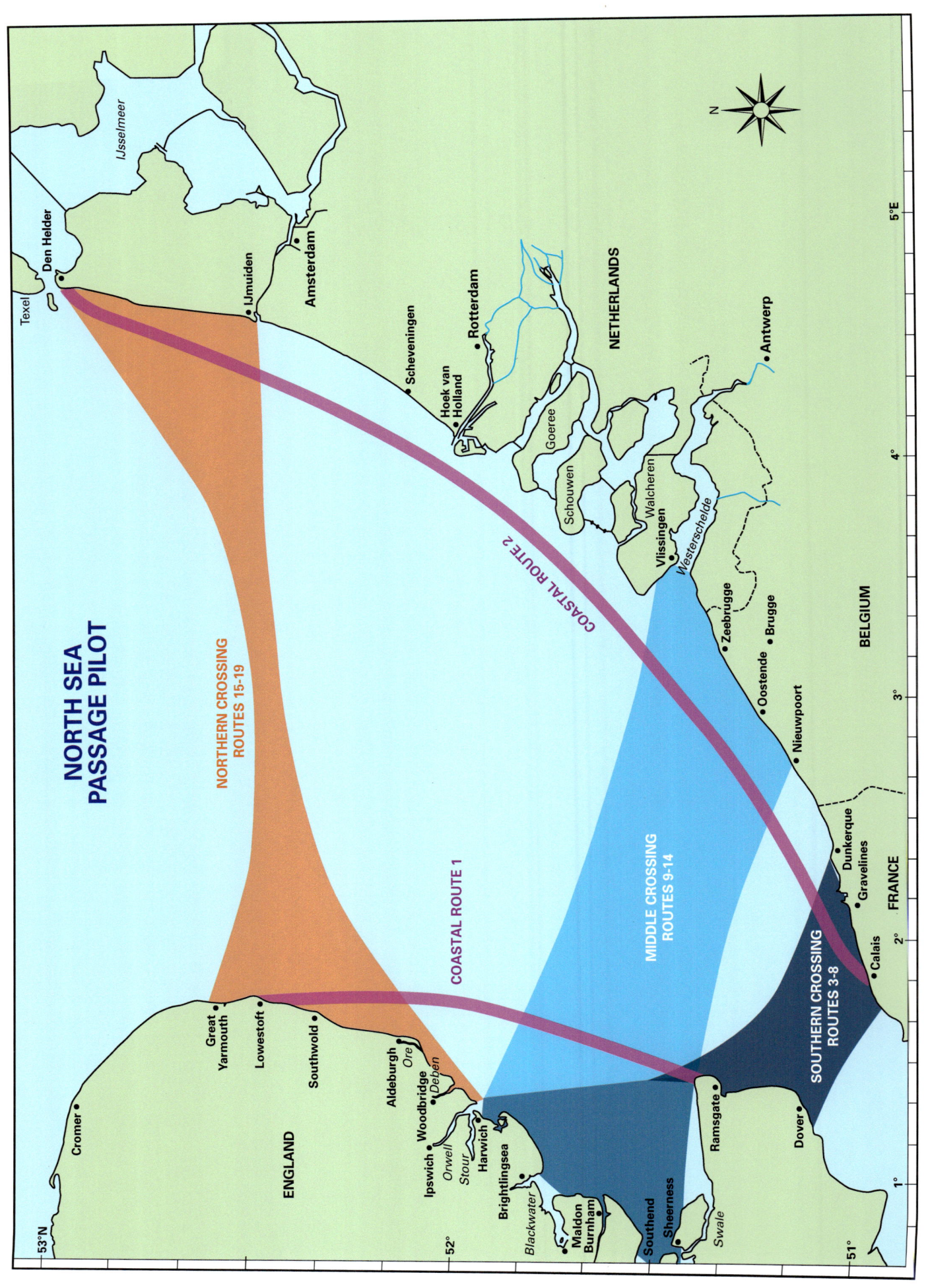

North Sea Passage Pilot

Routes between the east coast of England, Belgium, north France and the Netherlands

Garth Cooper

Imray Laurie Norie & Wilson Ltd

Published by
FB Imray Laurie Norie & Wilson GmbH
Ölzeltgasse 3/10, 1030 Vienna, Austria
+43 1 869 90 90
www.imray.com
2022 (Reprinted 2026)

All rights reserved. No part of this publication may be reproduced, transmitted, or used in any form by any means – graphic, electronic or mechanical, including photocopying, recording, taping or information storage and retrieval systems or otherwise – without the prior permission of the Publishers.

1st edition 1987
2nd edition 1991
3rd edition 1998
4th edition 2003
5th edition 2008
6th edition 2013
6th edition revised 2018
7th edition 2022

© Garth Cooper, 2022
Garth Cooper has asserted his right to be identified as the author of this work in accordance with the Copyright, Designs and Patents Act 1988.

© Photographs: Garth Cooper, unless otherwise credited

ISBN 978 178679 066 8 Printed book
ISBN 978 178679 390 4 PDF book

British Library Cataloguing in Publication Data.
A catalogue record for this title is available from the British Library.

PLANS
The plans in this guide are not to be used for navigation. They are designed to support the text and should always be used with navigational charts.

NOTICE: The UK Hydrographic Office (UKHO) and its licensors make no warranties or representations, express or implied, with respect to this product. The UKHO and its licensors have not verified the information within this product or quality assured it. The data in this publication has been derived in part from material obtained from the UK Hydrographic Office with the permission of the UK Hydrographic Office, Her Majesty's Stationery Office, Vlaamse Hydrografie and Dienst Der Hydrografie, Netherlands.

© British Crown Copyright, 2022. All rights reserved. Licence number GB AA - 005 – Imray
THIS PRODUCT IS NOT TO BE USED FOR NAVIGATION

© Copyright Vlaamse Hydrografie 2022 All rights reserved.

© Copyright Dienst Der Hydrografie, Netherlands 2022. All rights reserved.

CAUTION
Whilst every care has been taken to ensure accuracy, neither the Publishers nor the Author will hold themselves responsible for errors, omissions, or alterations in this publication. They will always be grateful to receive information which tends to the improvement of the work.

SUPPLEMENTS AND UPDATES
This pilot book will be amended at intervals by the issue of correctional supplements. These are published at www.imray.com and may be downloaded free of charge.

The last input of technical information was in Spring 2022.

Printed in the United Kingdom by Halstan & Co. Ltd

CONTENTS

Preface *vi*
Introduction *viii*
Preparations and passage making *10*
Regulations and paperwork *33*

ROUTES
Introduction *37*

I. COASTAL ROUTES
1. **UK Coast**
   Ramsgate to Lowestoft / Great Yarmouth *41*
2. **European Mainland Coast**
   Calais to Den Helder *44*
   Bad weather routes inland *46*

II. SOUTHERN CROSSING ROUTES
3. Ramsgate or Dover to Calais *49*
4. Ramsgate or Dover to Dunkerque *51*
5. Thames and Medway to Calais *54*
6. Essex rivers to Calais *55*
7. Harwich to Calais *58*

III. MIDDLE CROSSING ROUTES
8. Essex rivers to Oostende *61*
9. Essex rivers to Nieuwpoort *62*
10. Harwich to Nieuwpoort *62*
11. Harwich to Oostende *63*
12. Essex rivers to Zeebrugge *64*
13. Harwich to Zeebrugge *64*
14. Essex rivers and Harwich to Vlissingen *65*

IV. NORTHERN CROSSING ROUTES
15. Harwich to IJmuiden *67*
16. Harwich / Lowestoft to Den Helder *69*
17. Lowestoft to IJmuiden (Scheveningen coasting) *71*
18. Great Yarmouth to IJmuiden *72*
19. Great Yarmouth to Den Helder *72*

V. EUROPEAN MAINLAND PILOTAGE
Calais *73*
Dunkerque *75*
Nieuwpoort *77*
Oostende *78*
Blankenberge *79*
Zeebrugge *80*
The Schelde Delta *83*
Noord and Zuid Holland *85*
Scheveningen *86*
IJmuiden *88*
The Noordzeekanaal *90*
Den Helder *91*

VI. UK EAST COAST PILOTAGE
Dover *94*
Ramsgate *96*
Harwich *98*
Lowestoft *100*

APPENDICES
i. RYA recommendations for safety equipment for offshore cruisers *102*
ii. Rule 10 Traffic Separation Schemes *103*
iii. Coastguard and rescue facilities in the southern north sea *104*
iv. Charts *105*

GLOSSARIES *106*

INDEX *110*

PREFACE

I have sailed in a variety of waters round the world but am always drawn back to the grey, often roiling waters of the southern North Sea and more particularly to the southern East Coast and Thames Estuary, with regular forays into the Netherlands. So, when I was asked if I would take over *North Sea Passage Pilot* (NSPP) from Brian Navin, I felt a certain degree of dread at meeting the great man's standards and pride at being asked so to do.

No doubt, the years spent compiling *East Coast Pilot* (ECP) and my steadily increasing trips across the North Sea, were considered grounds to be appointed to take on the task. I hope you will judge I've done a reasonable job within the parameters that with any pilot guide it's a continuing and evolving product.

This edition differs from its predecessors in that developments in navigation aids have advanced, that the sea is now more cluttered than ever with man-made structures, designated sea lanes and roundabouts and there is a whole new set of regulations with which the cruising sailor must comply. I have also re-evaluated timings to a target speed of 6 knots through the water. The routes we discuss are primarily from the southern East Coast of the UK and the Thames Estuary to and from the near continent. I have assumed that most of us are familiar with these local waters, but those who aren't should refer to *East Coast Pilot* and *Cruising Guide to The Netherlands* (both published by Imray).

I've also taken the opportunity to streamline information and presentation while adhering to Brian's basic principles of accuracy and honesty.

I must put on record my grateful thanks to those who have helped me get this project off the ground, namely, Ian Jewry, Tim Thomas and Dick Holness, and the team at Imray.

My particular thanks to Willie and Lucy Wilson at Imray for their trust in me, to Jane Russell for keeping me focused, as any good editor should do, and to the design team for so calmly dealing with an often cantankerous and curmudgeonly author.

Brexit has finally been done; however, it's not all over by a very long way and it'll be several years at least for the dust to settle and our relationships with our continental friends to stabilise and clarify. Covid too has hit us hard, not least delaying production of this book, and has caused major disruption to our sailing. These two events will undoubtedly have major consequences on our ability to 'just pop over the other side'. Without doubt the level of bureaucracy will increase but hopefully the common interest in sailing will mean we'll still get a warm and friendly reception when we fetch up on continental shores.

Garth Cooper,
Morven, Levington,
Spring 2022

THE AUTHOR

Garth Cooper has been 'messing about' in boats for over seventy years. He learnt to sail a lugsail dinghy on Barton Broad at the age of five. He trained as a boat builder-designer on leaving school but gravitated into journalism after finishing his apprenticeship. After a spell on the *Kent Messenger*, he joined *Farmers Weekly* and went on to present Farming Today on BBC Radio 4. After a spell at university, he returned to broadcasting as a freelance for 17 years. He was editorial manager of a B2B publishing company in Norwich for six years before changing careers again and working for *Sailing Today* and editing *Anglia Afloat*. He is one of the authors of *East Coast Pilot*. For nearly 20 years he held several offices in the RYA East region. He's an active member of the East Anglian Sailing Trust, taking blind people cruising.

He currently sails a Contest 33, having owned a mid-sixties Holman classic for 24 years. His boats have included a Deb 33, an East Anglian, a Queen Bee 28 and a Wing 25, among others.

The author

The author's Contest 33, *Morven*

DEDICATION

This new edition is dedicated to the late Brian Navin and his family for their commitment to this project, which ran for six editions under his authorship from 1987 to 2018.

Brian's contribution to pilotage information was considerable and included coverage of the Netherlands, Germany and Denmark as well as *North Sea Passage Pilot*.

Garth Cooper is also co-author of *East Coast Pilot* (Imray)

INTRODUCTION

This book is intended for cruising skippers planning to sail or motor across the North Sea as comfortably as possible. In the following chapters we'll guide you and hopefully demystify what it means to cross this busy piece of water. This book is aimed at the first timer and as an aide-memoire to the more regular and experienced skipper, a great many of whom will hold RYA Yachtmaster Coastal or have experience to that standard. It does not include the several race passages across the North Sea, some of which follow long and tortuous routes to give race crews a good work out.

With today's larger, faster, and potentially more seaworthy boats a trip across to Oostende, Cadzand, the Westerscheldte or IJmuiden can often be accomplished within 24 hours, while Den Helder is two days and a night. The traffic in yachts crossing to and from the near Continent has increased tremendously in recent years.

On shortish trips like these astronavigation isn't necessary but the ability to follow a paper chart, and not rely solely on electronic aids, is essential. In the event of a power failure good old-fashioned dead reckoning navigation will often save the day.

This guide, together with suitable charts and a current nautical almanac, provides the necessary information for these medium-distance trips between the rivers, estuaries and ports in an area stretching from Great Yarmouth to Ramsgate on the UK side and Calais to Den Helder on the Continent.

Thanks to the increase in commercial traffic and hardware in the southern North Sea we are somewhat more restricted in our routes than we were even 20 years ago. On the other hand, the area is less lonely with all the gas and oil rigs, wind farms, special marks, support vessels and shipping traffic adding interest in an otherwise empty sea.

Long and tortuous race routes are not the focus of this guide

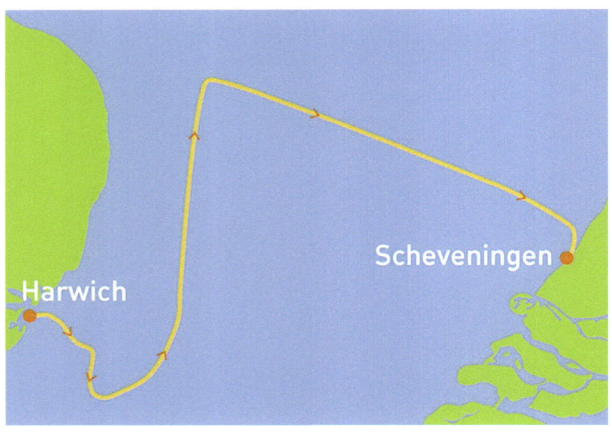

We've taken the opportunity to simplify and streamline the presentation of this edition to make it easier to follow. For example, we introduce two coastal routes, along the East Coast and along the continental coast, with key waypoints to branch off into local waters, ports and estuaries using local pilot guides. The number of cross-North Sea routes has been reduced in the light of man-made obstacles, traffic separation zones and a greater number of windfarms.

How to use this book

I hope to demonstrate that with a modicum of planning, and an understanding of the technical and legal requirements, making a passage to the near Continent is straightforward, sea state and weather allowing. We'll be taking you through the official requirements and regulations, how to behave in traffic separation zones, how best to use navigation aids and tidal and weather information. And, for those of you not familiar with planning a longish passage, how to work out a simple plan and the importance of keeping an up-to-date log.

This book has been designed to be used both as a route planning tool and as a running guide on the trip to get you into your chosen destination port. My aim is to get you safely across and into the harbour, at which point I hand over the baton to the relevant local area cruising guides. You will find there are references to *East Coast Pilot* and *Crossing the Thames Estuary* and for those of you planning to sail further into the Belgian and Dutch inland waterways, *Cruising Guide to The Netherlands*. All give detailed local pilotage for the various ports, rivers, and creeks in greater detail than I attempt to here.

At the beginning of each route description, you'll find a panel giving detailed information under the following headings:
  Distance and target duration
  Charts
  Recommended start times
  Expected arrival time
  Recommended return start time
  Expected arrival time return
  Tidal stream notes

In the individual UK and continental port information panels:
  Port radio
  Entry signals
  Customs
  Mooring and facilities

On page 5 is a list of useful publications to have on board. There's also a list of port and marina websites, which are worth looking at for current information on your destinations.

In addition, you'll need an up-to-date yachtsman's almanac with tide tables, and in Holland, an up to date *ANWB Wateralmanak 2* (plus a pocket Dutch dictionary). For legal reasons you must also carry a copy of the *ANWB Wateralmanak 1*, which includes copies of all the shipping regulations in force in the Netherlands, including the Inland Waters Police Regulations and Shipping Regulations on the Westerschelde. Sadly, these Dutch publications are not currently available in English and their expense constitutes a tax on sailing in Dutch waters.

Tidal streams and differences

All the routes discussed in this edition of North Sea Passage Pilot are optimised for tides, but some of them will require a flexible approach given the fickleness of the weather, mainly the wind strength and direction.

There's a list of times of changes in direction in tidal streams at various points near the coast, obtained from the Admiralty Sailing Directions, along with a list of HW time differences from HW Dover for the various harbours. Corrections are occasionally made to these time differences by the Hydrographic Department, so they cannot be regarded as accurate to within more than a few minutes. In any case, these times are averages and approximations, and in practice meteorological conditions can appreciably affect them.

Tidal streams are described by the direction in which they are running, for example south means a south-flowing stream. The timing of the change of direction of the stream is usually referred to HW Dover, unless stated otherwise. If a speed is quoted this will be the maximum speed, which is usually about three hours after slack water.

In the approaches to some harbours or rivers you may encounter a strong tidal set in what has traditionally been called 'the offing'. When this is significant it is noted under the title of the harbour as DS (Direction of Stream).

A good source of tidal data is Imray's Tides Planner app, which gives you up-to-date information in your locality on your smart phone or tablet. You can select which area you want to download.
www.imray.com/tides-planner-app/

Bearings and directions

The bearings given are all True. Directions are indicated by the usual abbreviations: W for west, NE for northeast, WSW for west-southwest, etc.

TIDAL DIFFERENCES ON DOVER

Location	Dover
Great Yarmouth	–0200
Harwich Haven	+0040
Lowestoft	–0133
Orford Haven	+0010
Queenborough	+0130
Ramsgate	+0030
Sheerness	+0130
Southwold	–0105
Woodbridge Haven	+0025
Calais	–0215
Dunkerque	–0115
Oostende	–0045
Zeebrugge	–0140
Scheveningen	+0321
IJmuiden	+0401
Den Helder	–0438

Chart datum

For planning purposes, we recommend C30 Southern North Sea. Depths are shown in metres (m) above Lowest Astronomical Tide (LAT), which normally equates with chart datum. Drying heights are given as such in the text but on plans the number is underlined. On the chartlets depths of more than 5m are coloured dark blue and depths less than this are coloured light blue. On many of the local plans on the continent the light blue extends out to the 5m contour. Drying heights are coloured brown and land is green. No distinction is made in dredged areas although the depth may be reduced by silting.

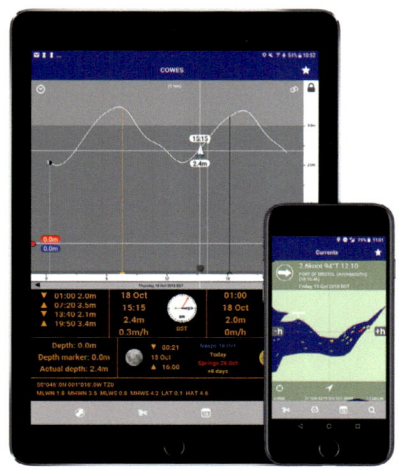

Imray Tides Planner app

INTRODUCTION

TIDAL STREAMS

The figures against the arrows denote mean rates in tenths of a knot at neaps and springs.

Thus 06,11 indicates a mean neap rate of 0·6 knots and a mean spring rate of 1·1 knots.

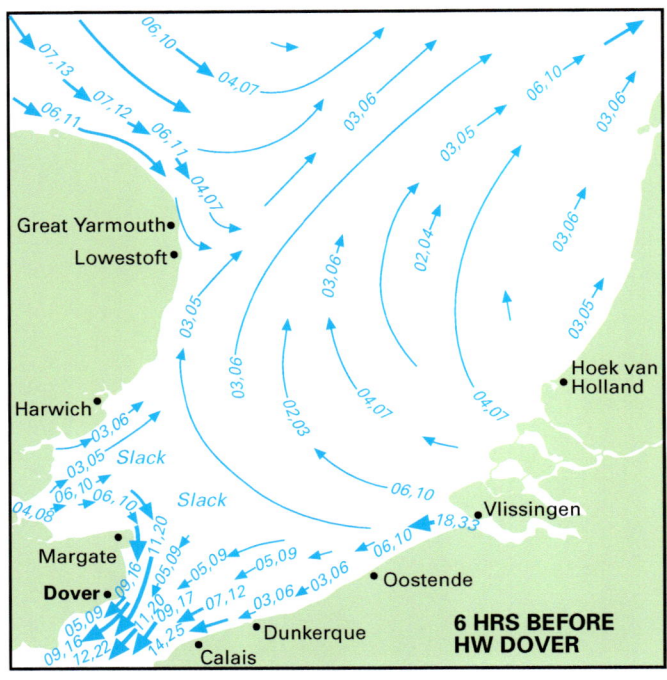

6 HRS BEFORE HW DOVER

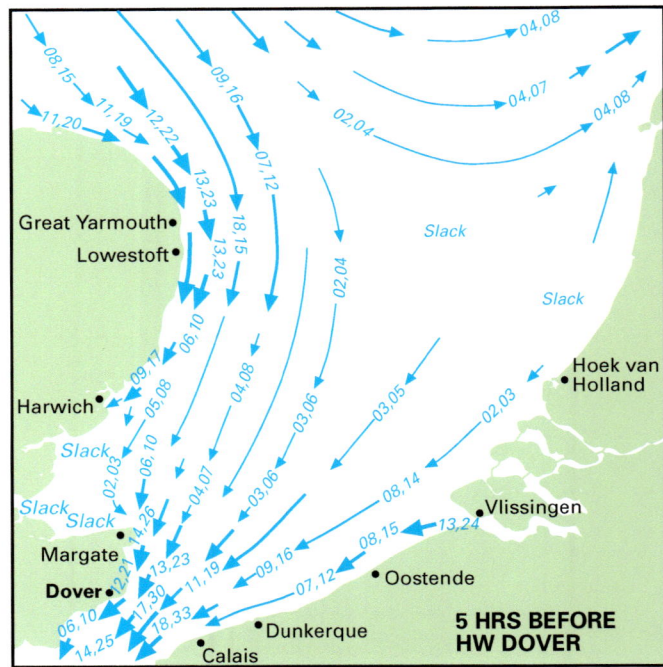

5 HRS BEFORE HW DOVER

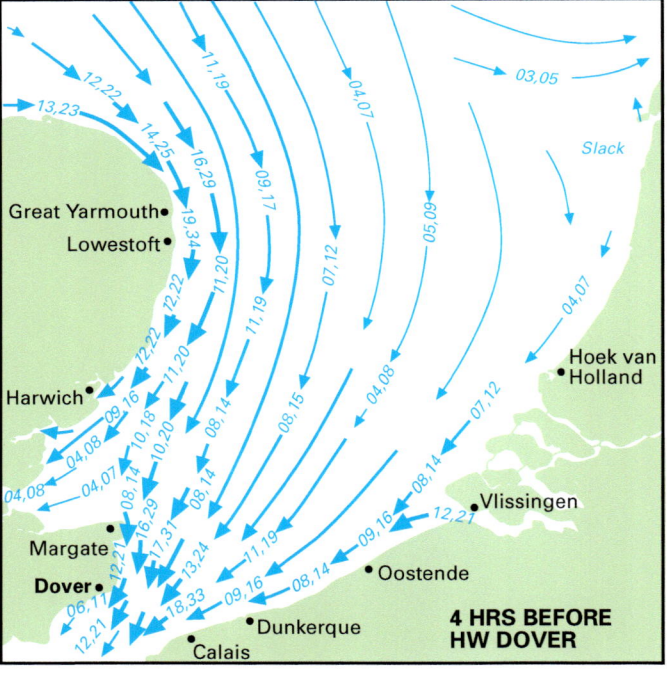

4 HRS BEFORE HW DOVER

3 HRS BEFORE HW DOVER

Tidal streams

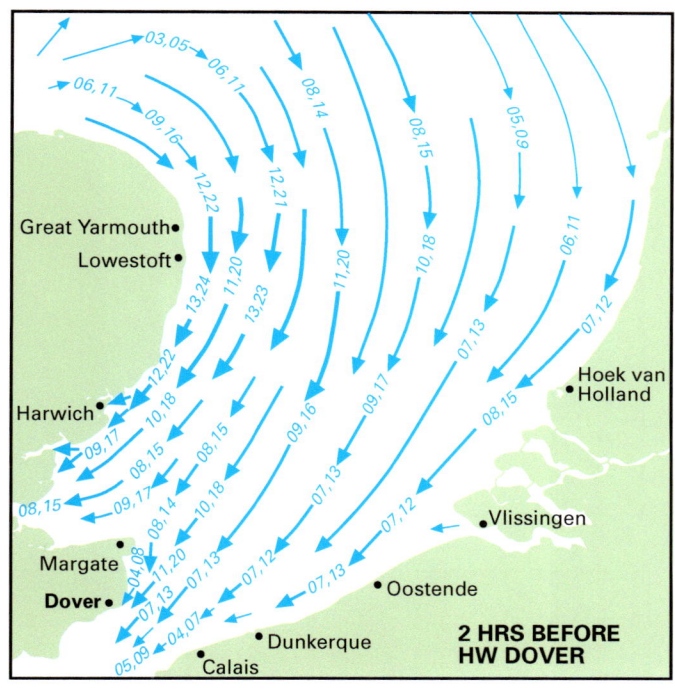
2 HRS BEFORE HW DOVER

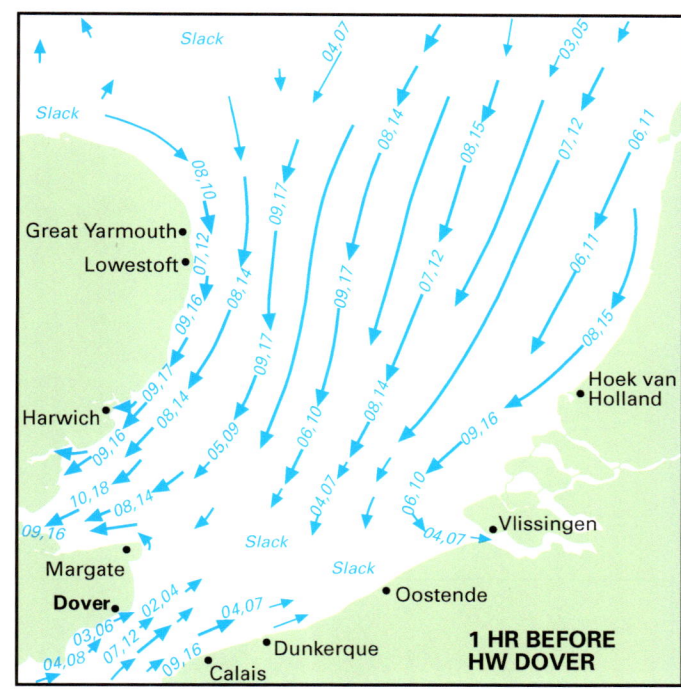
1 HR BEFORE HW DOVER

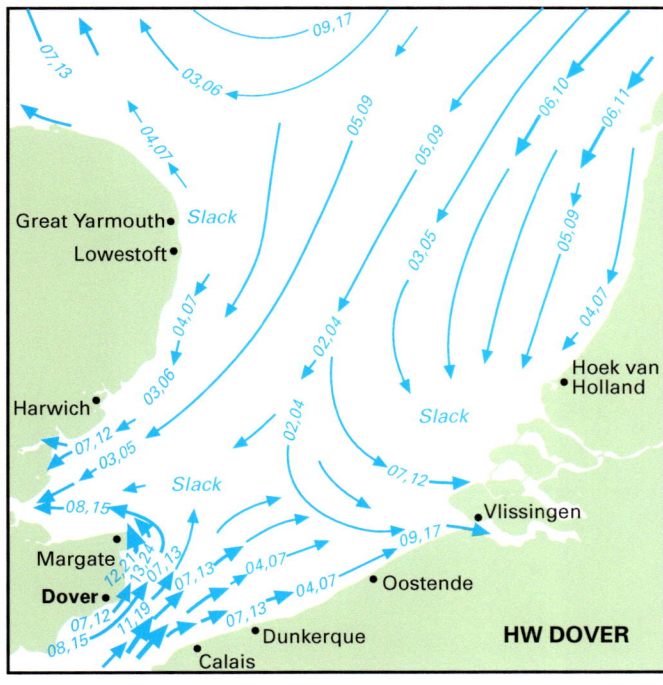
HW DOVER

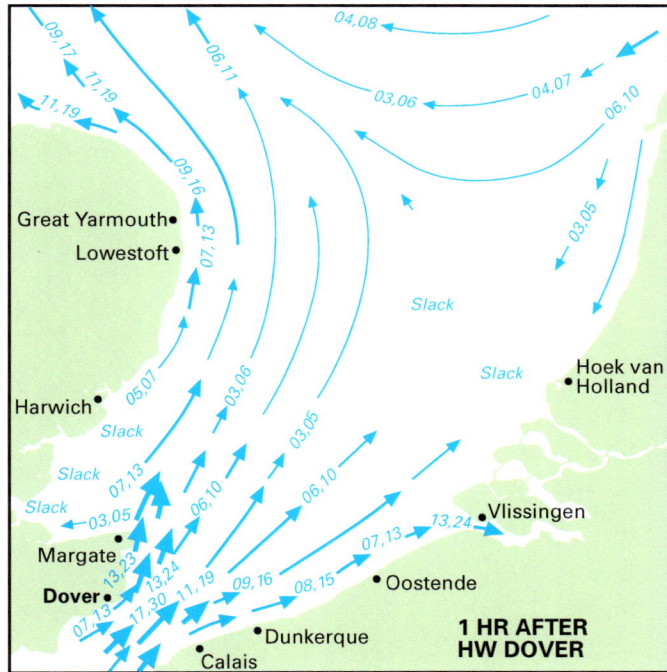
1 HR AFTER HW DOVER

NORTH SEA PASSAGE PILOT

INTRODUCTION

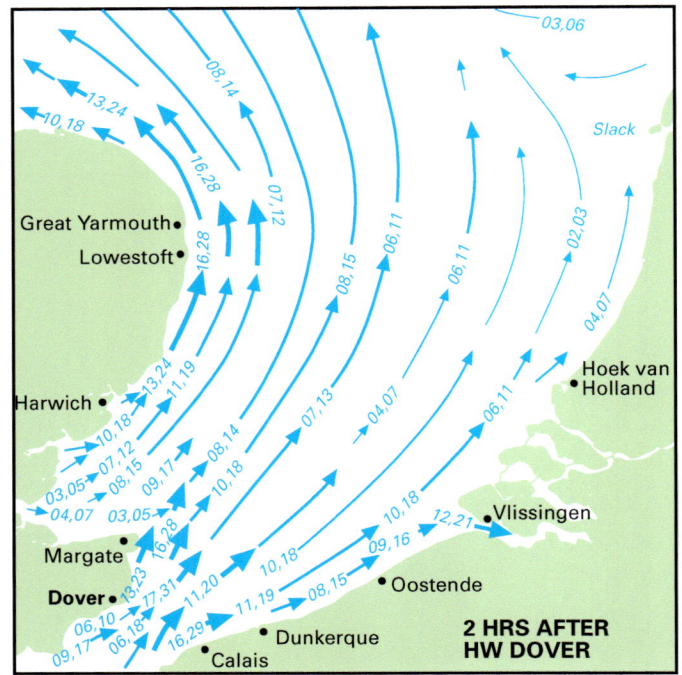

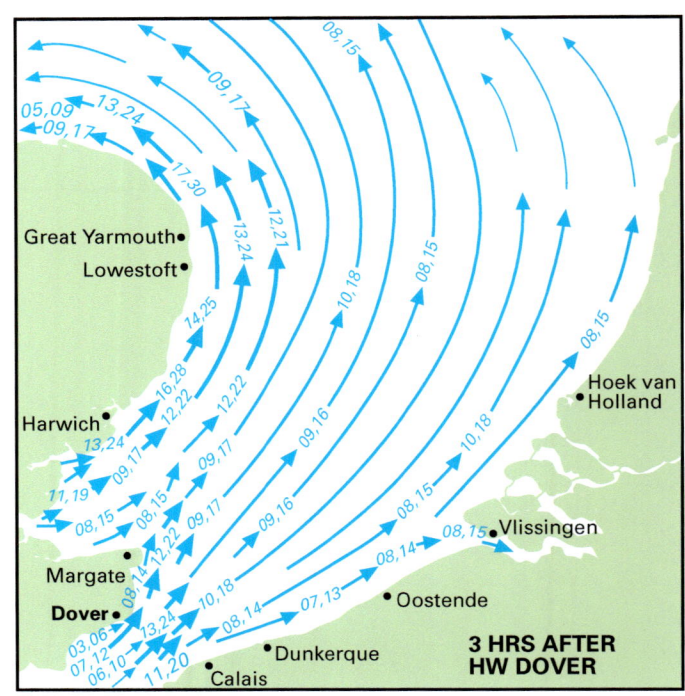

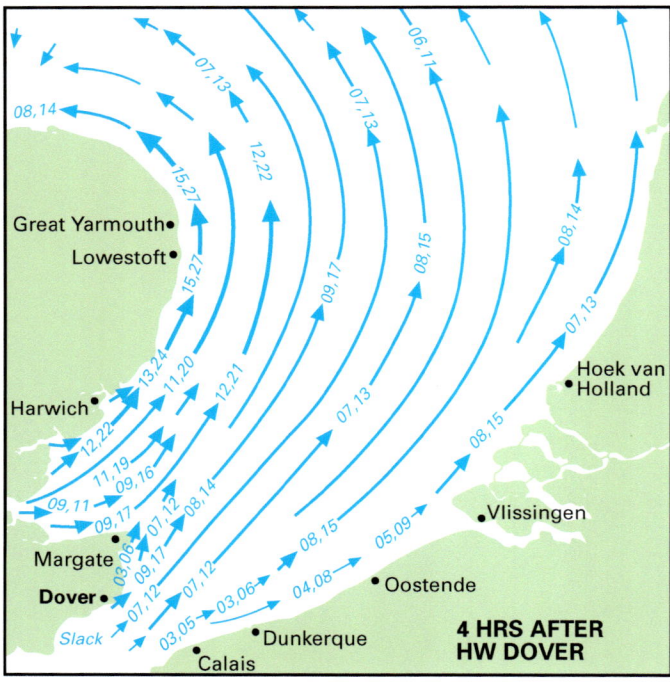

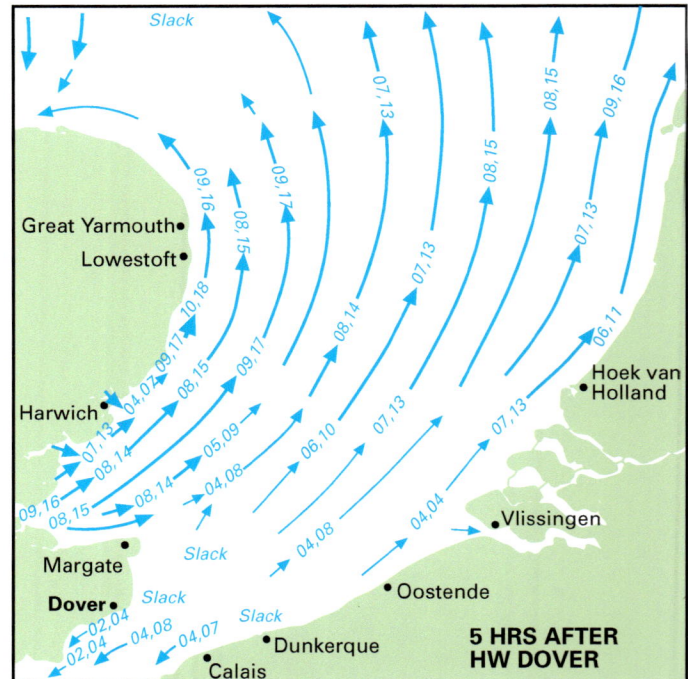

Useful reading

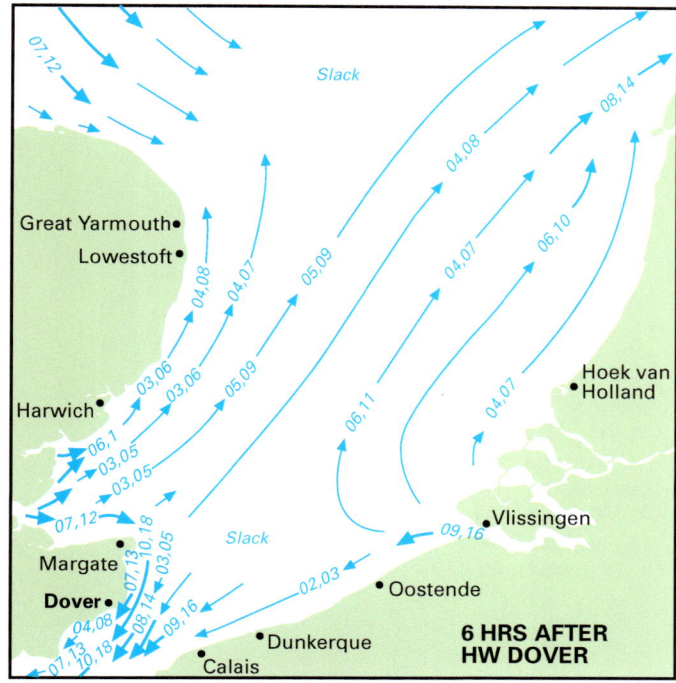

Winds

Winds are given as the compass point from which they blow unless they are described as off or onshore.

Entry times

Recommended entry times such as two hours before high water to 1·5 hours after (HW −0200 to HW +0130) is based on a draught of 1·5m and no significant swell or sea. Entry times are the target arrival time at your chosen port, working back from which will give you an approximate start time for the voyage.

Useful reading

Almanacs

The Cruising Almanac The Cruising Association (Imray)

Reeds Nautical Almanac (Adlard Coles Nautical)

Reeds PBO Small Craft Almanac (Adlard Coles Nautical)

Koninklijke Nederlandse Toeristenbond ANWB
www.anwb.nl

Wateralmanak 1. Reglementen in vaartips (Regulations and navigation tips)

Wateralmanak 2. Vaargegevens (Navigation data)

Pilot guides

East Coast Pilot, Garth Cooper and Dick Holness (Imray)

Cruising Guide to The Netherlands (Imray)

Most major ports produce their own harbour guides, and these are well worth getting hold of at the planning stage.

Planning charts

Imray C30 Harwich to Hook

Imray C25 Humber to Holland

For more detailed chart information see page 105.

UKHO

UK Hydrographic Office website (Notices to Mariners, tidal predictions etc): www.admiralty.co.uk

NP 5011 Symbols and Abbreviations used on Admiralty Charts

Other useful sources

Netherlands Hydrographic Office (Koninklijke Marine)
www.hydro.nl

Waterstanden en Stromen HP33 (Annual Netherlands tide tables and tidal stream diagrams). Also available as a CD – HP33D

Royal National Lifeboat Institution
www.rnli.org.uk
Safety on the Sea, Sailing, Sea Safety Guidelines

HM Customs and Excise
www.hmrc.gov.uk
Notice 8: Sailing your pleasure craft to and from the United Kingdom

Royal Yachting Association
www.rya.org.uk
RYA VHF Handbook G31
Boat Safety Handbook G103
Boating Abroad Advice

NORTH SEA PASSAGE PILOT 5

INTRODUCTION

HARBOUR AUTHORITIES AND USEFUL WEBSITES

Netherlands Board of Tourism
www.holland.com
Belgian National Tourist Office
www.visitbelgium.com
Great Yarmouth Port Authority
www.eastportuk.co.uk
Lowestoft Haven Marina
www.lowestofthavenmarina.co.uk
Southwold Harbour
www.eastsuffolk.gov.uk
Harwich Haven Authority
www.hha.co.uk
Port of London Authority
www.pla.co.uk
Port of Ramsgate
www.portoframsgate.co.uk
Dover Harbour Board
www.doverport.co.uk
Calais Port
www.calais-port.fr/en
Port of Gravelines
www.portvaubangravelines.com
Port of Dunkerque
www.dunkerque-port.fr/en/

VVW Nieuwpoort Marina
www.nieuwpoort.be/nieuwpoort/view/nl
Port of Oostende
www.portofoostende.be
Port of Blankenberge
www.blankenberge.be
Port of Zeebrugge
www.zeebruggeport.be/en
Ports of Vlissingen and Terneuzen
www.zeeland-seaports.com
Port of Rotterdam
www.portofrotterdam.com/en
Den Haag: Scheveningen-Port
www.denhaag.nl
Marina Scheveningen
www.jachtclub.com
Zeehaven IJmuiden
www.zeehaven.nl
Marina Seaport IJmuiden
www.marinaseaport.nl
Port of Amsterdam
www.portofamsterdam.com
Port of Den Helder
www.portdenhelder.com

SMALL CRAFT SYMBOLS

The following symbols are used on larger scale charts and plans, and are shown in magenta.

- Visitors' moorings
- Visitors' berths
- Yacht marina
- Public landing
- Slipway for small craft
- Water tap
- Fuel
- Pump-out facilities
- Customs
- Public house, inn, bar
- Restaurant
- Yacht or sailing club
- Toilets
- Public car park
- Hard standing for boats
- Launderette
- Caravan site
- Camping site
- Nature reserve
- Harbourmaster
- Travel hoist
- Public telephone
- Post office
- Building
- Airport
- Flagpole/flagstaff
- Castle/Fort
- Hospital
- Notice Board
- Wooded
- Beacon (with various topmarks)
- Mooring buoy
- Crane
- Chimney
- Radio/TV Mast
- Water tower
- Tower
- Monument
- Wind turbine
- Tilting bridge
- Lock

Tide Mill Marina, Woodbridge, up the River Deben on the UK east coast

SYMBOLS USED ON CHARTS

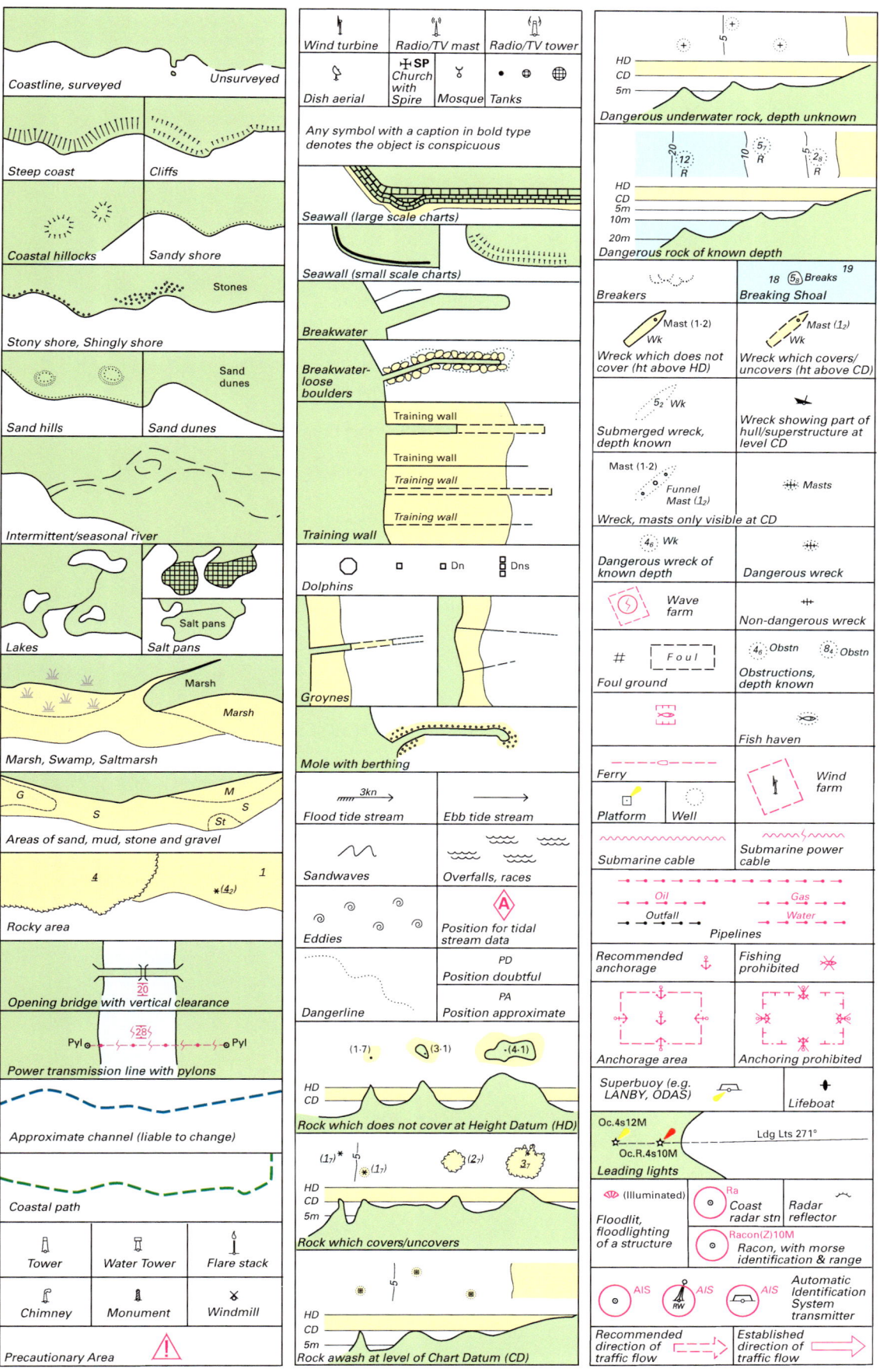

INTRODUCTION

KEY TO ABBREVIATIONS

Throughout the text and plans in this guide familiar abbreviations have been used for convenience.

Bn	Beacon
By	Buoy
CC	Cruising Club
CG	Coastguard
Ch	Channel
Conspic	Conspicuous
DSC	Digital Selective Calling
E	East, Eastwards, Easterly
ECB	East Cardinal Buoy
ECM	East Cardinal Mark (eg beacon)
F	Fixed light
Fl	Flashing light
ft	Foot, feet
G	Green
H	Hour, eg H+15 is 15 minutes past the hour
hr	Hour, hours
HW	High Water
HWN	High Water Neaps
HWS	High Water Springs
IDM	Isolated Danger Mark
IQ	Interrupted Quick flashing light
Iso	Isophase light
kn	Knot, knots
L.Fl	Long flash
LNG	Liquefied Natural Gas
LOA	Length Overall
LPG	Liquefied Petroleum Gas
LW	Low Water
LWN	Low Water Neaps
LWS	Low Water Springs
M	Mile (nautical mile)
m	metre
MHWS	Mean High Water springs
min	Minute
mins	Minutes
MLWS	Mean Low Water Springs
MMSI	Maritime Mobile Service Identity
MSI	Maritime Safety Information incl. inshore waters forecast, gale warnings and navigational warnings
Mo	Morse
N	North, Northwards, Northerly
NCB	North Cardinal Buoy
NCM	North Cardinal Mark (eg beacon)
NE	Northeast or Northeastwards
NW	Northwest, Northwestwards
Oc	Occulting light
ODAS	Ocean Data Acquisition System
PAYG	Pay As You Go
PH	Port Hand
PLA	Port of London Authority
Pt	Point
PWC	Personal Water Craft (jet ski)
Q	Quick flashing light
R	Red
S	South, Southwards, Southerly
s	second(s)
SC	Sailing Club
SCB	South Cardinal Buoy
SCM	South Cardinal Mark (eg beacon)
SH	Starboard Hand
SPB	Special Purpose Buoy
SW	Southwest, Southwestwards
SWB	Safe Water Buoy
SWM	Safe Water Mark
TSS	Traffic Separation Scheme
UKHO	United Kingdom Hydrographic Office (the Admiralty)
UTC	Universal Time Corrected (same as GMT – Greenwich MeanTime)
vert	vertical
VQ	Very Quick flashing light
VTS	Vessel Traffic Service
W	West, Westwards, Westerly; White
WCB	West Cardinal Buoy
WCM	West Cardinal Mark (eg beacon)
Y	Yellow
YC	Yacht Club

THE BEAUFORT SCALE

The Beaufort scale, which is used in Met Office marine forecasts, is an empirical measure for describing wind intensity based on observed sea conditions.

Specifications and equivalent speeds

Beaufort wind scale	Mean Wind Speed (Knots)	Mean Wind Speed (ms^{-1})	Limits of wind speed (Knots)	Limits of wind speed (ms^{-1})	Wind descriptive terms	Probable wave height (m)	Probable maximum wave height (m)	Seastate	Sea descriptive terms
0	0	0	<1	<1	Calm	-	-	0	Calm (glassy)
1	2	1	1-3	1-2	Light air	0.1	0.1	1	Calm (rippled)
2	5	3	4-6	2-3	Light breeze	0.2	0.3	2	Smooth (wavelets)
3	9	5	7-10	4-5	Gentle breeze	0.6	1.0	3	Slight
4	13	7	11-16	6-8	Moderate breeze	1.0	1.5	3-4	Slight - Moderate
5	19	10	17-21	9-11	Fresh breeze	2.0	2.5	4	Moderate
6	24	12	22-27	11-14	Strong breeze	3.0	4.0	5	Rough
7	30	15	28-33	14-17	Near gale	4.0	5.5	5-6	Rough-V.rough
8	37	19	34-40	17-21	Gale	5.5	7.5	6-7	V.rough - High
9	44	23	41-47	21-24	Strong gale	7.0	10.0	7	High
7.0	10.0	7	High	25-28	Storm	9.0	12.5	8	V. high
10	52	27	48-55	25-28	Storm	9.0	12.5	8	V. high
11	60	31	56-63	29-32	Violent storm	11.5	16.0	8	V. high
12	-		64+	33+	Hurricane	14+	-	9	Phenomenal

LIFE-SAVING SIGNALS

SOLAS CHAPTER V REGULATION 29

To be used by Ships, Aircraft or Persons in Distress when communicating with life-saving stations, maritime rescue units and aircraft engaged in search and rescue operations.

Note: All Morse Code signals by light (below).

1. SEARCH AND RESCUE UNIT REPLIES

YOU HAVE BEEN SEEN, ASSISTANCE WILL BE GIVEN AS SOON AS POSSIBLE

Orange smoke flare

Three white star signals or three light and sound rockets fired at approximately 1 minute intervals

2. SURFACE TO AIR SIGNALS

Note: Use International Code of Signals by means of light or flags or by laying out the symbol on the deck or ground with items that have a high contrast background.

Message	International Code of Signals		ICAO
I require assistance	V	✕ ...—	V
I require medical assistance	W	▢ .——	X
No or negative	N	▦ —.	N
Yes or affirmative	C	▤ —.—.	Y
Proceeding in this direction			↑

3. AIR TO SURFACE REPLIES

MESSAGE UNDERSTOOD

Drop a message. OR Rocking wings. OR Flashing landing or navigation lights on and off twice. OR T — OR R .—.

MESSAGE NOT UNDERSTOOD

Straight and level flight. OR Circling. OR R .—. P .——. T —

4. AIR TO SURFACE DIRECTION SIGNALS

SEQUENCE OF 3 MANOEUVRES MEANING PROCEED IN THIS DIRECTION

Circle vessel at least once.   Cross low, ahead of vessel rocking wings.   Overfly vessel and head in required direction.

YOUR ASSISTANCE IS NO LONGER REQUIRED

Cross low, astern of vessel rocking wings.

Note: As a non preferrred alternative to rocking wings, varying engine tone or volume may be used.

5. SURFACE TO AIR REPLIES

MESSAGE UNDERSTOOD - I WILL COMPLY

Change course to required direction. OR T — OR Code & answering pendant "Close Up".

I AM UNABLE TO COMPLY

International flag "N". OR N —.

6. SHORE TO SHIP SIGNALS

SAFE TO LAND HERE

Vertical waving of both arms, white flag, light or flare

OR K —.—

LANDING HERE IS DANGEROUS ADDITIONAL SIGNALS MEAN SAFER LANDING IN DIRECTION INDICATED

Horizontal waving white flag, light or flare. Putting one flare/ flag on ground and moving off with a second indicates direction of safer landing.

S ... Landing here is dangerous.
R .—. Land to right of your current heading.
L .—.. Land to left of your current heading.

PREPARATIONS AND PASSAGEMAKING

Requirements of skipper and crew

Before attempting a passage involving long periods out of sight of land and often at night, skipper, crew, and boat must be adequate for the job. The recommended complement is a crew of three: a competent skipper, a second in command, and one other active and useful crew member. On larger yachts at least one additional member is needed to enable two distinct watches to be established. Seasickness is a scourge of almost all of us. Even the strongest of us can feel queasy and below par when the cold, wet and the incessant rolling wears us down. There's a wide range of proprietary products and mechanical devices for combatting the scourge. It's really a case of finding what works for you. It's important for the safe working of the ship that crews are kept as free of the vomiting scourge as possible.

It's becoming increasingly important in Europe for a skipper to have some sort of 'certificate of competence' in the use of his vessel. Many readers of this book will have achieved Yachtmaster qualifications, at least to the level of Coastal Skipper. Generally recognised is the International Certificate of Competence (pleasure craft) awarded by examination by an RYA appointed examiner on the owner's own vessel; it needs renewing every five years, though no further examination is required. You'll need the inland waterways (CEVNI) endorsement to navigate the canals and lakes on the Continent. A necessary document includes a Radio Operator's Certificate.

Both skipper and crew should be physically fit; the prospect of a heart attack or seizure in mid North Sea is a daunting one. Eyesight standards should be reasonable, and if you suffer from colour blindness you'll be at a disadvantage when distinguishing and interpreting lights, especially at night. If contact lenses are worn, a pair of waterproof goggles are also useful for bad weather. It's essential for all crew, including the skipper, to make known any medical conditions and medications before setting off.

Finally, if any potential crew member feels competent only to sail in inshore waters and inland waterways there is always the wide range of ferry and air services across the North Sea from which crew can join or leave; the routes from Harwich and Dover provide reasonably priced foot-passenger services to Hoek van Holland, Zeebrugge, Oostende, Dunkerque, and Calais.

Requirements of the boat

A crucial question a skipper must answer before setting off is: 'Is the boat sound and suitable for the voyage?'

It goes without saying that a good programme of winter maintenance should ensure that important aspects such as soundness of hull, the strength of deck and rigging fittings, keel and keel bolts, condition of sails, and the reliability of the engine should be thoroughly checked. A reliable engine is essential for avoiding danger, conforming to the traffic separation schemes, and manoeuvring into harbours. It's worth having a professional rig check and getting the motor serviced. Take spare oil, coolant, alternator belt (and pump belt if separate) and raw water pump impeller. Check the sails are in good order, that there is a tested lifejacket for each crew member.

You should always carry the proper safety equipment, charts and tide tables and a copy of the International Regulations for Preventing Collisions at Sea. Many officials ask to see these, especially in France. And a warning here, if carrying pyrotechnic flares as part of your safety equipment, they must be in date, as must lifejacket servicing certificates. And take a liferaft; you can hire one for the duration if you don't want to buy one. Ensure the liferaft has been regularly serviced and is within its service date.

Check your fenders; ideally you should have eight on board plus, maybe, a large fender ball for use in locks. A fender board is also useful. You'll also need good quality long warps, enough for the four corners plus springs. It's not a bad idea to have a long towing warp aboard as well. An extra-long or an additional extension electricity lead, along with a long hose with universal connections, are sensible components of the store's locker. A set of engine spares is a high priority.

Don't forget to fill the fuel tank and carry at least ten litres of white diesel as spare fuel (see page 35). Top up the water tank and, after some discussion with the crew, fill the store cupboard and fridge. On this latter point, you also need to check on what types and amounts of foodstuff purchased in the UK you can take into the EU, even if it's for personal consumption (stories of ham sandwiches being confiscated from lorry drivers abound).

While there are recognised statutory and recommended minimum standards of equipment for cruising vessels, there is still the question of what additional useful equipment to take. A summary of the minimum RYA 'recommendations' for yachts of below 13·7m (45ft) in length is listed in Appendix I. Larger vessels are required to carry a wide range of safety equipment, fire appliances, and other equipment. Smaller vessels should carry an appropriate proportion of the items of equipment listed. A VHF radio, (including DSC) with the relevant operator's licence is essential in an area with such a comprehensive coverage of port and coast radio stations, Coastguard Rescue Centres, and heavy shipping traffic; nowhere in this area of the North Sea is a vessel likely to be out of range of another ship or shore VHF station, a confidence-inspiring situation for the lone yacht on a night passage.

Electronic position-fixing equipment (GPS)

The legal enforcement of the Traffic Separation Schemes, the development of offshore oil and gas fields and increasing governmental regulation of offshore areas are placing a premium on the need for a yachtsman to have a continuous accurate position-fix in the busy area covered by this book, and electronic position-fixing equipment (GPS) provides the experienced yachtsman with an invaluable means of navigating. **But it is an aid and not a substitute for seamanship;** thorough navigational knowledge, and above all the keeping of a proper log of the passage and making frequent conventional estimates of position are essential. An eye on the depth can also help fix a position by referring to the depth contours on the chart.

Electronic navigation is now common, but you must constantly check your position by traditional navigation techniques and whenever possible by eye. You should also run a paper chart plot with position entries every hour at least; every half hour in foul weather. It's also recommended that you have a hand-held receiver as a back-up to your main system and a swung magnetic compass as well. Be warned: Satellite-derived positions are sometimes more accurate than the chart upon which you are plotting.

GPS is referenced to the World Geodetic System 1984 (WGS84).

Radar

Whether to invest in radar (not on the RYA list) is probably the most difficult question of all: In a small, short-handed yacht with a lively motion in heavy seas, the need to concentrate on a small screen is often of less importance than a good lookout, and competent steering and yacht-handling. But in calm foggy conditions radar can be worth its weight in gold, although some of the cheaper automatic radar warning devices are more practicable for the smaller vessel. In the hierarchy of equipment, a full-blown radar set is probably left to the end.

AIS

AIS is a boon when crossing shipping lanes, especially at night, and several of the more important marks at sea are now fitted with AIS transmitters to aid navigation. But if you rely on AIS it's important to understand its limitations. A useful guide has been published by the Royal Institute of Navigation and is free to download at www.rin.org.uk/page/ENav. Printed copies are available from www.imray.com.

Typical North Sea summer cruising

The typical North Sea cruising holiday extends for 2–3 weeks and is one of two options: An offshore passage to a chosen cruising ground and coast-hopping or cruising inland during the bulk of the remaining period before a return passage; or coast-hopping throughout, possibly with a Dover Strait and/or Thames Estuary crossing. Experienced sailors are more likely to opt for the direct route between the Delta or Noord Holland and the Norfolk, Suffolk, and Essex coasts, whilst the Oostende–UK east coast passage is also a popular way of avoiding the tricky Thames Estuary crossing. Those with less experience, and/or more time, tend to do more coast-hopping, and the Dover Strait in season is crowded with all nationalities of cruising yacht heading in both directions.

There are several interesting cruising destinations in the southern North Sea, most of which have dense concentrations of boats and facilities. On the English side these are Dover and Ramsgate; the Medway and Swale; the Thames to St Katharine's Dock, London (also a route for vessels with removable masts into the English inland waterways); the rivers Crouch and Roach, Blackwater and Colne, Orwell and Stour, Deben, and Ore; and Southwold, Lowestoft, Great Yarmouth, and the Norfolk Broads. In France and Belgium there is a string of North Sea harbours from Calais to Zeebrugge with entrances to another extensive inland waterway system.

Blackwater to Calais at dawn

PREPARATIONS AND PASSAGEMAKING

The Netherlands has the highest concentration of high-quality yachting facilities of all: the Schelde Delta itself leads to massive inland waterway system, while the North Sea ports of IJmuiden and Den Helder give access to the IJsselmeer and the Frisian canals, lakes, Waddenzee, and the Friesland islands.

Passage planning

Before you set off, you'll need to develop a passage plan. It's straightforward and basic common sense, and something in which you can involve the crew. For this you'll need the latest up-to-date charts, both paper and electronic (this can be on a chart plotter, a hand-held GPS, an iPad, tablet or even on your mobile 'phone), a tidal atlas, tide tables (for most crossings, tides are based on Dover) and a current almanac.

There are four planning objectives:
1. To avoid hazards en route (shoal patches, TSSs and DWRs)
2. To time the passage, in the given weather conditions, for entry to the destination on the flood and in daylight
3. To minimise the overall distance and time at sea
4. To simplify the navigation and thus the chances of error.

Working your tide is crucial, especially in the coastal zones. In the North Sea the flood runs SW and the ebb runs NE; there are some local exceptions you need to watch for, for example the ebb out of the Scheldt runs in a WSW direction, the same as the sea flood along the Belgian coast. On most of the routes across the North Sea you will be crossing the tide and need to take this into account. On some routes however, especially where the trip is over seven hours long, you'll need to factor in the need to punch into some tide. For a short-handed or family crew, it may pay to choose an over-tide stop, if available. With a larger crew capable of working a watch system, punching on may be sensible.

Always remember that the aim is to be off your destination port just before HW to ensure an easier entry. Also, aim to arrive in daylight, particularly if it is your first ever visit. For this reason, many North Sea crossings take place overnight. Your route should take account of natural hazards such as sand

Passage Plan Morven						Log:	Engine:
Date:18.10.21		Crew: 4.			Final:	11,456	
From: Harwich		Towards: Ijmuiden			Initial:	11,321	170hrs
Tidal Data: 2 N, 1 S		Time zone UT +/- hrs: +1			Run:	135	
HWLW	Port:		Port:		Port:	Port:	
10.15	Walton	4 m	Hoek	0201 2.2m			
Tidal gates:							
2 n 1 S							
Weather forecast:							
S 3-5 smooth/slight occ rain. Mod/poor							
24hrs: S 3-4 rising 5-6 mod rain/drizzle poor/good							

Time:	Mark	Dist M	Notes:
0800	SYH		Slip berth (Harwich VTS VHF Ch 71) Punch flood
0900	Landguard	3	Dept Landguard and punch last of flood towards N Shipwash
10.15	Tide Gate		Tide turns N
11.30	N Shipwash	15	New course 065° for NW EA1. Tide ebbing NE
16.35	Tide Gate		Tide turns S
16.30	NW EA1	35	Skirt WF and then set course due E to clear Y DWR
19.30	Clear DWR	16	Set course 080° CMG for IJMW 1 at entrance to Ij Guel Keep N of MN4
24.30	Tide gate		Tide Turns N
02.30	IJMW 1	42	Course due E follow S edge of Ch; Y buoys. Beware Y post 1M out
06.30	Ijmuiden	24	Arrive Ijmuiden harbour VHF 61
22.5hrs		135	AV Speed 6 Knots

A plan gives you targets and expected times along your route

Weather

Good passage planning is crucial

banks in the coastal zones, wind farms, gas and oil rigs, and a small number of exclusion zones. In addition, you should plan a course that allows you to cross commercial shipping lanes at right angles to the line of travel of the big shipping. Simply sailing in a straight line from A to B is no longer possible.

There's a simple five-stage passage-planning routine you can follow before setting off, preferably the day before but thoroughly re-checked against the weather forecast on the day of the passage (see below). It pays to involve the whole crew in your deliberations:

1. Mark your proposed route on the chart, aiming for a point a mile or two up-tide of your destination, the course to be made good (CTMG), correcting if necessary, for a right-angle passage across the shipping lanes. Enter a waypoint on the chart plotter for each expected alteration to the rhumb line course. It's worth noting which way the tide is pushing you when laying in the courses crossing the shipping lanes.
2. Measure approximate distances to and from the departure and arrival harbours via this route.
3. List times of HW Dover on day(s) of passage and for the local HW/LWs at the departure and arrival harbours and for the course changes.
4. Estimate an average speed for the passage assuming reasonable but not excessive use of engine to keep up to the average.
5. With electronic position-fixing equipment a series of waypoints along the route can be loaded into the machine and marked on the chart. As well as displays of bearings, distances off, and lat/long fixes, most machines also have a function which displays the distance off track to the next waypoint (cross track error) and the side of the track to which the vessel has deviated, and if waypoints have been marked on the main CTMG you get an instant picture of the vessel's deviation in relation to the above passage plan.

Weather

Weather and wind conditions vary and seldom remain the same for more than a few hours on any passage. Across the seasons as a whole, pressure averages 1015 millibars throughout the region but with the generally eastward passage of depressions driving in on the Jet Stream, and intervening high pressure ridges through or to north and south of the region, it can fluctuate hourly, falling as low as 950 millibars in a deep depression and bringing a series of rapid changes in wind strength and direction.

Less frequently, more stable conditions may last for up to a week or more due to the spreading of high-pressure air from (usually) the Azores region of the Atlantic in summer (June to August) when the Jet Stream swings N of the area, and Siberia in winter (December to February), with pressure sometimes reaching 1050 millibars, and usually with lighter more variable conditions. Spring (March to May) and autumn (September to November) are the most variable seasons.

In terms of wind strength and direction an early cruising season from April to August, is preferable to a late one, say from July to November. However, the early season approach does tend to suffer slightly more from the danger of fog, with less chance of fog during July, August, September, and October, although a reduction in air pollution in the last 40 years has reduced the fog problem considerably.

Fog is a hazard to be avoided in the traffic separation schemes but is thankfully rare in the sailing season; 5 per cent frequency (1·5 days a month) and is often a brief coastal feature in quiet anticyclonic conditions due to night-time temperature inversion on the land and fog drifting onto the sea but clearing during the morning. There tends to be a slightly higher fog frequency nearer to

Confused seas

NORTH SEA PASSAGE PILOT

PREPARATIONS AND PASSAGEMAKING

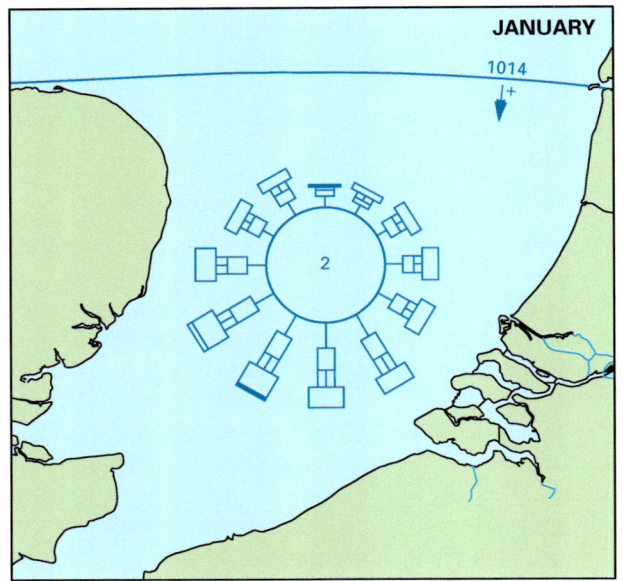

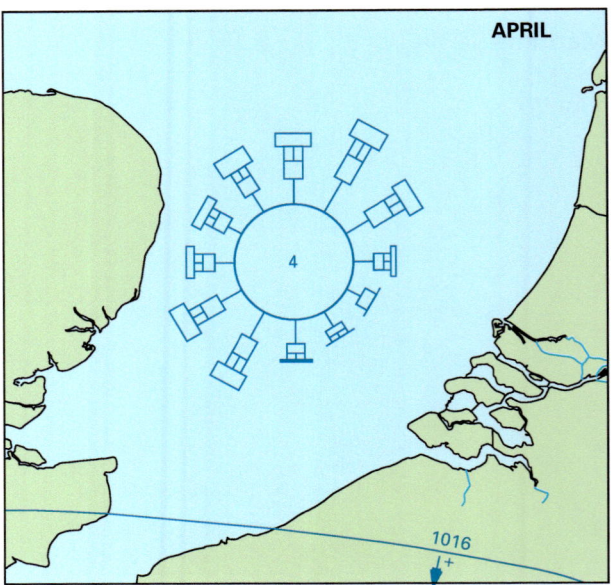

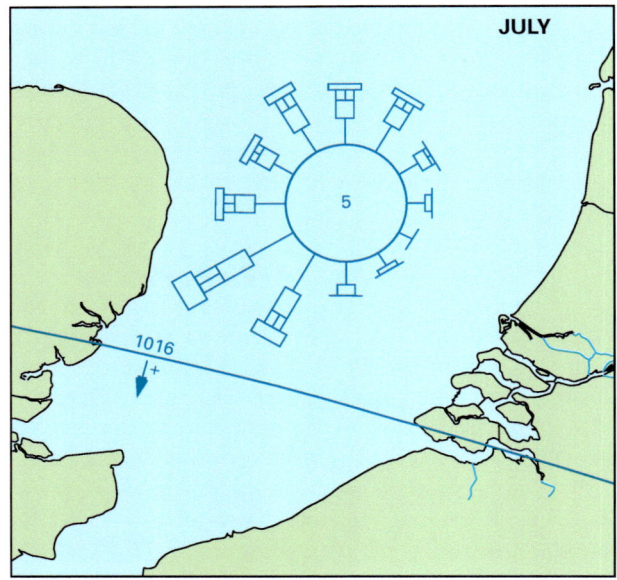

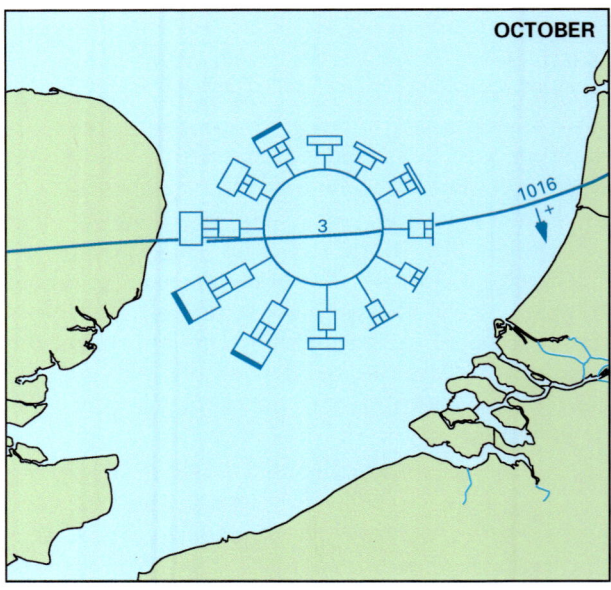

Wind distribution by season

Frequency of wind from any direction
Subdivided by Beaufort Force

the Dover Strait particularly on the French/Belgian coast stretching up as far as the Delta.

The average frequency and strength of winds gives a useful guide to holiday timing, providing you're prepared to wait a few days for the right conditions. The prevailing is from SW to NW with a N to NE component mainly from February to May. As the coasts on each side lie in these directions, winds near the shore tend to be stronger, and rougher conditions are often encountered at the end of a passage. On the continental side both W to SW and N to NE winds create rough conditions and on the English side, including the Thames Estuary, NE to E winds produce the worst lee shore conditions. In autumn and winter most winds come from the SW quadrant, so sailing from the English coast to Holland is usually a 'downhill' run but difficult for the Dutchman or returning Englishman in the opposite direction.

14   NORTH SEA PASSAGE PILOT

Weather

Maritime Safety Information (MSI) broadcasts
The Maritime and Coastguard Agency states that NAVTEX is the primary means for broadcasting MSI but many leisure sailors use marine VHF, public service radio, harbour notice boards and, increasingly, the internet.

UK inshore waters forecasts and MSI on VHF
After an initial announcement on VHF 16 it is then transmitted on one of VHF 62, 63 or 64.
Around Northern Ireland, the Western Isles of Scotland, Shetland, and Southwest England VHF 10 is also used.

Coastguard Operation Centre (CGOC) & Area	Inshore Forecast Areas 24 hour forecast, 24 hour outlook. Valid up to 12M offshore	Broadcast times LT and schedules				Shipping Forecast Areas
		B	C	A	C	
ABERDEEN Cape Wrath to Berwick	Cape Wrath to Rattray Head inc Orkney. Rattray Head to Berwick	0130 1330	0430 1630	0730 1930	1030 2230	Fair Isle, Cromarty, Forties, Forth, Tyne
HUMBER Berwick to Bawdsey	Berwick to Whitby, Whitby to Gibraltar Point. Gibraltar Point to N Foreland	0150 1350	0450 1650	0750 1950	1050 2250	Tyne, Dogger, Fisher, Humber, German Bight, Thames
DOVER Felixstowe Ferry to Beachy Head	Gibraltar Point to N Foreland. N Foreland to Selsey Bill	0110 1310	0410 1610	0710 1910	1010 2210	Humber, Thames, Dover, Wight
SOLENT Beachy Head to Exmouth	N Foreland to Selsey Bill. Selsey Bill to Lyme Regis. Lyme Regis to Land's End inc Isles of Scilly	0130 1330	0430 1630	0730 1930	1030 2230	Dover, Wight, Portland, Plymouth
SHETLAND Shetland, Orkney and N coast of Scotland	Shetland Isles and 60M offshore. Cape Wrath to Rattray Head inc Orkney	0110 1310	0410 1610	0710 1910	1010 2210	Viking, Cromarty, Fair Isle, Faroes

Note
1. Near area boundaries, it is advisable to monitor the adjacent area forecast.
2. During Casualty Working, the transmission may be delayed. Monitor VHF 16.
3. Further information and a list of aerials with their working channels is available online at MCA/064.

Schedule A
Full maritime safety information broadcast, including new inshore forecast and outlook, gale warnings, general synopsis and shipping forecast for appropriate sea areas, WZ navigation warnings, SUBFACTS and GUNFACTS where appropriate, three-day fisherman's forecast (October to March).

Schedule B
New inshore forecast, new outlook, gale warnings.

Schedule C
Repetition of inshore forecast and gale warnings as per previous Schedule A or B broadcast plus new strong wind warning.

UK COASTGUARD FORECASTS AND MSI ON MF			
Aerial	Frequency/KHz	Times (UTC)	
Aberdeen	2226	0730	1930
Cullercoats	1925	0750	1950
Shetland	1770	0710	1910
Broadcasts are preceded by a call on 2182kHz Content is Schedule A			

Weather forecasts
Choose your weather carefully and allow enough time to delay departure by a couple of days if needed to allow bad weather to pass. Shipping forecasts up to 24hrs ahead tend to be reliable, although particularly unstable weather patterns with fast-moving deep depressions sometimes leave the forecasters guessing beyond 12hrs ahead. Before a passage it is vital to monitor both the shipping and inshore waters forecasts. At the same time, you should obtain a seven-day tidal prediction for any selected ports you need.

BBC weather forecasts on Radio 4
The shipping forecast:
Radio 4 LW, 198kHz, at 0048*, 0520*, 1201, 1754 LT (*also VHF and MW.) Areas and terms used are described below.

Internet-sourced weather
The internet is a valuable source of weather information and is often readily accessible even several miles out to sea and is an additional source of GMDSS MSI forecasts and synoptic charts. Although outages are rare, it is not an operational system and should not be relied upon. URLs can change with no warning, content may change. As with any weather forecast, it's sensible to always check date and time of origin. A major benefit is being able to read forecasts and save them; this is useful particularly when in a foreign language. MyCA and Frank Singleton's websites give fast

direct links to information provided by national weather services. Otherwise, type the following into a browser address bar to enter national weather service websites:

metoffice.gov (UK)
met.ie (Ireland)
meteofrance.fr (France)
dmi.dk (Denmark)
knmi.nl (Netherlands)
meteo.be (Belgium)
dwd.de (Germany)

For those with limited bandwidth, perhaps using a satellite phone, the free Saildocs service uses email to provide texts of many GMDSS forecasts. For details send a blank email to info@saildocs.com. Free MailASail services provide GMDSS texts and synoptic charts as small email attachments. For the menus of texts send a blank email to weather@mailasail.com with subject help-text; for charts put the subject as help-graphic.

There are several excellent weather forecasting websites and apps, including:

www.windguru.cz
www.windy.com
www.predictwind.com.

You can get weather updates on a rolling three-hourly basis up to a week ahead. Different websites and apps rely on different weather models such as GFS (Global Forecasting System), ECMWF (European Centre for Medium-Range Weather Forecasting) and others. Many of the popular apps and websites rely on data from the same model. As a rule of thumb, it is sensible to monitor forecasts generated by a variety of models; when the forecasts from different models align there is more certainty in the weather predictions; when the forecasts differ it is a useful warning that the weather systems may be less stable and predictable.

VHF weather bulletins

Inshore Waters forecasts:
Follow the 0048 and 0520 shipping forecasts on Radio 4.

The 0520 forecast on Radio 4 is followed by reports of actual weather from coastal stations and light vessels. Reports are from locations shown on the UK sea area chartlet. Some of the stations are automatic and measure visibility but not 'weather' i.e., there are no reports of rain, drizzle, showers etc. The 0048 forecast on Radio 4 is followed by an extended list of stations. Some coastal reports are broadcast on NAVTEX 490kHz. There is a Met Office service, ☏ 0370 900 0100 or Fax 0370 900 5050 for details. Alternatively, use www.weatherquest.co.uk, University of East Anglia, ☏ +44 1603 507 605.

GMDSS services from other countries:
Routine forecasts are given in UTC unless otherwise stated. Bulletins for open sea areas will usually be in English. Meteorological terms in other languages are usually recognisable with some practice. Useful multi-language glossaries are found in the Yachtsman's 10 Language Dictionary (Adlard Coles Nautical).

Oostende Radio: VHF 27. 0720, LT, 0820, 1720 UTC. Forecasts for Thames, Dover. In English.

Dutch Coastguard: 0940, 2140. Forecasts for Dogger, Humber, Thames, and German Bight. In English. MF. 1,890 kHz (Appingedam), 3,673 kHz (Den Helder Coast Guard). 0805, 1305, 1905, 2305 LT. Inshore waters to 30 M offshore. In English. VHF Appingedam VHF 83, Schiermonnikoog VHF 23, Westkapelle VHF 83. On VHF and MF, warnings 4-hourly from 0333.

France: The French CROSS stations broadcast inshore waters forecasts (in French). Forecasts cover up to 20M offshore. Transmissions are a pre-recorded synthesised voice from each transmitter in sequence.

NAVTEX

There are four NAVTEX stations covering the region, broadcasting navigational warnings and weather information in English by facsimile: Cullercoats (G on 518kHz and U on 490kHz, from the Tyne-Tees coast), Niton (E and K on 518kHz, and T and I on 490kHz from the Isle of Wight), Oostende (T and M on 518kHz) and Netherlands Coastguard (IJmuiden, P on 518kHz).

Tidal streams

Crossing the North Sea can involve several tidal changes, depending on speed and distance to cover. Harwich to IJmuiden, for example, around 100M, will involve three, or possibly four, tide changes, depending on speed: ebbing at the start, a S-going flood, and a N-going ebb, and for slower boats finishing on a S-going flood. Most North Sea passages are made cross tide.

In general, the tide starts moving down the North Sea into the Dover Strait at around HW Dover −5hrs and turns northwards at HW Dover +1. On the Norfolk coast, it tends to turn about an hour earlier than these times and on the opposite north Dutch coast about an hour later. In the central area spring tides seldom exceed 2kn, but on the Norfolk coast 'bulge' the streams tend to be much stronger than in the Dutch 'bight': At HW Dover −4 the East Anglian S-going stream averages 1·9kn neaps to 3·0kts springs; on the Dutch coast north of Europoort it reaches its maximum up to 3hrs later at HW Dover −1, when the average is 0·8–1·5kn, about half the rate of the Norfolk coast. The N-going stream reaches its fastest across the whole of the northern part of the region at about HW Dover +3 at similar rates to the S-going, though a little slower on the East Anglian coast at 1·7–3·0kn.

In the Dover Strait itself the tide turns about 2hrs earlier than in the northern part of the area, the SW-going stream starting approximately HW Dover +5 and the NE-going at HW Dover –1. The funnelling effect of the Strait creates much stronger rates: the SW-going reaches 1·8–3·3kn in the middle of the Strait at HW Dover –4; the NE-going reaches 1·7–3·1kn HW Dover +2.

Dover mean Springs range is 5·9m but can reach as much as 6·6m, and at Dover entrance in these conditions the rate can reach as much as 4·6kn compared with a mean of 4·1kn; off the Norfolk coast a 3·4kn mean can be associated with 3·8kn in practice. At the other extreme Dover mean Neaps range of rate is 3·3kn but can be as small as 2·1kn in practice, producing on the northern Dutch coast tidal sets as low as 0·5kn maximum.

Tidal diamonds and tidal atlases

Although tidal diamonds provide tidal set and rate information to use during a passage, this information cannot be fully appreciated without the use of tide tables and tidal atlases. Almanacs provide adequate tide tables and tidal charts, but it is well worth investing in the three more robust Admiralty Tidal Stream Atlases for use in planning, and on passage when actual times of day can be pencilled on the corners of each hourly page for quick reference. These Admiralty atlases cover:

1. Thames Estuary (with co-tidal chart) (based on HW Sheerness) NP 249
2. Dover Strait (based on HW Dover) NP 233
3. North Sea – southern portion (based on HW Dover) NP 251,

Inside the front covers is a table for calculating the rate of tidal stream, on the assumption that the rates vary with the range of tide. Or, use Imray's Tides Planner app.

A valuable source of tidal information is carried on Imray charts. On the backs of the covers for the four charts covering this area – C1, Thames Estuary; C8, Dover Strait; and C30 and C28 covering the S North Sea – are hourly tidal streams diagrams complete with direction and rates. Tidal stream data is also given at the tidal diamonds on the charts.

For the inlets of the Schelde Delta and the Schulpengat on the Dutch coast it's also advisable to buy *HP33 Waterstanden en Stromen* (Dutch Hydrographic Office) since the Admiralty tidal atlases do not adequately cover these areas.

It is a matter of simple mental arithmetic to estimate tidal rates from an atlas or tidal diamond using the average springs and neaps rates found there.

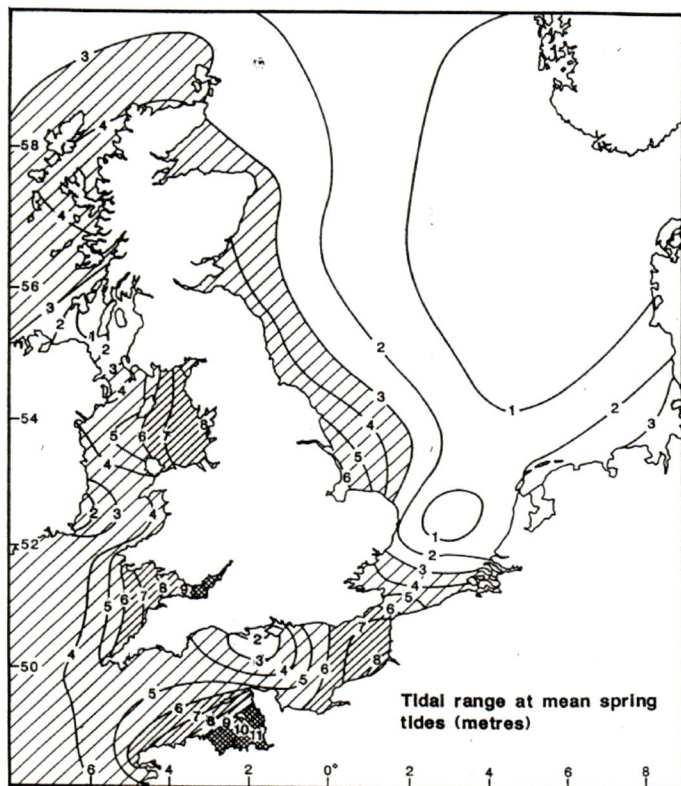

Tidal range springs

Tide times and depths

Knowing your depth is critical for approach navigation but also can be extremely useful in estimating position from soundings while crossing the longitudinal North Sea banks well offshore. In the northern part of the offshore area, where the tidal range is only 1m or less it's less critical, but accurate estimation is important in the area bounded by the Dover Strait and S of a line from Harwich to the Schelde and including the Thames Estuary; this area is littered with shoals and has a tidal range between 2m in the centre of the southern North Sea to 5·5m at the bottom end where it merges with the Dover Strait.

Tidal movements can be calculated more easily by using HW at Dover as the base time: local HW on the continental coast is progressively later; Dunkerque/Oostende area is approximately +1hr, Vlissingen +2, Hoek van Holland +3, but at the very N of the area IJmuiden/Den Helder is HW Dover –4·5hrs.

On the UK east coast Orfordness has HW at the same time as Dover, while it's 2 hrs earlier at Great Yarmouth, so that from Orfordness south westwards as well as from North Foreland westwards along the N Kent coast, local HWs are progressively later than Dover.

Fluctuations of tide level and tidal surges

Accurately predicting tidal depths and tidal sets and drifts is particularly important in navigating this shallow region. To compound the problem of estimating depth, strong or prolonged winds and unusually low or high barometric pressures can raise or lower the height of tide from its predicted level. Winds blowing with the ebb can lower LW and prolong the ebb, and those blowing with the flood can raise HW and prolong the flood, while winds blowing against the tides can have the opposite effects.

Small yachts tend to avoid bad weather and dash across the North Sea with good shipping forecasts so tidal streams and depths can be predicted with acceptable accuracy, but allowance for margins of error must always be made, particularly on trans-North Sea passages involving the longer distances and crossing shoals.

Log keeping

Sailors used to short-distance coastal cruising in familiar waters may have grown used to minimising the number of routine tidal calculations, logbook and chart entries. An offshore or unfamiliar North Sea passage requires a little more recording and log keeping. An example of a detailed log is shown below. Should the electronics go down then a regularly kept log should place you within five or six miles down the track from your last charted position. We have heard of instances where authorities have asked to check the log to make sure you've done the trip you claim. The EU is playing hard ball on the 90-days in any one 180-day period and proving you've arrived legally can be supported

Log of an actual trip

Voyage from **Den Helder** to **Levington Marina** Date **30/31 May**

Time	Remarks	Log	Course	Wind
1015	Den Helder Ent. – Engine on / Full sail			NNW3
1025	TR reported Scheveningen Radio			"
1100	WP1 (Kap Hoofd) 0.3 to port			"
1125	SG / WP2 Log streamed A/C 245° True	0	245°	"
1505	WP3 / TX1 Abeam 2.0 to starboard	16.0	"	"
1603	WP4 / Texel Abeam 3.3 to starboard	21.5	"	NW2
1922	UN12 (yellow buoy) close to port	37.0	"	"
1955	WP5 (M08 buoy) 4.3 to starboard	39.5	"	0
2100	Topped up diesel tank			"
2315	WP6 (Brown Ridge) 2.1 to starboard (sounding confirmed)	53.5	"	S2
0100	Engine off / Full sail 1.0 South of track plan	62.0	"	S3/4
0250	WP7 (DWR entry) 3.9 to starboard	69.9	"	"
0342	A/C 286° true to cross Deep Water Route	73.3	286°	"
0515	WP8 (DWR Departure) close to	80.5	"	"
0540	A/C 245° True for Shipwash Light Vessel		245°	SW2
0715	Engine on / Full sail. On track	87.2	"	SW3
0915	A/C 230° True. Sails off. Track plan 0.8 to port	96.5	230°	"
1037	WP9 Close (en route for Shipwash Lt V)	101.1	"	"

continued.
Voyage from _____ to _____ Date _____

Time	Remarks	Log	Course	Wind
1150	Track planned 0.3 to port	106.1	"	SW4
1342	1 reef in mainsail / Roll in jib. Track planned 0.8 to port	113.3	"	SW5
1515	WP10 (Shipwash Lt V) 0.4 to port	120.2	"	"
1531	N Shipwash buoy close to port	121.6	"	"
1546	NE Bawdsey buoy close starboard A/C 245°	123.0	245°	"
1615	TR reported Orfordness Radio / Link call home			
1715	Cutler buoy close starboard	128.5	"	"
1844	Platters buoy / Crossing of Harwich Channel started	133.7	–	SW3
1920	WP11 (Landguard Pt) 0.4 to starboard / Log taken in / Engine off	135.0	–	"
2015	Arrive Levington Marina	–	–	–

by an accurate log. There is another factor in play here; that of safety. Knowing where you if the rare calamity overtakes you, when perhaps the GPS is not working, you can get help to you more quickly by referring to the logbook.

Watchkeeping

An essential component of any passage plan is watchkeeping. Compared with a well-crewed offshore racer, discipline in a smaller, often family-crewed, cruising yacht is usually more relaxed and the watchkeeping system looser. The problem on these short passages with limited crew numbers is the shortage of time to adapt to a new sleeping timetable, and few people get much sleep during off watches which tend to be short and frequent. Ideally you should start the watchkeeping system as soon as you are cleared away for sea.

A good system for a crew of three on overnight passages is the three/three or three/two method; three 3hr or 2hr watches (depending on the crew's preference as some prefer short lookout/helming periods) rotated for each member, including the skipper, as follows:

a. Two or three hours ON watch (at the helm if not on autohelm)
b. Two or three hours OFF watch (lying down essential even if not asleep)
c. Two or three hours STANDBY (cooking, helping with sail changes, or relaxing)

This order should be strictly kept as the previous on-watch member must be allowed to 'switch off' and sleep immediately after finishing their watch. The standby member can prepare a hot drink and food half an hour before going on watch. Inevitably the

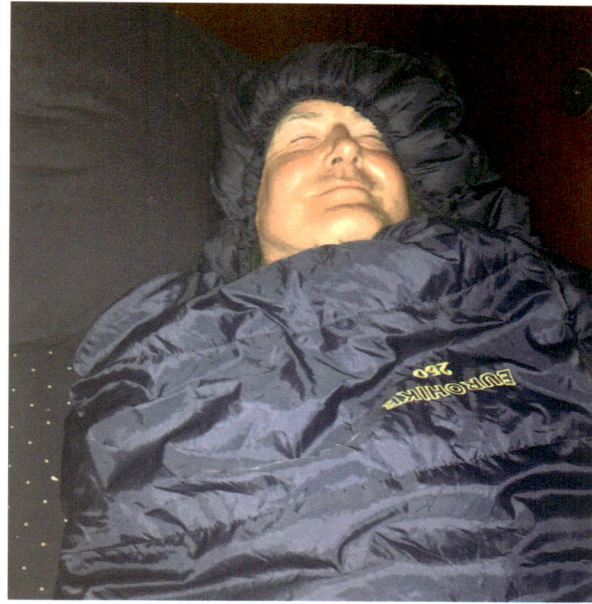

Crew members need time off watch

skipper of this three-person crew will find him- or herself navigating or on lookout 'out of hours' depending on likely dangers, but the opportunity of a complete scheduled 'off' watch is still important. It is essential that at least two of the crew are 'up top' (in the cockpit) when crossing shipping lanes.

With four crew it is probably better if the navigator/skipper still operates the system above, exempting themselves from any continual watch and instead snatching sleep during longer non-navigational periods. The skipper has a duty to self and to crew to juggle the three somewhat contradictory balls of conserving his or her own strength, putting the crew at ease, and remaining vigilant.

Keeping watch is an essential discipline

PREPARATIONS AND PASSAGEMAKING

With a yet larger crew of five or more a four-hour watchkeeping system can be operated, with two watches of two persons each, within which helm/lookout/cooking can be rotated, but again the skipper/navigator should be exempt. But the best laid watch systems usually degenerate a little on a short passage, being strictly maintained initially and during the hours of darkness but slipping a little as the other side is reached and spirits rise, even though the weather often blows up when closing these 'wind-parallel' coasts. This is a cue for skippers to be on their toes since they need all their pilotage skills to get into that unfamiliar harbour.

Things can be tough for the husband-and-wife cruising crew, which is all too often the norm. We suggest that one or two additional able-bodied crew are drafted in for at least the crossings out and back.

Crew safety

The general rule on personal safety on board, and it's a good one to follow, is to wear lifejackets while underway, but not down below, as a swamped boat can cause a lifejacket to inflate and trap the wearer under the coachroof. In addition, crew who leave the safety of the cockpit for deck work should be tethered. At night and in rough weather the crew working the cockpit should also all be tethered. If the boat has been properly prepared and secured for night sailing, there should be little reason to go forward on deck, with the exception perhaps of reefing at the mast. A good practice is to shorten sail before dusk, a slight drop in speed is worth it for the comfort and the knowledge that unless if blows up in the night the crew won't have to leave the safety of the cockpit. On a lot of occasions, the wind tends to drop during the night only to freshen again with the dawn. It is generally not a good idea to run a spinnaker after dark.

Marine communications

Most yachts engaged in coastal cruising or short offshore passages will have a VHF radio, preferably fitted with DSC. Usage is intended to be brief, clear and to allow other vessels to use VHF in turn. You may send a message to another vessel, a water-taxi, or an authorised shore station such as the CG, harbour control or marina. You must not call an individual person by name but must use a vessel's name or call-sign and your boat name. Low power (1watt) should be used in harbours and is compulsory on European inland waterways.

All radios must be licensed; OFCOM issues free lifetime licences for ship's radios online (with an alternative hard copy for a fee). These must be carried on board but not necessarily displayed, and must list all the radio and radar equipment. A fixed

Wearing lifejackets while underway but not when below is a good safety rule to follow

Radio and coastguard stations

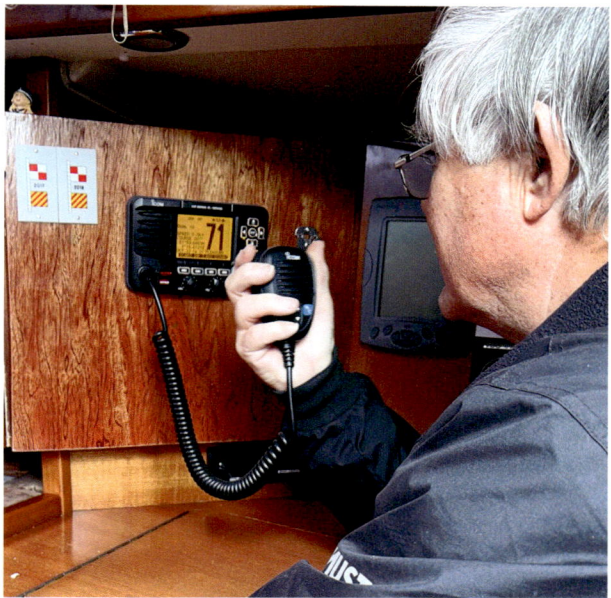

Used correctly VHF is an indispensable tool

MAYDAY Distress Call

If the radio is fitted with Digital Selective Calling it will have a red distress button on the front of the set. Carry out the following procedure:

1. Make sure the set is turned on and, if a separate GPS is connected, make sure that is turned on as well.
2. Lift or slide open the cover over the RED distress button.
3. Press the RED button momentarily once.
   If time allows scroll down on the screen and select the nature of the distress.
4. Press and hold the RED button for 10 seconds. This will send your boat identity and GPS position to the CG and all ships within range. The screen will show that the alert has been sent.
5. Wait no more than 15 seconds and send a voice MAYDAY following the standard procedure.

The set will now automatically be on Channel 16 on HIGH POWER. If time doesn't allow you to scroll the screen, the automatic distress call will still be sent, but without giving the nature of the distress.

If your set does not have a RED distress button, just carry out the voice procedure. The minimum information required is your vessel's name and position.

penalty of £100 will be payable for not being registered. Details at www.ofcom.org.uk/manage-your-licence/radiocommunication-licences/online-licensing-service

VHF 16 is for Calling and Distress only. Call on a working channel if you can. Monitor VHF 16 for Distress calls and port channels when in harbour areas. Boats with a DSC radio should enter the MMSI number of the coastguard station for the area in which they are sailing. Mayday calls made using the RED button alert all DSC radios within range. Intership channels are VHF 06, 08, 72, 77. If sailing in company, arrange the VHF in advance (usually VHF 72, 77 or 06, for yachts).

The Global Maritime Distress and Safety System (GMDSS) includes INMARSAT, Search and Rescue Transponders, EPIRBs and Navtex (see Meteorology section). It provides for a worldwide co-ordinated Search and Rescue Service of coastguards, lifeboats, and helicopters. In Europe there are Centres every 100M with VHF aerials every 25M. Once in contact with the CG they will co-ordinate all SAR action.

Radio and coastguard stations

VHF radio allows you to communicate with other stations up to a maximum effective range of about 10M for other vessels and between 30 and 50M for shore stations throughout the area except for a limited north-central area of doubt. However, even here in the DWRs and the approaches to the Texel TSS there is usually a commercial vessel within range listening on Ch16 or communicating on other channels. The GMDSS semi-automatic communication system also means that vessels with DSC apparatus can directly communicate with each other and with coastguard stations on VHF via their own unique nine-digit Maritime Mobile Service Identity (MMSI) number.

COASTGUARD OPERATIONS CENTRES

Station	MMSI	Telephone
United Kingdom		
Dover	002320010	+44 1304 210008
London	002320063	+44 2083 127380
Humber	002320007	+44 1262 672317
Belgium		
Oostende	002050480	+32 59 701100
Netherlands		
Den Helder	002442000	+31 223 542300

The coasts of the region are covered by a network of about 40 inshore and offshore lifeboat stations, plus summer auxiliaries, operating within rescue networks, and in addition to the operation of DSC VHF radio, a MAYDAY call on Ch16 reaches stations either direct or is relayed by other vessels to bring help rapidly. Again, the area between the Norfolk and Noord Holland coasts is the more difficult since a vessel can be up to 55M from shore-based help, nearly four hours even at an average 15kn, so rescue by helicopter or by nearby ships coordinated by the coastguard services is a more likely option here. In the area between Harwich and Vlissingen the potential distance is up to 40M and nearer to the Thames Estuary and Dover Strait narrows to about 10M maximum, although the very heavy traffic in this area also means a good chance

PREPARATIONS AND PASSAGEMAKING

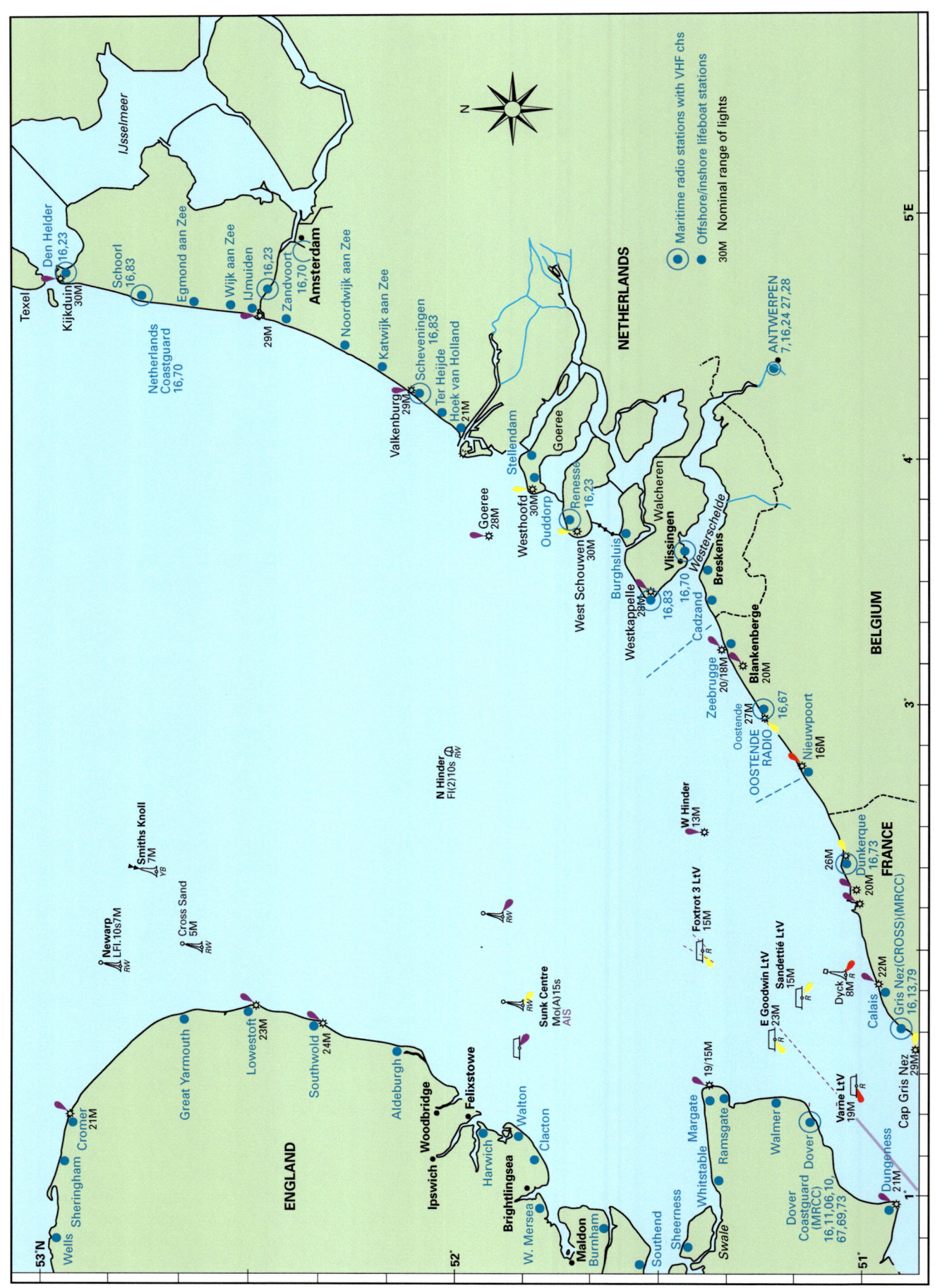

Coast Radio and Lifeboat Services

of assistance from passing ships. If you have an MF radio, range is no problem on any of these passages.

Even more widespread are the port radio stations (also detailed in yachtsman's almanacs and the Admiralty List of Radio Signals, Volume 6). There are 52 of these, 24 on the English and 28 on the continental coasts, and some with subdivisions with separate call signs. Most are for port operations only, but many of the VTS (Vessel Traffic Services) stations (including Harwich, Thames and Medway, Dover Strait, Scheldemonde, Nieuwe Waterweg, Noordzeekanal, Den Helder) put out regularly timed information broadcasts about hazards, weather, traffic movements or at specified times when visibility is less than 1000m. All these services are worth listening to if your vessel is in the vicinity but listening on any one of the ordinary port operations channels provides a very useful guide to the state of traffic movement providing the language can be understood, sometimes it is in English; certainly, most of the stations have operators who will respond to a request in English, which is advisable when entering or leaving harbour.

Rescue services

In an emergency, VHF is preferred to mobile phones for summoning assistance because the latter only have a range of about 10M, cannot be located by direction finding equipment, and cannot alert nearby vessels.

MAYDAY is the International Distress Call on VHF 16 using high power (25 watt). All other radio traffic must cease until the emergency is over unless related to distress working, you should remain silent if you hear emergency working on Ch16. It may only be used when a person or a vessel is in grave and imminent danger needing immediate assistance. All vessels are required to monitor VHF 16 and, if practical, proceed to the casualty to render assistance.

DSC sets send repeated distress messages once the red button has been pressed. These include the vessel's identity and GPS position, to the coastguard. This transmission has a slightly better range than normal VHF and should carry 50M. It will also switch all DSC radios to VHF 16 on all stations within range and turn on an alarm.

VHF and ATIS on EU inland waterways

In the inland waterways of France, Belgium, and the Netherlands, your VHF radio must be ATIS (Automatic Transmitter Identification System) enabled, and on entering the waterways you should switch it on, this will be checked by harbour authorities on arrival. In UK territorial waters the set should be ATIS-deactivated.

As a UK yachtsman visiting these countries you need to check well in advance if your set is ATIS compliant and, if not, arrange for it to be adapted or replace it with an ATIS-compliant VHF set capable of being activated and deactivated for ATIS. You will then need to contact the Ofcom website www.licensing.ofcom.org.uk to obtain an ATIS number (your MMSI number plus the prefix 9, making a 10-digit number) and a Notice of Variation to your ship radio licence. You should also download a copy of the Basel Arrangement detailing the rules for use of VHF on the inland waterways of the member countries, which you must have on board, as well as your ship radio licence and operator certificate. From then on, when your VHF set is activated in these inland waterways, every call you transmit will include your ATIS identification number.

If your set isn't compliant, restrict its use to essential traffic only; it's better to do this than remain silent!

Wind farms and support vessels

Wind farms are now a fact of life when crossing the southern North Sea. The nearest to the UK shore are Scroby Sands off Great Yarmouth and the Gunfleet Sands off Clacton. The London Array is in the very middle of the Thames Estuary, while the Gabbards affect those of us who aim for the Dutch coast. The Kentish Flats wind farm has been expanded and needs care to pass in the shallows off the E entrance to the Swale. Thanet wind farm NE of North Foreland is being extended. You can sail through UK wind farms so long as you keep 50 metres clear of turbines and 500 metres from maintenance boats working on towers, and you do so in clear daylight.

On the continental side the number of wind farms continues to grow. Off the Dutch coast you'll encounter the Egmond aap Zee, Luchterduinen, Gemini and Princess Amalia wind farms. Off the Belgian coast the Belwind, Northwind and Thornton Bank wind farms. In general, it is illegal to pass through Dutch and Belgian windfarms, although there are a couple of exceptions including the Egmond aap Zee and the Luchterduinen either side of the IJmuiden approach channel.

As if that weren't bad enough, craft wishing to leave to the north of our area, say beyond Lowestoft or across to the North Dutch or Friesland coasts, will eventually run the gauntlet of a new, massive, multi-thousand tower wind farm stretching from just south of Lowestoft to as far north as the Dogger Bank, with a width greater than half that of the southern North Sea. The construction of the southern end of this huge East Anglian One development affects the route to IJmuiden.

To aid ship safety, the towers in all wind farms are painted yellow up to 12m above sea level, and the corner towers, plus those at some key points down the sides of the farm, have yellow flashing lights, also at 12m. There is, however, some doubt that at this height these lights will be visible to crews of recreational craft

PREPARATIONS AND PASSAGEMAKING

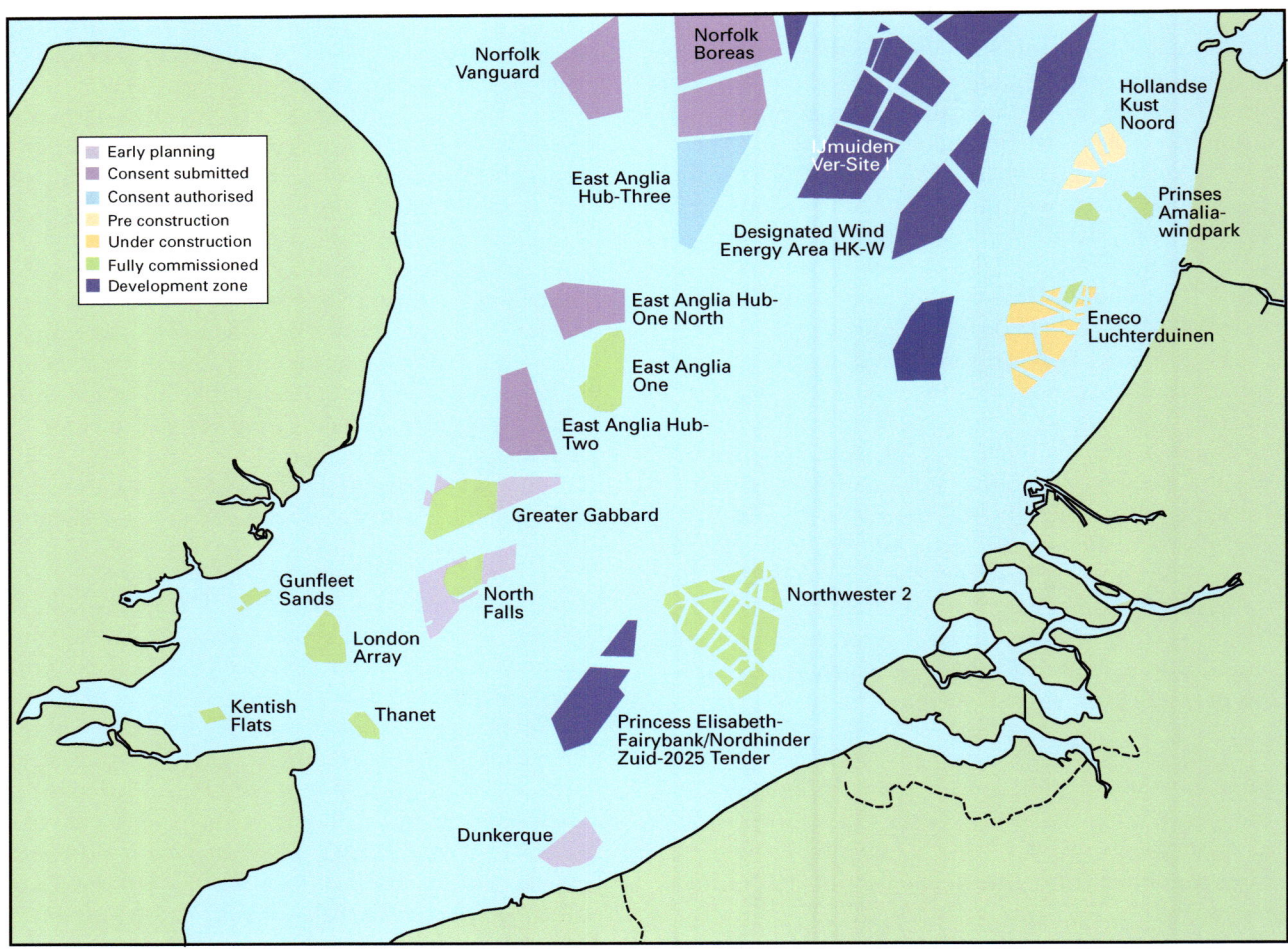

Wind farms in the southern North Sea

navigating in fog or dirty weather. The farms emit sound signals in fog.

It has been generally agreed that the rotor tip clearance will be 22m above MHWS and at this height 96 per cent of yachts will, if forced into the arrays, pass underneath without being struck by a rotor. Unfortunately, on the Gunfleet, just off Clacton, the clearance is only 20m, reducing the number of yachts able to go through without danger of being struck by the rotor tips.

General advice to sailors is to avoid the farms as much as possible, but to be aware of their positions, marks, and lights, which are shown on current charts.

Oil and gas platforms

In the northern part of the area covered by this book frequent navigational hazards which also provide an aid to navigation are the oil and gas production platforms and associated structures, as well as wind farms. You are prohibited from going within 500m of such obstructions. These structures usually have illuminated nameboards on each side, display an all-round white light flashing Morse Code 'U' (dot-dot-dash – You are running into danger') every 15 seconds, range 10M or 15M, synchronized with red lights also flashing (U), range 2M, and finally a fog signal also sounding 'U'.

Traffic Separation Schemes (TSS)

Usually, traffic separation schemes (TSSs) are confined to narrow straits and turning points round headlands. In the North Sea the many banks and shoals dictate a much more widespread network of interconnected routes. In general, the controlling depth for the fairways in the TSSs is 21m but there are a few shallower patches within some lanes, mostly marked by light buoys. The position of the TSSs is a critical factor dictating the direction of any passage across the southern North Sea. The boundaries of the TSSs are determined by the depths of water in the region, and these boundaries in turn determine the positioning of many of the major lights and radio beacons. TSSs concentrate through-traffic in the region into approximately 10M-wide bands in two opposing 5M-wide lanes, with several lanes branching off, and shallow-area variations on this theme. The schemes consist of two opposite-

Traffic Separation Schemes

CAUTION: WIND FARMS AND THE PASSAGE ROUTES

None of the routes in this book cross any of the current and developing wind farms but many pass close to their boundaries. The Marine and Coastguard Agency's (MCA) advice to mariners navigating near offshore renewable energy installations offers three options, depending on the vessel's characteristics (type, tonnage, draught, manoeuvrability etc.) and the weather and sea conditions:

A. Avoid the area completely: In general, it is not allowed to sail through Dutch and Belgian windfarms.
B. Navigate around the edge of the area, or
C. In the case of a wind farm, navigate, with caution, through the array.

As well as danger from wind farm maintenance and service vessels in the vicinity of a wind farm, small pleasure craft face the danger of drifting onto the wind farm structures which may have a scour protection of boulders and/or concrete mattresses placed round their bases as well as undersea electric cables which endanger anchoring. Most wind farms are sited on shoals. An inshore wind farm, therefore, should be treated similarly to a shoal area in terms of pilotage, so you should make every effort to avoid them.

It is impossible to leave a wide offing to some wind farms on some passages and there is frequently a need to pass close to the boundary of an operational wind farm or a wind farm under construction.
However, all the passages demonstrated avoid directly navigating through an array and you should always avoid doing so if possible. Your passage plan should be based on up-to-date large-scale charts showing the boundaries of the wind farm areas so you can make appropriate allowance for sea and wind conditions, treating the farms as dangerous shoals while on passage. It's a good idea to hatch them in or mark the boundaries with marker pen on your charts before setting out.

There are six wind farms in the area to be factored into route plans (see plan opposite). The River Crouch to Calais, for example requires navigating past the Gunfleet and London Array farms via Fisherman's Gat Precautionary Area. Harwich-Calais route passes between the Gabbard and London Array, and east of the Thanet farms. The Southend-Calais routes pass the Kentish Flats and Thanet farms.

You must keep 500m clear of windfarm construction vessels off the UK coast

going lanes of traffic leaving each other port to port, with a traffic separation zone (TSZ) in between.

A yacht taking two hours to cross the 10M width of the two lanes in the Dover Strait could meet, on average, 20 ships crossing its path – maybe 10 in each lane, or one every six minutes. But statistical averages can deceive, and ships can sometimes be widely spread, or in other cases bunched so that a series of vessels in line cross a yacht's track followed by a long gap. Similarly, although the cross-channel ferries average one every 10 minutes, in summer the frequency can be much higher.

The main destinations for incoming North Sea commercial traffic are the Thames Estuary's commercial ports of Tilbury, Harwich, and Felixstowe, and on the continental side Antwerp, Europoort/Rotterdam and Hamburg. Since both sides of the North Sea are strewn with treacherous sandbanks the traffic lanes tend to be well offshore to allow clearance of the 20m contour.

The Thames Estuary is the most crowded sailing area in the UK after the Solent. It has a charm and character that makes it unique, but the commercial traffic using the Thames is so continuously heavy that

PREPARATIONS AND PASSAGEMAKING

the Port of London Authority (PLA) is the largest port authority in the country. Felixstowe is the largest container port in the UK, one of the busiest in Europe, and accommodates the very largest cargo ships in the world. The Thames Estuary is the funnel through which much of this shipping travels to reach either Harwich in the north section or the Thames in the south. Approaching the Continental coast also needs some care, with the approaches to Scheveningen, Hook and Vlissingen all blanketed by the notorious Maas traffic management schemes. Commercial traffic into these ports and the Westerschelde is heavy and leisure vessels need to keep well clear.

North of the turn-off for Europoort and heading for the Texel Separation Scheme, through traffic as well as ferry traffic reduces considerably, probably to about half or less than in the Dover Strait. This is because the southern North Sea is wedge-shaped: at the southwest corner the Dover Strait is 20M wide from South Foreland to Cap Gris Nez and at the northern exit from Great Yarmouth to Den Helder is over 100M. On the western side from Ramsgate, across the Thames Estuary to Lowestoft is about 75M; and on the eastern side following the concave bay formed by the coastline of Belgium and Holland from Cap Gris Nez to Den Helder the distance is nearly 200M.

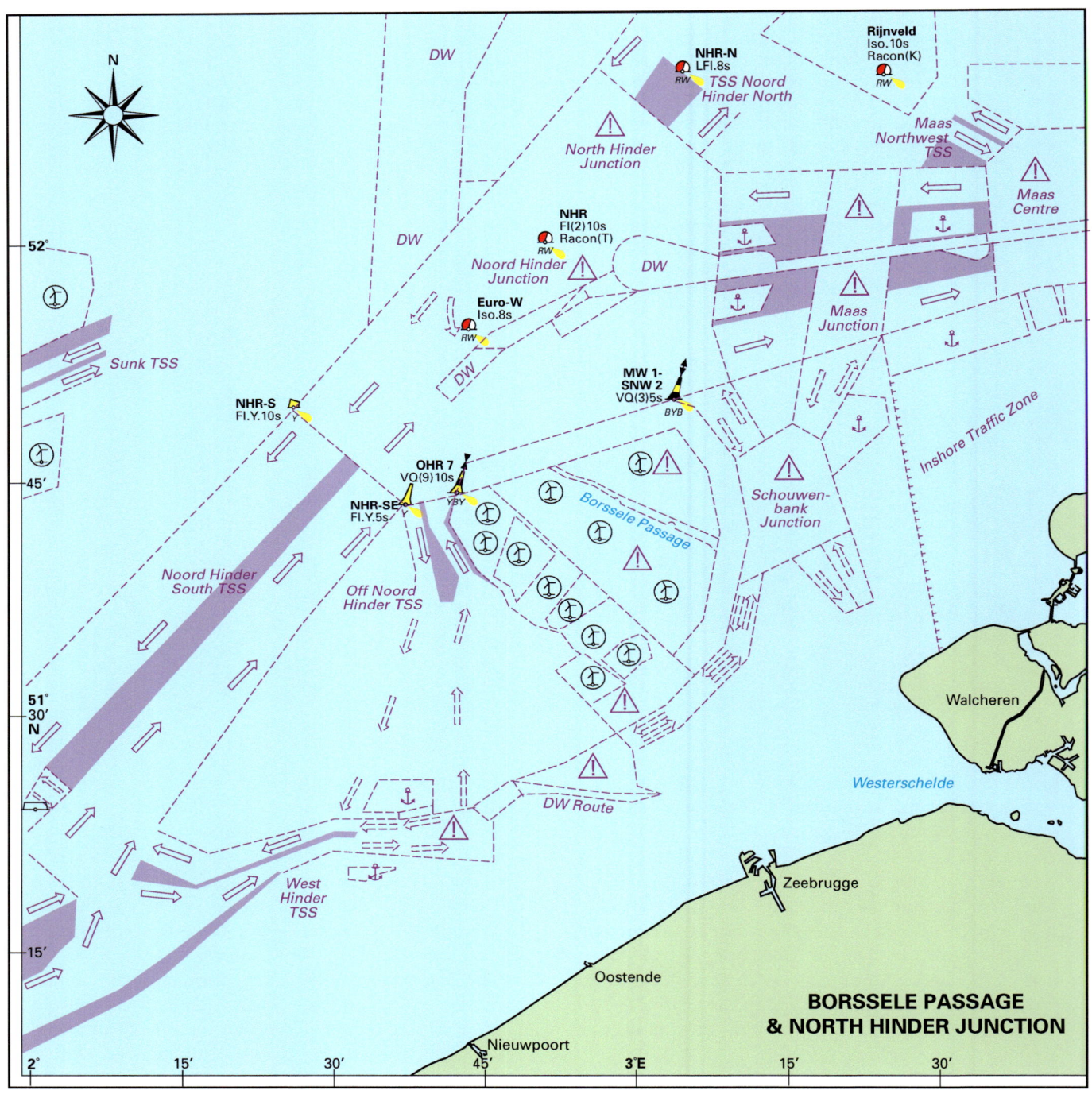

BORSSELE PASSAGE & NORTH HINDER JUNCTION

The main TSS leads northwards through the Dover Strait with a branch heading NE past the West Hinder Lt towards the approaches to the Westerschelde, with a second eastern offshoot further N near the Noord Hinder Lt buoy to Europoort. This junction point, known as the Noord Hinder Junction Precautionary Area, is the maritime equivalent of a traffic roundabout, with a 1M diameter circle round the Noord Hinder buoy acting effectively as a traffic 'island' (albeit somewhat complicated by the nearby DW vessel anchorage as well as the entrance to the Eurogeul DWR); it is an area in which vessels should be particularly careful and is to be avoided by yachts, if possible.

There is a second such area, the Maas Precautionary Area, just off Europoort, where another 1M diameter circle, Maas Centre, marked on its S side by a RW Iso.4s light buoy, acts as the roundabout. Yachts heading into the Nieuwe Waterweg for Rotterdam or coast hopping past Europoort cannot avoid entering this latter precautionary area and should keep to the landward side of it, crossing the traffic at the roadstead into Europoort at as close to a right angle as practicable. The officially recommended procedure is to call Maas Control (VHF 3) before crossing, give name of vessel, position, course, and maintain a listening watch, follow a track close west of a line joining buoys MV, MVN (south of the entrance) and Indusbank N (north of the entrance), and cross under power and in company when possible.

On the UK side of the North Sea the Sunk Traffic Scheme is complicated. It consists of an eastern 'Outer Precautionary Area' and a western 'Inner Precautionary Area' with three short Traffic Separation Schemes – North, East, and South – focusing on 'Sunk Centre', another 1M diameter anticlockwise 'roundabout' with a light float in the centre. To further complicate matters there is a north-south 'Two-Way Route' for local traffic on the west side of the Outer Precautionary Area and the South TSS, and a recommended route for the North Sea ferries to and from Harwich which passes south of the South Galloper bank. There are also 'Inner' and 'Deep Water' anchorages designated within the two Precautionary Areas. Commercial vessels must communicate with Sunk VTS (VHF 14). Harwich VTS (VHF 71) is the communications channel in the vicinity of the Harwich Deep Water Channel and the harbour itself. Yachts and small vessels are recommended to monitor these VHF channels as well as Ch 16 while crossing the area. It is not necessary to call Harwich VTS and announce your presence; if you have AIS they'll monitor you and they have excellent high-definition radar as well.

It is vital to keep a good lookout behind as well as ahead.

There are two more TSS in the region; one on the approach to IJmuiden, while the other is the Off Texel TSS which clips the most northern yacht passage covered in this book. Yachts heading for Den Helder should aim to approach well to the south to give a wide berth to this scheme.

Deep Water Routes (DWR)

As some of the largest commercial ships can draw as much as 24m (78ft) when laden, the 20m minimum depth for the traffic lanes is clearly not enough and

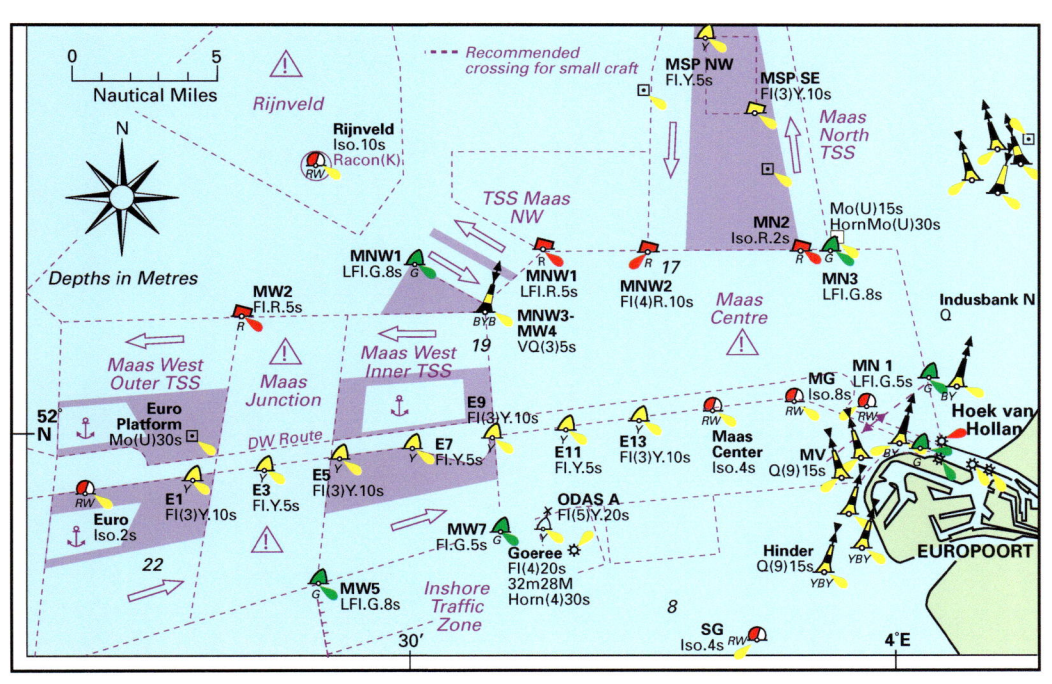

The Maas Junction is complicated and crowded with fast moving big ships. It is essential to cross in the yacht channel and only under guidance from Maas Control

PREPARATIONS AND PASSAGEMAKING

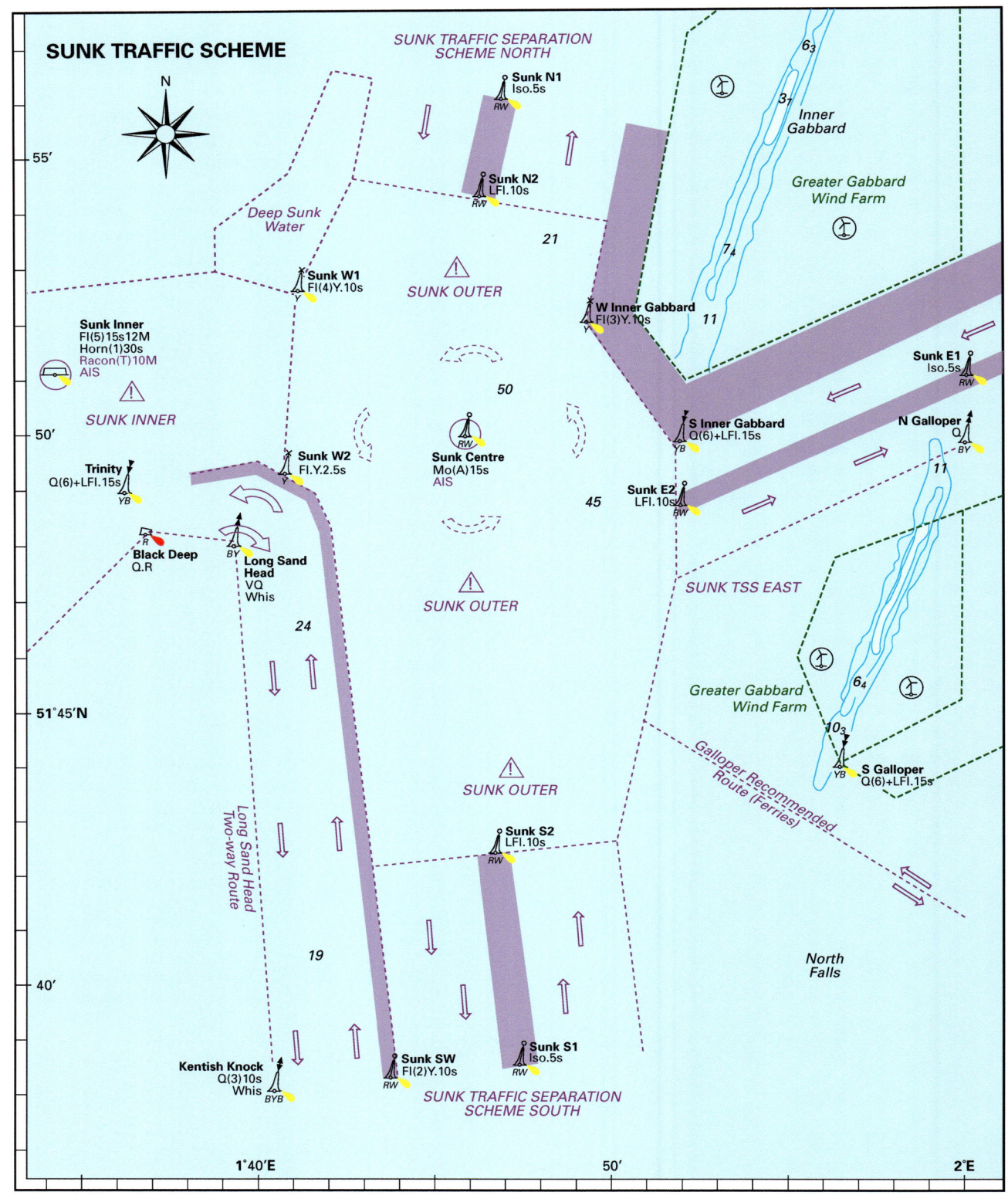

28 NORTH SEA PASSAGE PILOT

additional Deep Water Routes (DWRs), generally of 30m depth and over, have been added. Some DWRs are within the normal lanes but separated from the other shallower draught traffic. There is one northwest of the Sandettié Bank TSZ, while another forms the approach to and the Eurogeul route itself into Europoort and is in the middle of the TSZ between the two shallow-water lanes. The most extensive DWR is outside the shallower water schemes and leads northwards from the Noord Hinder Precautionary Area, with an additional northeastern branch leading into the German Bight. These separate DWRs are not divided into two lanes, although the ColRegs apply here as in the TSSs.

There is a buoyed, lit Deep Water Channel from the Sunk Inner, at the southern end of the Shipwash shoal, curving north then westwards into the Orwell estuary. There are also W-going and E-going normal-draught traffic lanes marked by a few outer buoys on either side of this channel from just off Landguard Point to about 5M offshore. Ingoing and outgoing leisure vessels must keep outside the southern edge of the channel and east going traffic lane. If you are crossing the channel, do so as near to right angles to the channel as possible, halfway between the Platters (S card) and Rolling Ground (G) buoys east of Landguard Point. A Precautionary Area stretches from the end of the channel just S of the Shipwash Sand E-wards out to sea and S-wards towards the Long Sand, with the Sunk Lanby in roughly the middle of the area. It's here that pilot boats collect, so extreme caution should be exercised crossing the area and VHF 16 should be monitored.

Inshore Traffic Zones (ITZs)

Near to coasts, special inshore traffic zones (ITZs) are designated. Rule 10(d) of the International Collision Regulations applies (see below). There is one ITZ in the area, south of Europoort and one off the two entrances of the Delta tributaries, the Haringvliet and Grevelingenmeer.

Collision avoidance

The skipper should be thoroughly conversant with the ColRegs, and is advised to brush up on these immediately before the passage, particularly Rule 10 dealing with traffic separation schemes and the rules dealing with lights, which are easy to forget yet so necessary at night in the TSSs. Observance of these rules is mandatory, and prosecution can follow noncompliance.

The rules state that we should, as far as is practicable, avoid crossing traffic lanes, but if we must, then do so on a heading that is at right angles (90°) to the flow of restricted traffic. The rule is mandatory in TSSs but is advisory for DWRs. Getting across as quickly as possible will almost certainly require firing up the engine. You can sail across but do NOT TACK; you'll get fined for doing so. You'll need to double check your position and make any necessary course adjustment to recover your route after crossing.

The safest action is to keep well out of the way of approaching ships. Often, they're going faster than 22kts, take a heck of a long time to stop and don't change course too quickly. With AIS you can identify them and, if needed, call them direct to ascertain their intentions. Any avoiding action should be

Motoring across the DWR at dusk. Keeping the mainsail up enhances the visibility of the yacht

PREPARATIONS AND PASSAGEMAKING

taken early on and not left until it is too late. Most often the safest action is to pass well clear of their stern, even if this means slowing down or altering course.

A correctly mounted radar reflector, preferably active, and bright, reliable navigation lights will help you to be seen, but never assume that a ship has seen you. Even if you transmit on AIS it is possible that the ship is not monitoring Class B signals and will therefore not have your vessel on its screen.

Aids to navigation

The small-yacht navigator tends to confirm his reckoning with as many visual fixes as possible, and Light Vessels, floats, Lanbys and the occasional light tower are particularly useful at night, although the dipping distance of the average Light Vessel from a yacht cockpit or foredeck is only about 11M (the nominal range quoted on the charts is usually 15M). In good visibility their loom over the horizon may be seen well beyond 11M.

There are few remaining long-distance offshore lights in the region on the assumption that most vessels use electronic position-fixing equipment so do not require such length of range. The Goeree Light Tower (28M) and the marks bunched near the Dover Strait (15M) have ranges as befits their importance in the TSSs, while Sunk Centre has a 16M range off the East Anglian coast. Surprisingly, the West Hinder Light Tower has only a 13M range and the Noord Hinder is only an HFP buoy.

There are 20 major onshore light locations: five on the English and 15 on the continental coasts. These vary in range between 20M and 30M: Lowestoft, Cap Gris-Nez, Dunkerque, West Kappelle, West Schouwen, West Hoofd, Maasvlakte, IJmuiden and Kijkduin (photo below). The elevations of these lights are in some cases quite high, so the dipping distances are usually above 19M, being particularly long on the Dutch coast and enabling ideal night-time or dawn approaches.

Kijkduin light tower

SOUND SIGNALS

In confined waters especially, ships will use their sirens to inform nearby craft of their planned movements. It pays the small boat skipper to know what these signals are. A short blast (•) is 1 second; a long blast (–) is 4–6 seconds.

•	I am turning to starboard
• •	I am turning to port
• • •	My engines are going astern
• • • • •	I am uncertain of your intentions
–	I am coming round the bend
— •	I am overtaking to starboard
– – • •	I am overtaking to port
– • – •	I agree you can overtake

In restricted visibility, at intervals of not more than 2 minutes

–	I am making way through the water
—	I am underway and stopped
– • •	I am restricted in my ability to manoeuvre

Vessels at anchor or aground ring bells, sound gongs or sound • – • for five seconds every minute.

Racons and AIS

Radar transponder beacons emit a Morse characteristic 'flash' on a vessel's radar screen when triggered by the vessel's radar emission and many of these have ranges of 8M or more. There are about 50 racons in the area covered by this book. We have not included lists of these, but they are marked on most charts by a surrounding circle and the symbol 'Racon' followed by the appropriate Morse character under the symbol for the buoy or light.

More and more buoys and marks are being fitted with AIS transponders, particularly important turning marks and separation zone marks for commercials; such as W. Hinder, Foxtrot 3 and Hinder 1. These are all marked on charts with the letters AIS in red italics below them.

International Port Traffic Signals

NAVIGATIONAL LIGHTS AND SHAPES

Rule 25 Motor Sailing
Cone point down, forward

Rule 26 Fishing/Trawling
A shape consisting of two cones point to point in a vertical line one above the other

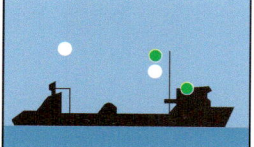
Rule 26 Vessel Trawling
All round green light over all-round white, plus side-lights and sternlight when making way

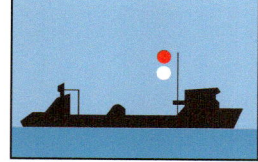
Rule 26 Vessel Fishing
All-round red light over all-round white, plus side-lights and sternlight when making way

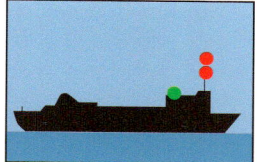
Rule 27 Not under command
Two all-round red lights, plus sidelights and stern-light when making way

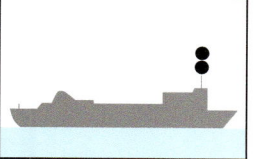
Rule 27 Not under command
Two black balls vertically

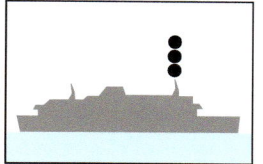
Rule 30 Vessel aground
Three black balls in a vertical line

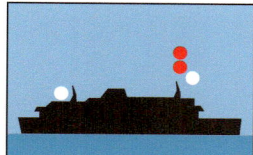
Rule 30 Vessel aground
Anchor light(s), plus two all-round red lights in a vertical line

Rule 30 Vessel at anchor
All-round white light: if over 50m, a second light aft and lower

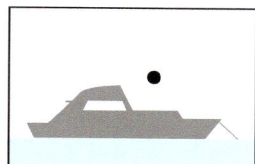
Rule 30 Vessel at anchor
Black ball forward

Rule 24 Towing by day - Length of tow more than 200m
Towing vessel and tow display diamond shapes

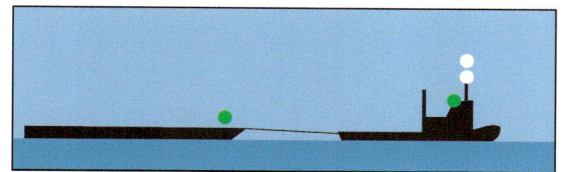
Rule 24 Vessels being towed and towing
Vessel towed shows side - lights (forward) and sternlight
Tug shows two masthead lights, sidelights, stern-light, yellow towing light

Rule 27 Dredger

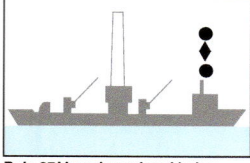
Rule 27 Vessel restricted in her ability to manoeuvre
Three shapes in a vertical line - ball, diamond, ball

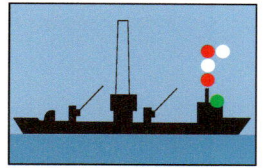
Rule 27 Vessel restricted in her ability to manoeuvre
All-round red, white, red lights vertically; plus normal steaming lights

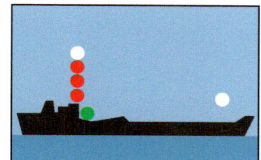
Rule 28 Constained by draught
Three all round red lights in a vertical line, plus normal steaming lights.
By day-a cylinder

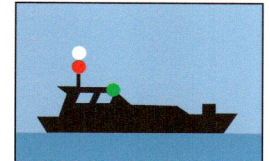
Rule 29 Pilot boat
All-round white light over all-round red; plus side-lights and sternlight when underway or anchor light

Rule 27 Divers down
Letter 'A' International Code

International Port Traffic Signals

A unified system of Port Traffic Signals (PTS) that is simple and easy to commit to memory, and uses only lights by day or night, is almost universal. The main message will always be given by three lights shown vertically. Provision is made for small vessels navigating outside the main channel to disregard the main message. This signal will be useful at large ports with a wide access channel.

Auxiliary signals may be added, as required, to the right of the column carrying the main message using either white or yellow lights. An auxiliary signal may, for example, be added to message No. 5 to give information about the situation of traffic in the opposite direction, or to warn of a dredger operating in the channel (see illustration).

Three red lights indicate 'Do Not Proceed'. Green lights indicate 'Proceed". A single yellow light displayed to the left of the column carrying main messages No.s 2 or 5, at the level of the upper light, may be used to indicate that 'Vessels which can safely navigate outside the main channel need not comply with the main message'. Local auxiliary signals employing only white and/or yellow lights are displayed to the right of the column carrying the main message. A chart of all the PTS is shown below.

Before entering harbour it's advisable to contact port control or the local VTS service by VHF (Harwich is an exception in discouraging small craft from this except in emergency) but it is essential to know the International Traffic Signals and to obey those exhibited as you enter a harbour, and particularly those of the large ports in the southern North Sea where, unlike Harwich, the entrances are physically constricted. Failure to obey these signals could result in large fines. The following ports display the signals (see where under appropriate port): Great Yarmouth, Lowestoft, Ramsgate, Dover, Calais, Dunkerque, Nieuwpoort, Oostende, Zeebrugge, Vlissingen, Den Helder.

Harwich is an open bay, and the rivers Deben and Ore are also without signals, while Southwold occasionally uses closure signals. Gravelines is an

PREPARATIONS AND PASSAGEMAKING

open channel with entry to the marina through a lock. IJmuiden is a wide entrance without an outer signal station where care must be taken before entry to the outer yacht harbour or approach to the signals for the locks. Scheveningen has an open outer entrance and special signals on an inside entrance. Blankenberge, Breskens, Cadzand and Terneuzen have yacht harbours without signals and are to be entered with care.

Hoek van Holland is another exception with a double outer entrance, one arm leading to the Nieuwe Waterweg and the other to Europoort and has special horizontally laid out signals.

IALA/IAPH/PIANC PORT TRAFFIC SIGNALS

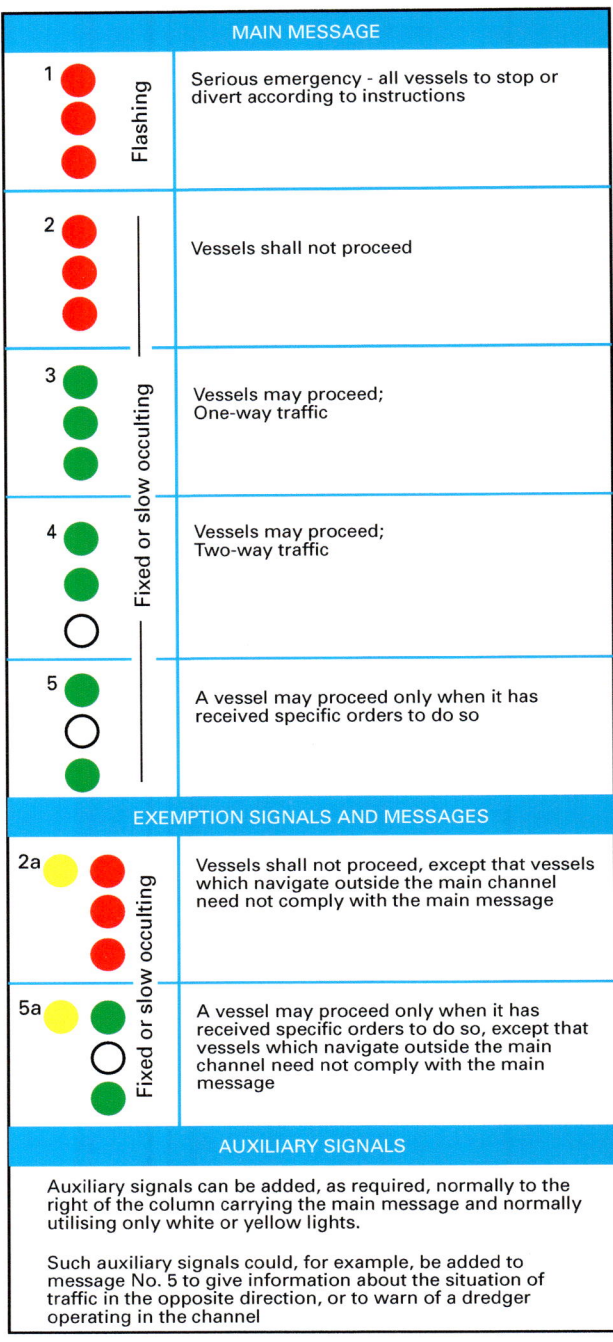

REGULATIONS AND PAPERWORK

Customs requirements

Sailors of all nationalities should ensure that they conform to local customs procedures before they embark on a foreign trip. Now that Great Britain has assumed third country status, UK sailors will need to complete Part 1 of form C1331 and post it to the Border Force office in Dover. Coming back, you'll need to fly the yellow Q flag, fill in Part 2 of the C1331 form and call up National Yachtline on ☏ 0845 723 1110 and follow instructions carefully. (As you do already when returning from the Channel Isles).

The address for the Border Force is:

UK Border Force
Yacht Reports
Freight Clearance Centre
Lord Warden Square
Western Docks, Dover
CT17 9DN

Delayed sailing

If there are any delays to your departure, or if any details on the notification change, you should contact Border Force by writing to the address that the original C1331 was sent. You should also inform the Border Force of abandoned voyages by endorsing part 2 of the C1331 with the words 'voyage abandoned' and then forward to the address that Part 1 was sent.

Passports and Schengen forms

Many of us will have several years to run on the EU red coloured passports. Issued in the UK they are still valid. However, there is a rumour that they will be withdrawn before too long, so if you've only a year or so to run it may pay you to apply for one of the new blue UK passports to save a potential hassle at the border check.

UK vessels visiting the EU must complete a crew list form in triplicate and submit one copy to the immigration office at the port of entry (the

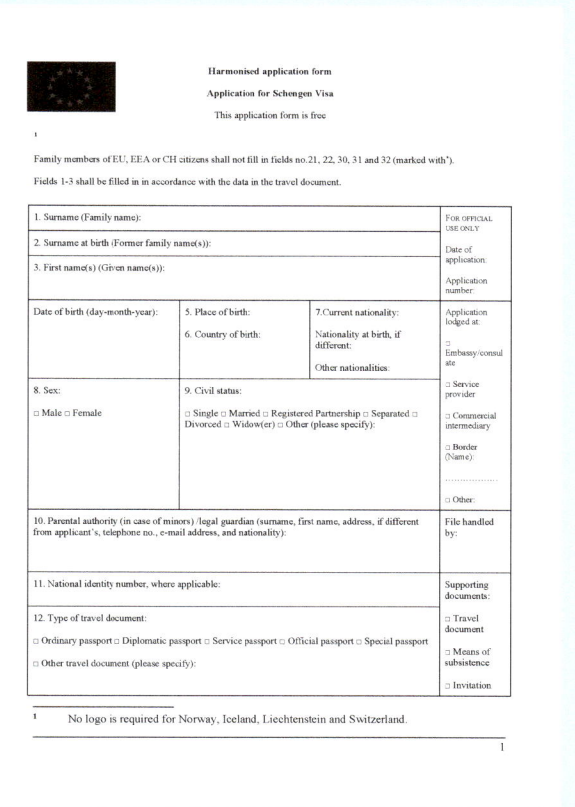

Examples of C1331 and Shengen Visa forms

REGULATIONS AND PAPERWORK

Ship's papers checklist:
- Ship's Registration docs
- Schengen forms (crew list) in triplicate
- Insurance docs
- VHF Licence
- Radio Operator's certificate
- Copy International Regulations for Prevention of Collisions at Sea
- Life raft and lifejacket service certificates (must be in date)
- 'Q' Flag
- Volumes 1 (including the Binnenvaart Politie Reglement (BPR) and 2 of the Dutch Wateralmanac
- Proof of competency (skipper)
- Fuel bills
- Ship's Log

Individual crew members:
- Passport (with at least six months left to run)
- EHIC/GHIC and private travel and health insurance as well
- Competency certificates
- Proof of financial soundness (EU requires visitors to show they have with them or access to a minimum of €55 a day to support themselves, some countries insist on seeing bank statements for the past six months)

Harbourmaster will tell you where this is) so make sure that you back this up with full original documentation, not photocopies, of all the requirements listed in the section below. The Schengen forms can be obtained from the RYA www.rya.org.uk.

You'll need to specify your return port and date when you check into the Schengen Area, as your passport must be stamped going in and out again to comply with the 90 days in any rolling 180-day period. Miss it and you may find they won't let you back in again in the future! Which is why you'll need to enter the EU and leave the EU at one of the designated ports where they have immigration officers stationed. Note that visitors to the EU must show proof of a valid return ticket on a specific date, this can be difficult for crews joining a boat via ferry or airport and you may have to furnish them with a letter designating the expected date and port from which you will be returning.

Schengen forms or crew list will be scrutinised and failure to log them with the immigration authorities on arrival will be met with stern disapproval. The generally laid-back approach to them in recent years is sadly no longer tolerated. You'll need three copies, one to leave with the immigration officer of your entry port and two on board to be scrutinised by harbour officials as you cruise.

Future changes to conditions for visa-free travel

From December 2022, non-EU nationals who do not require a visa to enter the Schengen area, will need to request prior authorisation to visit Schengen countries. This authorisation is not the same as a visa. You can apply for authorisation via the European Travel Information and Authorisation System (ETIAS). You can only apply online. The exact date on which these changes will come into force is not yet clear. You can find more information on the website of the European Commission, www.europa.eu.

Netherlands: The official ports of entry are Amsterdam, Delfzijl, Den Helder, Eemshaven, IJmuiden (Seaport Marina), Rotterdam, Terneuzen and Vlissingen. You must make sure you obtain immigration, customs, and passport clearance, for which you may need to visit another office. Yachts must be registered and are required to carry a copy of the Binnenvaart Politie Reglement (BPR) which is included in Volume 1 of the Dutch Wateralmanak. Skippers in charge of vessels of over 15m in length and/or capable of 20km/h (11 knots) or more in speed must possess: either a Dutch licence of competence to use the lakes, rivers and canals, or a Dutch licence of competence to use the Schelde Estuary, IJsselmeer, Waddenzee, Eems and Dollard. (Each of the above can be obtained in The Netherlands by special examination in Dutch).

UK sailors can produce the RYA International Certificate of Competence (ICC), or as an alternative the ICC plus the RYA shore-based Day Skipper course completion certificate. You should check with the RYA and/or with the Dutch Embassy if your vessel is in this category.

Belgium: Basically, there two ports of entry for UK yachts to log into Belgium, Oostende and Zeebrugge. As in the Netherlands, local certificates are required for fast vessels on the inland waterways and skippers of vessels more than 15m in length and capable of more than 20km/h (11 knots) under power must hold an ICC.

France: Entry ports in the north sector include Dunkerque, Calais and Boulogne. Only in inland waters is a certificate of competence required – for all vessels except those less than 5m in length and not capable of more than 20km/h (11knts). For those in charge of vessels less than 15m in length the ICC has been accepted by the authorities together with a copy of Code Européenne des Voies de la Navigation Intérieure.

Other official requirements

Insurance

It's vital you insure your boat and carry a marine insurance cover note. Most UK marine policies automatically cover the English Channel and the waters of the North Sea, but if you intend to cruise at all inside the extensive waterways of Holland, Belgium and France, it's worth checking on the extent of your coverage for inland waterways.

To minimise any legal problems of customs and other types of clearance in foreign ports, the boat must be registered with its national registration authority, be appropriately marked, and carry aboard the registration documents. In the UK there are two types of register but essentially the Part 1 Register is for larger vessels and special cases and is expensive. The Small Ships Register, administered by the MCA, is the easiest method of registering. Both Part 1 and SSR registrations need renewing every five years.

Travel/health insurance:

Before you travel, make sure you've got a valid European Health Insurance Card (EHIC) or UK Global Health Insurance Card (GHIC) or travel insurance with health cover. You may not have access to free emergency medical treatment and could be charged for your healthcare if you do not have an EHIC or GHIC when visiting an EU country. If you have an EHIC it will still be valid while it remains in date; when it runs out apply for a GHIC.

All crew members must also have suitable travel and health insurance, which must include a get you home clause, in addition to GHIC/EHIC cards. Loss of personal papers, credit cards, cash and luggage must all be covered.

Netherlands: 'Black water' discharge ban

The discharge of 'black water', i.e., toilet waste, into territorial coastal and inshore surface waters is banned. This applies to pleasure craft with a length of 2·5–24m which are not older than 1950. These craft should be installed with holding tanks (fixed or flexible), dry or chemical toilets or, what is marginally feasible in the inland waterways, their crews could choose not to use their boats' toilets but use facilities ashore. Since 2009, marinas with over 50 mooring places are required to have pump-out stations. The Regioteam Zulver Zeeuwe Water publishes a brochure (in English as well as Dutch) on the website www.vuilwater.info which gives a detailed background to the measures including a list of the Zeeland ports with facilities and suggestions on the design of holding tanks and toilet installations.

Red diesel fuel in Belgium, the Netherlands and France

Marine red diesel is still on sale to leisure vessels in the UK, despite the Government's plans to phase it out following a judgment from the European Court of Justice. It was announced in the 2021 budget that now that Britain has left the EU, red diesel will continue to be legal in yachts in the UK.

The CA's Regulations and Technical Services group (RATS) has received information from HMRC that they agree with the Istanbul Convention of 1990, which allows vessels to make visits to the EU27 and elsewhere, without import prohibitions or restrictions on propulsion fuel. This includes visiting craft with UK red marine diesel, or red dye traces, in the engine tank(s).

You'll have to pay the 100 per cent tax on any fuel purchased in the UK and keep receipts (fuel station till receipts are not recognised but the printed ones issued by most marinas are), log the date of refuelling and subsequent engine hours. Do not carry red diesel in anything other than the main tanks, nor buy any outside the UK.

Ship's stores

When we were members of the EU, we could fill the ship's store with a wide range of foods. Now we will have to declare and open our food stores to inspection and, if we have banned foods onboard, expect to have them confiscated.

You can no longer take products of animal origin, such as any food or drink containing meat or dairy, or plants and plant products (salads) into the EU. There are certain exemptions to this rule for quantities of powdered infant milk, infant food, confectionary, specialised foods, and pet feed. You can, however, bring a limited quantity of fruit and vegetables as well as eggs, egg products and honey. Restricted quantities of fish or fish products are also allowed.

In essence, you'll need to feed the crew going over but ensure the cupboard is bare on arrival. Shopping at some ports of entry will need carefully researching before you go.

Pets

You can no longer use a pet passport issued in Great Britain (England, Wales, and Scotland) for travel to an EU country or Northern Ireland. You can still use a pet passport issued in an EU country or Northern Ireland.

When travelling to an EU country or Northern Ireland, your pet needs a microchip, a valid rabies vaccination, an animal health certificate (unless you have a pet passport issued in an EU country or Northern Ireland), and proof that your dog has received tapeworm treatment if you're travelling on to Finland, Ireland, Northern Ireland, Norway or Malta. These requirements also apply to assistance dogs.

Check the rules of the country you're travelling to for any additional restrictions or requirements before you travel.

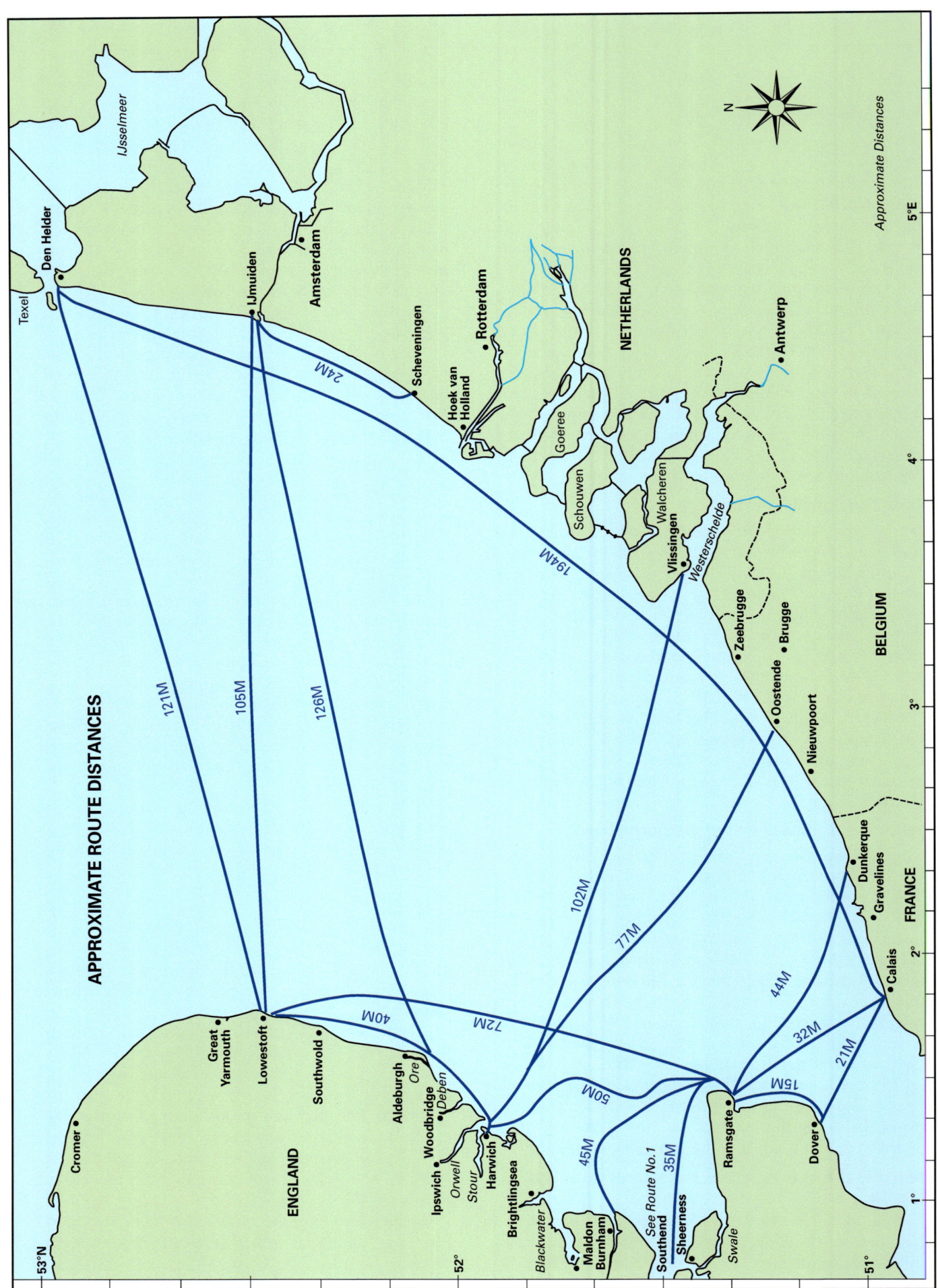

ROUTES

Introduction

Because of the increase in obstacles, such as wind farms and gas/oil installations, coupled with a major two-way deep-water route (DWR) right up the middle of the southern North Sea feeding commercial ships in and out of Antwerp, Rotterdam, Harwich and on into the Baltic, we're not left with a great deal of choice in our routes. It basically boils down to four tight areas – the most complicated is the English Channel area with a need to cross double DWRs and keep off the tails of several nasty shoal banks. The core route here is E. Goodwin LtV to Ruytingen SW (north of Calais), with variations to allow for the weather. Other core routes are: Long Sand Head (in the outer Thames Estuary) to West Hinder (off the Belgian coast); North Shipwash (off the Suffolk coast) to IJM1 (off IJmuiden); South Holm (off the Norfolk coast) to Schulpengat (Den Helder approach).

Anyone coming out of the Thames or Medway and heading for the southern ports should seriously consider an overnight in Ramsgate. Having said that, there's no easy way of getting from Ramsgate to the Schelde, so go to Dunkerque and have a break and join the coastal spine route taking the tide up the coast. For most family crews (namely husband and wife) coming out of the Essex rivers or Harwich, tiredness will have set in by the time they reach MBN buoy, so a stop at Oostende is both practicable, sensible and tide neutral. The timing is dependent on the ebb down the Swin.

These routes are by no means immutable, but provide simple passages, prominent marks, minimal hazards, minimal time within the traffic lanes, and minimal potential confusion from turning traffic by avoiding the major precautionary areas.

Plans

Plans are not to be used for navigation.

Courses on the plans

These are courses to make good (CTMG) uncorrected for tides between departure and destination points (the rhumb lines) and not the actual ground tracks which vary with time of start, tidal streams, and weather conditions. Bold lines are the CTMGs between major marks charted. Pecked lines are CTMGs across TSSs where the course to steer should be as close to a right angle to the traffic as is practicable. Do not crab across.

Distances

Nautical miles along the CTMGs charted with no allowance for tides.

Average speed

All plans and related timings are based on an assumed average of 6 kts uncorrected for tides. This represents an average-sized auxiliary sailing yacht (11m+) which sails whenever possible and motors if necessary to keep up this average. The navigator of a yacht which averages a significantly different speed from this, say half a knot or more, should recalculate the listed duration and tidal sets before planning a passage.

Tidal streams

Tidal times are expressed in hours, rounded to the nearest half hour. Passages are planned to achieve a favourable tidal set near hazards and in the coastal approaches. Once again, the navigator of a yacht which averages a significantly different speed from 6kts should re-estimate start times to achieve this objective. This can be done usually by subtracting or adding a few hours to the listed start times after comparison of the recalculated 'duration' with the listed figure.

Marks

Only major departure, turning and arrival marks are listed in detail. Groups of channel buoys are described in general terms.

Approach clearance

Except where otherwise stated, the conventional clearance is 0·5M approaching large sea marks and buoys. The major thing to keep in mind is not the charted course but the actual position of the vessel and the position of dangers in relation to its track. Above all keep a constant lookout around the full horizon; this is particularly important with the increasing use of automatic steering, radar and electronic position-fixing equipment which allow vessels to precisely home in on the marks.

Clearance in buoyed channels

Closer approach than 0·5M to marks in channels is often essential to avoid danger. The assumption here is that the cruising yacht always crosses a channel at right angles, keeps to the extreme starboard edge of a channel in either direction or, if depths permit, keeps just outside the edge of the channel.

Passage plans

Start times are only recommended; there may be other possibilities depending on the weather, and the best speed that can comfortably be maintained by the boat and other strategic objectives. The notes, however, should help to give the feel for a route even if a different start time is selected.

ROUTES

I. COASTAL ROUTES 1 AND 2

In this edition of NSPP we have introduced two coastal routes, one on the UK East Coast and the other on the mainland Europe coast. The one on the UK side runs from Ramsgate to Lowestoft Roads and on the mainland Europe side from Calais to Den Helder. Each route features a series of 'key points' where yachts can turn to take a direct route into their chosen port, river or estuary. In the information blocks we've also added 'Key Tidal Gates', points to be at when the tide turns to get the best assistance from the tidal streams.

II. SOUTHERN CROSSINGS: ROUTES 3 TO 7

The routes from Dover, Ramsgate and the Thames Estuary all converge on a single route into Calais with a spur on to Dunkerque, along the Coastal Spine, Route 2. These passages are so close together and use virtually the same crossing points on the world's busiest TSS, that we've bundled them together. The latter part of these routes is the basic guidance for several other routes which feed into them. They also cross the strongest tidal streams in the region and are often a beam reach across a wind funnelled by the Dover Strait, so sea conditions, particularly with wind against tide, are often rough. They are passages which require careful homework.

The Strait has heavy commercial through traffic and a considerable ferry cross traffic from outside as well as within the area, so vigilance is essential. The Goodwins, Varne bank, and the Ramsgate and Calais channels are well buoyed.

III. MIDDLE CROSSINGS: ROUTES 8 TO 14

If you are aiming for Belgian ports east of Oostende, then you need to take account of the peculiarity of the tidal flows on this coast. From West Hinder to Oostende you'll have around 3hrs of NE running ebb, before the powerful outflow from the Scheldt overpowers the North Sea ebb. For example, you may find that you'll have to struggle against a strong foul tide getting into Zeebrugge. It could mean a bit of a battle to go further east into the Scheldt or ports east of Zeebrugge. The sensible option is to break the journey at Oostende or Zeebrugge, if you can make it comfortably, and take advantage of a favourable tide next day.

For those yachts with radar, the Racon marks (all lit) in this area are Harwich Deep Water Channel No.1 (YM), Sunk Centre Lanby, Barrow No.3 (ECM), S Galloper (SCM), W Hinder Lt beacon, Oost Dyck Radar Tower, KB (NCM), MOW.0 (Y) Lt beacon, MOW 3 (Y) Lt beacon.

Caution: Traffic Separation Schemes
All the outward passages follow the outer southern edge of the West Hinder TSS to the lit KB (NCM). Watch out for the Oostdyck Anchorage in this area. The return passages here are reciprocal to the outward passages but in this direction take extreme care to keep at least 1M S of the buoys marking the edge of the E–going commercial traffic lane with its oncoming traffic.

Caution: wind farms
All passages involve skirting wind farms off the Essex and Kent coasts (Gunfleet, Greater Gabbard, London Array and Thanet) and S and N of the Belgian Belwind and Bligh Bank farms (see page 25).

Borssele Passage
Off the Dutch coast, to the North West of the Schelde Delta is the Borssele wind farm, through which runs a designated yacht and small craft passage. In earlier issues this formed part of a route from the N Shipwash (NCM) over the top of the Sunk Gyratory System and across to the west tip of the island of Walcheren, the north bank of the Schelde. We have not included this route as it is long, and the landfall end is difficult (the Botkil Rassen is damagingly hard!). Knowledgeable and experienced skippers may wish to use this route, but we don't recommend it for first timers or family sailors.

Netherlands 1800 Series Small Craft Charts
All these passages go to the Belgian and Dutch coasts and the compact Dutch Hydrographic Office Series 1801 charts or Imray 2120 Netherlands Chart Atlas are most useful for pilotage in the approaches and entrances to these harbours.

V. NORTHERN CROSSINGS: ROUTES 15 TO 19

Despite the distance and time involved, these passages are the simplest and least hazardous of any. They cross only the deep-water routes and the gap between the Noord Hinder and Texel TSSs, after the bulk of traffic has already turned inshore towards Antwerp and Hoek van Holland, and traffic on both coasts is lightest. There are fewer banks on either side, except those off Great Yarmouth and Lowestoft, and minor hazards are the offshore oil and gas platforms and wellheads, which are well marked and lit, therefore assisting position-fixing. One slight navigational complication: you should alter course to a right-angled heading across the DWRs.

On the UK East Coast, traffic is heaviest to the south near Harwich with its ferries and commercial ships. It is lighter near Lowestoft and Great Yarmouth where small coasters, fishing fleets and servicing vessels for oil and gas fields operate and on the Dutch side there is a similar amount and kind of traffic as well as Dutch naval traffic from Den Helder, and commercial traffic to IJmuiden.

On the minus side there are fewer vessels from whom to request aid, but even so a well-found yacht is far safer in deep water away from tricky shoal-water areas. The return passages cross the prevailing winds at a more acute angle, so it pays to study the weather forecasts carefully to avoid long periods of thrashing to windward. As with all North Sea crossings, a lee shore on the opposite side is a major hazard to be avoided.

The two critical requirements for any of these more northerly passages are for a favourable north or south tidal set during the course alteration across the DWRs, and for a favourable set into the destination harbour. On the diagonal passages into Harwich and Den Helder a flood tide is needed and on the more right-angled passages it helps to strike the coast N or S of the destination leaving an hour or two of fair tide towards the haven.

For those yachts with radar the marks (all lit) with Racons in this area are: Cross Sand (RW pillar), Smiths Knoll (SCM), BR/S (RW), P9-6 Platform (WCM) at south end of Texel YSS, SG (RW pillar) at entrance to Schulpengat.

PILOTAGE

For detailed pilotage on the East Coast refer to our sister publication *East Coast Pilot* and for pilotage on the coast of mainland Europe see *Cruising Guide to The Netherlands*, which includes the Belgian coast as well. Our two coastal spine routes, from Ramsgate to Great Yarmouth (Route 1) on the UK side and from Calais to Den Helder (Route 2) on the mainland Europe side, are for much of the time within sight of land.

WARNING SUNK SAND: CROSS-ESTUARY PASSAGES

www.crossingthethamesestuary.com and www.eastcoastpilot.com are useful for checking on the latest information reported for cross-estuary passages. Up to date chartlets, courtesy of Roger Gaspar, of the passage through the Sunk along with waypoints can be downloaded from these websites. Crossing the Estuary by the shortest routes possible is always a risk, so a number of rules should be adhered to: pick good weather; keep your eye on the echo sounder and constantly plot your position via GPS; navigate on a carefully timed rising tide which often means pushing the tide out of the surrounding rivers for a considerable period; back off and go the long way round if there appears to be any doubt – if you do go aground there is more chance of getting off if the tide is still rising; and finally report any potential chart corrections you feel should be made to the chart provider.

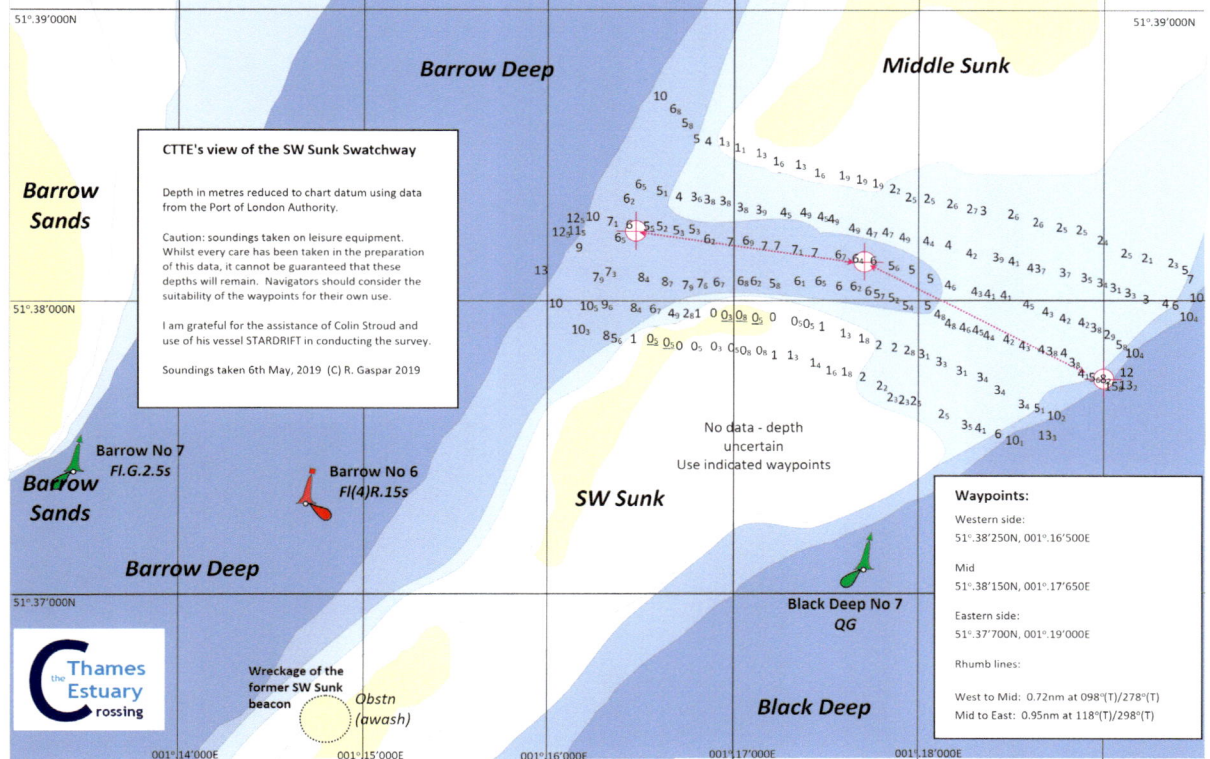

1. UK COAST RAMSGATE TO LOWESTOFT / GREAT YARMOUTH

Distance
Lowestoft 74M, Great Yarmouth 84M
Duration
14/18 hours
Charts
Imray C29, C25, 2100, C1, C8
Admiralty SC 5606, 5605, 323, 1828, 1827
Recommended start time outward HW
Dover +2
Arrival time outward
Local LW –2
Key tidal gate
Sunk Area
Recommended start time return
Local LW
Arrival time return
Dover –2
Key tidal gate
Sunk Area
Recommended stopover(s)
Greater Harwich, Shotley, SYH, Titchmarsh
Tidal streams
2+ Knts along coast

Heading north

The total distance on this route is over 70M and involves having to butt against a foul tide at some point – where to accept this is a matter for you. The ideal is to arrive at **E Barnard** (ECM) (south of Lowestoft) at HW Dover +1 or later, to take advantage of the fair tide to make the 10M from here to Gt Yarmouth, as the flows through the Stamford and Corton channels are quite strong. To achieve this, you'll need to leave Ramsgate at HW Dover +2 to take the N-flowing (ebb) tide to the west corner of the Thanet windfarm, and aim for the **Kentish Knock** (ECM). Then keeping the Long Sand Head two-way route to starboard, head for **Long Sand Head** (NCM). Your next mark will be **Storm** (SCM) across Sunk Precautionary Area (listening to Sunk VTS on VHF 14) to, **E Shipwash** (ECM), **N Shipwash** (NCM), then keep two miles off the coast to **E Barnard** (ECM). Take particular care to avoid Aldeburgh Ridge just north of Orfordness, and the proliferation of lobster pots off Sizewell power station.

N Shipwash NCM

The ebb will run out somewhere around the Sunk, so from about Long Sand Head you'll be fighting the flood to around Southwold.

You could split the journey by diverting to Harwich at Long Sand Head (note sand extends beyond rhumb line). Head to **NE Gunfleet** (ECM), then **Medusa** (G) and up the Medusa Channel. This option to split the journey would be sensible for the family-crewed boat. You could leave Ramsgate at HW Dover –1 to HW. If you break the journey north, then leave Harwich at local HW–1 and punch the last of the flood up past Felixstowe. Perhaps leave earlier still if aiming for Great Yarmouth and take the full five and a half hours of ebb up to Lowestoft. From **Landguard** (NCM) hang a left along the recommended yacht track to cross the deepwater shipping channel between **Rolling Ground** (G) and **Platters** (SCM) to run alongside the north side of the shipping lanes to **S Bawdsey** (SCM). Then cross the Shipway Channel to its eastern side and follow the red buoys to **N Shipwash** (NCM) (Racon). Keep an eye out for commercial shipping in the Shipway. Continuing northwards, stand well off the coast to **E Barnard** (ECM), south of Lowestoft, taking particular care to avoid Aldeburgh Ridge just north of Orfordness and the proliferation of lobster pots off Sizewell power station.

Divert at **N Shipwash** for the NW corner of Anglia One windfarm en route for IJmuiden (Route 15).

Just inside Lowestoft Outer Harbour

1. COASTAL ROUTES

Heading south

The route from Lowestoft Roads to Ramsgate will see you travel down the Stanford Channel to **E Barnard** (ECM) and follow the coast south about 2–2·5M off. You should leave Lowestoft at local LW to take the flood down as near to Long Sand Head as you can. As on the northward journey keep a sharp eye out for lobster pots off Sizewell Power Station and keep well east of the Aldeburgh Ridge. Aim for **N Shipwash** (NCM), followed by **E Shipwash** (ECM). Your next mark will be **Storm** (SCM) and across the Sunk Precautionary Area, followed by **Long Sand Head** (NCM), **Kentish Knock** (ECM), **NE Spit** (ECM) to Ramsgate.

East Barnard buoy

ALTERNATIVE DIVERSIONS

Ramsgate to East Coast rivers from Medway to Ore, or in changeable weather

(See plan on pages 56–57)

For **Thames** and **Medway**, leave at HW Dover -6 and punch a foul tide to North Foreland to take advantage of the west-going flood into the Thames. Keep two miles offshore to avoid the worst of the overfalls round N Foreland.

For the so called 'Overland Passage' (close inshore along the north coast of Kent) **to East Swale**, turn west once past N Foreland, and follow details in *East Coast Pilot*. For the deeper water route up the Thames and Medway, turn at **E Margate** (PHM) and follow outside the line of red buoys marking the Princes Channel to **Sea Reach No.1**. For the Medway head to the **Medway** (SWM). Keeping south of the Princes Channel will save you crossing this busy channel at the western end.

For the **Crouch and rivers further North**, leave Ramsgate at HW Dover −1 and head for **Outer Fisherman** (ECM), then through Fisherman's Gat to **Black Deep No.8** (WCM).

For the **Crouch, Blackwater, and Colne** (southern rivers), there is an unmarked swatchway across the Sunk Sand just north of **Black Deep No.7** (see page 39 for details.)

If you choose this route, then a start time of HW Dover +2 or 3 will get you **Outer Fisherman** (ECM) at slack LW with the rest of the passage on a rising tide. This shortcut takes you up Barrow Deep to **Barrow Deep No.5** (across to **N Middle** (NCM), and on to Swin Spitway, or down the Whitaker Channel to the Crouch.

For the more cautious, or for the more northern rivers, go up Black Deep to **Sunk Head Tower** (NCM), then to **NE Gunfleet** (ECM). This equates to approximately 36M or 6hrs. Turn down The Wallet for the southern rivers, or west to **Medusa** (G) and the Medusa Channel for Harwich. It should be noted that the flood starts at **NE Gunfleet** at HW Dover −5, so leaving Ramsgate at HW Dover −1 allows 8 or 9 hrs for this section. While leaving Ramsgate at HW Dover −1 is good for Harwich, it may be a bit too early for the run down into the Essex rivers via Sunk Head. For these rivers a start time of HW Dover or even HW +1 would be better.

For the **Deben and Ore**, aim just west of Roughs Tower (wartime anti-aircraft fort) to cross the Harwich shipping channel at **Cork Sand Beacon** (R post). Maintain dual listening watch to Harwich VTS on VHF 71. Both these rivers have very shallow, moving sand bars, and local chartlets are published annually on www.eastcoastpilot.com, so you need to plan these passages to arrive at the river entrances at local HW −2 to HW.

For cruises starting from the Thames/Medway, make a course up the Middle Deep or Barrow Deep with an overnight perhaps at Harwich, before joining the route at **N Shipwash**. From the Crouch a jaunt up the Barrow Deep, unless planning to over tide at Harwich. From Blackwater/Colne up The Wallet, outside the Cork and join the route at **Storm** (SCM) across the Sunk Precautionary Area. For more detail refer to *East Coast Pilot* (Imray).

Lowestoft's Lake Lothing

42 NORTH SEA PASSAGE PILOT

UK coast Ramsgate to Lowestoft / Great Yarmouth

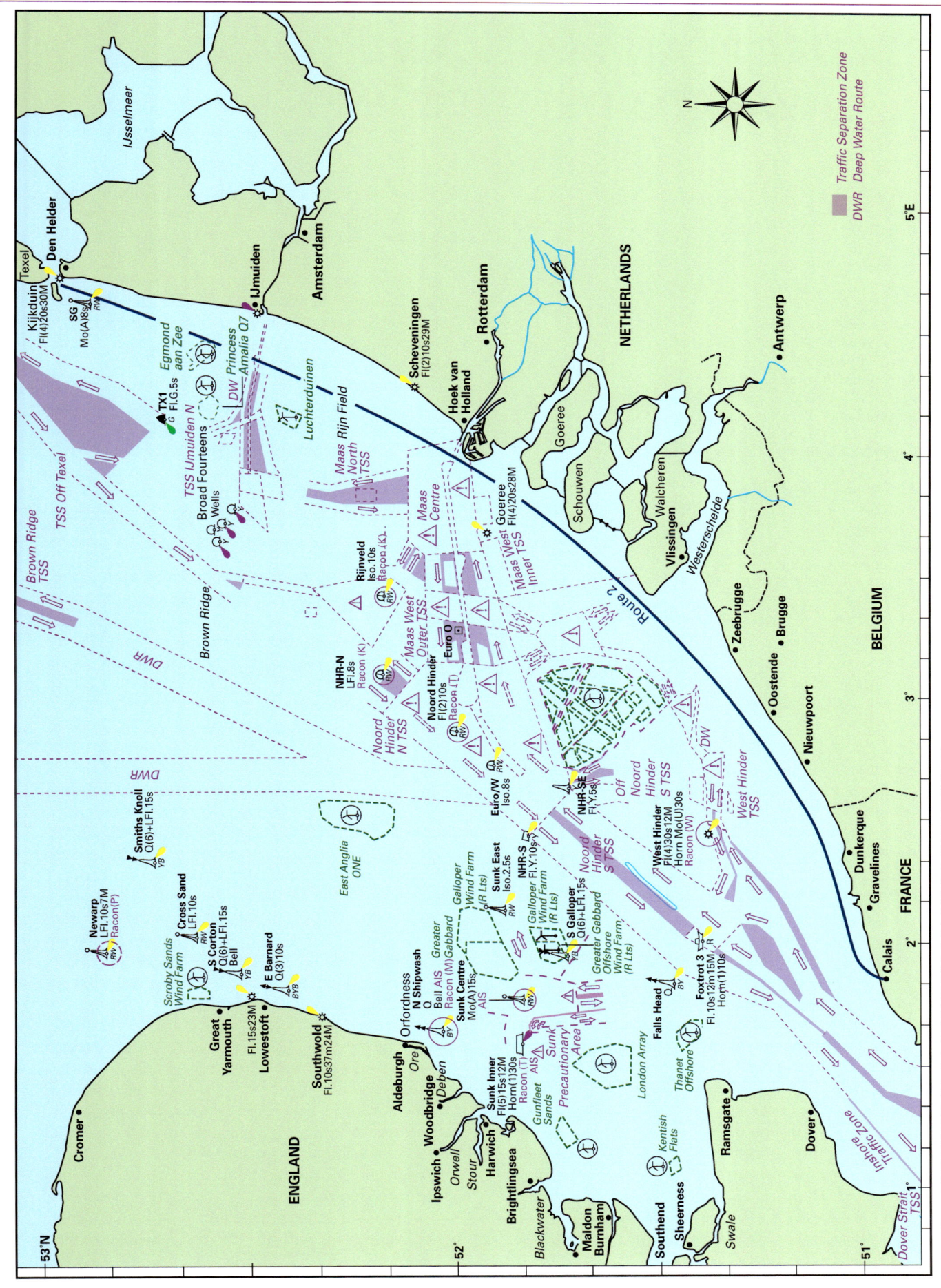

ROUTE 2 CONTINENTAL COAST FROM CALAIS TO DEN HELDER

NORTH SEA PASSAGE PILOT 43

I. COASTAL ROUTES

2. EUROPEAN MAINLAND COAST
CALAIS TO DEN HELDER

Distance
174M
Duration
30hrs
Charts
Imray C30, C25, 2110 chart pack, 2120 chart pack
Admiralty 1406, 1408
Dutch NV series 1800
Recommended start time outward HW
CA4/ HW Dover −1
Arrival time outward
Aim to pick up flood at entrance to Schulpengat
Key tidal gate
NE Akkaert, Hoek, IJmuiden, entrance to Schulpengat
Recommended start time return
Local HW DH +1
Arrival time return (critical)
Local HW −1 Calais
Key tidal gate(s)
Various
Recommended stopovers
Oostende, Scheveningen, IJmuiden
Tidal streams
Are not strong compared with the east coast. Tides run NE/SW.

Tides on the Continental coast are generally weaker than on the UK East Coast; there is less of a penalty for taking a foul tide. The tidal flow in the Westerschelde is generally counter to the North Sea streams and its impact can extend to the vicinity of Oostende. Planning passages here requires careful consideration of the tidal streams (see section on passages to and from Vlissingen on page 65). As a guide, leave departure ports around local HW to take advantage of the North Sea ebb.

The distance from Calais to Den Helder is almost 200M, so it's probably best to undertake this route in stages, especially as it's a lee shore in prevailing winds and can get quite bouncy. In bad weather, there is the option of the Standing Mast Route on inland waterways from Vlissingen to Amsterdam and beyond.

The basic coastal route runs from Calais to Oostende and then, keeping well outside the Raan Bank, to Scheveningen and then on to Den Helder. Staging ports will depend to some extent on personal preference, but the leg between Oostende and Scheveningen is long and not easily divided, except by diverting into inland waters, and has the added stress of crossing the very busy Rotterdam (Europoort) shipping channel. At the southern end you'll need to take special note of the tides.

The Raan sandbank on the northern point of the Westerschelde entrance should be given a wide berth, particularly in bad weather, passing close to **NE Akkaert** (ECM). Then follow just inshore of the well-marked inshore traffic zone.

Vessels crossing the Maas must do so at right angles, and only between **MV** (WCM) and **MN1** (G) They are required to report to Maas Entrance VTS on VHS Ch 03, with name, position, and course. From here to IJmuiden is roughly 36M.

The IJmuiden harbour entrance sticks out about a mile from the coast, and half-a-mile further out there is a large yellow beacon to be avoided.

Twenty miles north of IJmuiden, the **Petten** WCM, approximately three miles offshore, marks the edge of a shallow patch, 5M short of the **SG** (SWM) at the start of the channel into Den Helder.

Approach routes and tidal timing

The smooth sandy coast from Hoek van Holland to Den Helder is virtually unbroken. Throughout most of its length it falls steeply to soundings of 10m at only 1·5M offshore, but then slopes very gently to 20m 25M offshore in the south and slopes more steeply to reach 20m 5–10M offshore in the north, near Petten nuclear power station. The North Sea beyond is a flat basin with wide areas of 20–40m soundings and a steeper rise on the opposite UK coast.

The prevalent southwesterlies rake the Dutch coast at an acute angle and are deflected along it. Although there are no offshore banks or boulders to create tide rips, in winds over Force 4 rolling, often breaking seas do occur, which can be dangerous, especially in wind-over-tide conditions with the S-going stream. This is the case particularly near the 2M offshore strip northwards from IJmuiden to the Schulpengat. Strong northerly winds can be almost as bad when they are channelled along the coast in opposition to the N-going tidal stream.

There are only three harbours of refuge. Scheveningen and IJmuiden have north-facing entrances and provide shelter from winds from the SW quadrant but in northerlies the swell running into the entrances can be dangerous. Den Helder is well protected from most quarters but the approach through the Schulpengat can be difficult in southerly winds funnelling into the channel.

Onshore marks, as on the rest of the southern North Sea coast, are unmistakable and well charted by the Dutch Hydrographic Office: Towns, factories,

European mainland coast from Calais to Den Helder

water towers, church towers and spires rising from the flat shore – the steelworks north of IJmuiden is typical, also Petten nuclear power station, and the various high light towers. There are also several offshore platforms, some near Scheveningen and the Rijn Field near IJmuiden. Many of these features are well lit, and since the long-distance onshore lights are at 10–15M intervals there is usually no necessity to navigate blind at night, even some distance offshore.

In fog, anchoring is not usually feasible on most of this coast without running dangerously close inshore, other than inside the Schulpengat near Noorderhaaks island and the Westgat. When caught by fog, standing well off is often advisable, making sure to keep well away from the approach channels to the harbours, and particularly from the IJmuiden-Geul.

The distance from Hoek van Holland to Den Helder is 67M, a 12-13hr passage taking two tidal streams. Intervening distances are as usual more convenient for single-tide passages; Hoek to Scheveningen 14M, Scheveningen to IJmuiden 25M, and IJmuiden to Den Helder 34M.

To achieve a full stream into the Schulpengat means starting from Hoek van Holland entrance 3hrs after HW giving 2hrs of fair to slack tide, 6hrs of foul and a further 5hrs of fair to slack tide into Den Helder, arriving just after HW Den Helder. In the opposite direction, starting with a full S-going tide at HW Den Helder (6hrs before HW Hoek), or possibly an hour earlier, gives a slant of 6hrs of fair tide to begin, 6hrs against and a final 1hr of fair tide.

From Scheveningen to IJmuiden (25M) a start at –0200 HW Hoek holds 6–6·5hrs of N-going tide, and in the reverse direction a start +0300 on local HW (+0430 HW Hoek) means a similar period of S-going tide.

From IJmuiden to Den Helder (34M) you should start at –0300 HW IJmuiden (–0200 HW Hoek and –0100 LW Den Helder) which means half an hour of pushing the tide and then a full flood up to Den Helder. In reverse it is best to start –0100 HW Den Helder with the same tidal pattern as from IJmuiden, pushing a little then a full flood, arriving –0230 HW IJmuiden (–0130 HW Hoek).

Chenal Intermediaire PHB

Heading north

Leave Calais to **CA2** (R) and head north-eastwards to **DW5** (G) and enter the buoyed Passe de l'Ouest, passing the big commercial port of Dunkerque Ouest. Continue in the buoyed Chenal Intermediaire channel to Dunkerque itself. Here the buoyed channel continues for another seven miles to **E12** (SCM). From here aim for **Oostende Bank E** (G). Be careful of the marine farm in the Westdiep just east of the Nieuwpoort Bank buoy. From here you can continue to follow the coast round and drop down to Zeebrugge or continue into the Scheur Channel and round into the Westerschelde.

To continue up the coast, head from **Oostendebank E** to cross the Zeebrugge traffic lane at right angles close to **VG5** (G) and **VG6** (R) and head for **WP1** (G). Heading northeast up the Schooneveld and Steendiep, pick up the buoys marking the inshore shipping route and sail straight up to **MV** (WCM), followed shortly after by **MV C** (WCM)lt. Approaching **MV** you need to call up Maas Central on VHF 03. You need to leave **MV C** well to starboard and aim directly to **MN1** (G). You will be in the designated yacht channel across the busy Hook/Rotterdam traffic lane and must have your engine on.

On passing **MN1** aim for **Indusbank1** (NCM); from here you follow the coast about 2·5M off all the way to **SG** (RW) (Racon), the entrance buoy to the Schulpengat leading to Den Helder. Take special

Approaching IJmuiden from SW

1. COASTAL ROUTES

care crossing the entrance into IJmuiden and don't run into the large yellow post topped with a radio transmitter. Take care to stand off when passing the **Petten** (WCM) about five miles south of **SG**. (See the section on Mainland European Pilotage on page 73 for details of port entries).

Heading south

Coming south from Den Helder leave at local HW and take the ebb down the Schulpengat to **SG** (RW) (Racon) passing well clear of the **Petten** (WCM) about 5M further south. Staying about 2·5M off the coast, and passing inshore of the Egmond wind farm, set a course for **Eveline** (WCM) crossing the IJ Geul at right angles. From here to the **Indusbank N** (NCM) north of the Maas channel it's a clear run. At **Indusbank** aim for **MN1** (G) calling up Maas Central on VHF 03 for permission to cross. Motor sail to **MV C** (WCM) and pick up the buoys marking the inshore traffic route and following them southwestwards down the Steendiep and Schoonveld to **WP1** (G) followed by **VG6** (R) and cross the Zeebrugge traffic lane at right angles to **VG5** (G). You can turn east here to enter Zeebrugge or northeast into the Scheur Channel and the Westerschelde.

From **VG5** aim for **Oostendebank E** (NCM) (from where you can head eastwards into Oostende). Then continue on to **E12** (WCM) at the start of the buoyed Passe de Zuydcoote channel towards Dunkerque about 7M away. Be careful of the marine farm in the Westdiep just east of the Nieuwpoort Bank buoy. The inshore channels to **DW5** are well buoyed. It's a straight run then to **Calais Approaches** (WCM) and the channel into Calais.

Note For any route terminating at Calais make sure you arrive at least one hour before local HW, to ensure you have time to lock into the marina. You may have to wait outside if ferry traffic is heavy.

BAD WEATHER ROUTES INLAND

On entering the Dutch inland waterways to use the bad weather routes below you should have on board an ATIS-enabled VHF radio set which you should activate.

In bad weather it pays to go inside, Vlissingen to Rotterdam, Rotterdam to Amsterdam, and then Amsterdam to Den Helder. The routes are long but rewarding, especially for young crews, and they can be a holiday on their own. There are many opening bridges en route but some delightful wide-open sailing lakes in Dutch windmill countryside. Crossing the IJsselmeer requires caution particularly for deeper draught yachts since there are many soundings of less than 3m. In strong winds a nasty choppy sea can build up, and it is possible to become embayed on one of the many potential lee shores. However, there are many interesting harbours of refuge.

Storm off Scheveningen entrance

Buoy in Passe de Zuydcoote

E12 buoy at the start of the Passe de Zuydcoote

Yacht convoy up the Noord Holland Kanal on one of the mast-up inland routes

European mainland coast from Calais to Den Helder

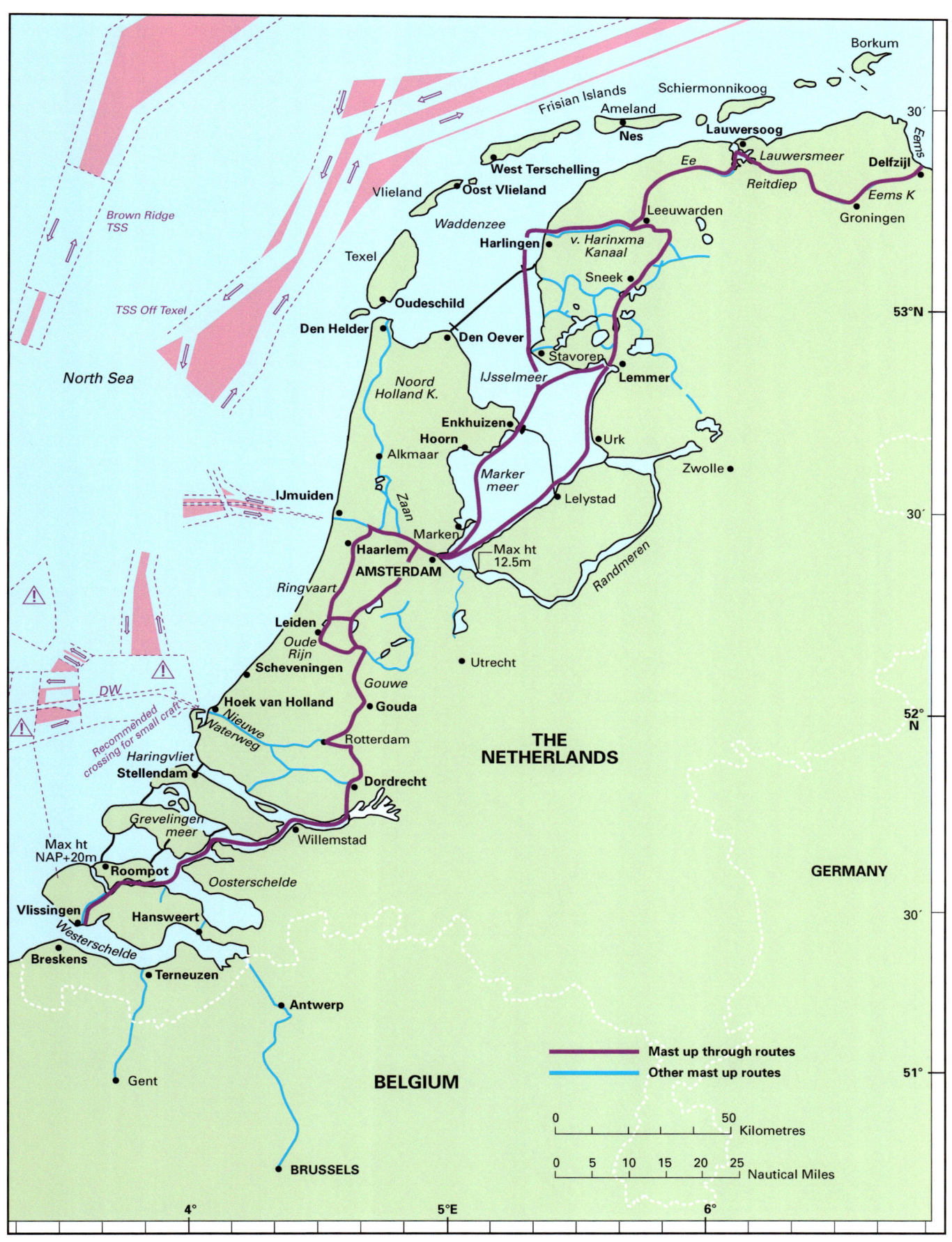

II. SOUTHERN CROSSING ROUTES

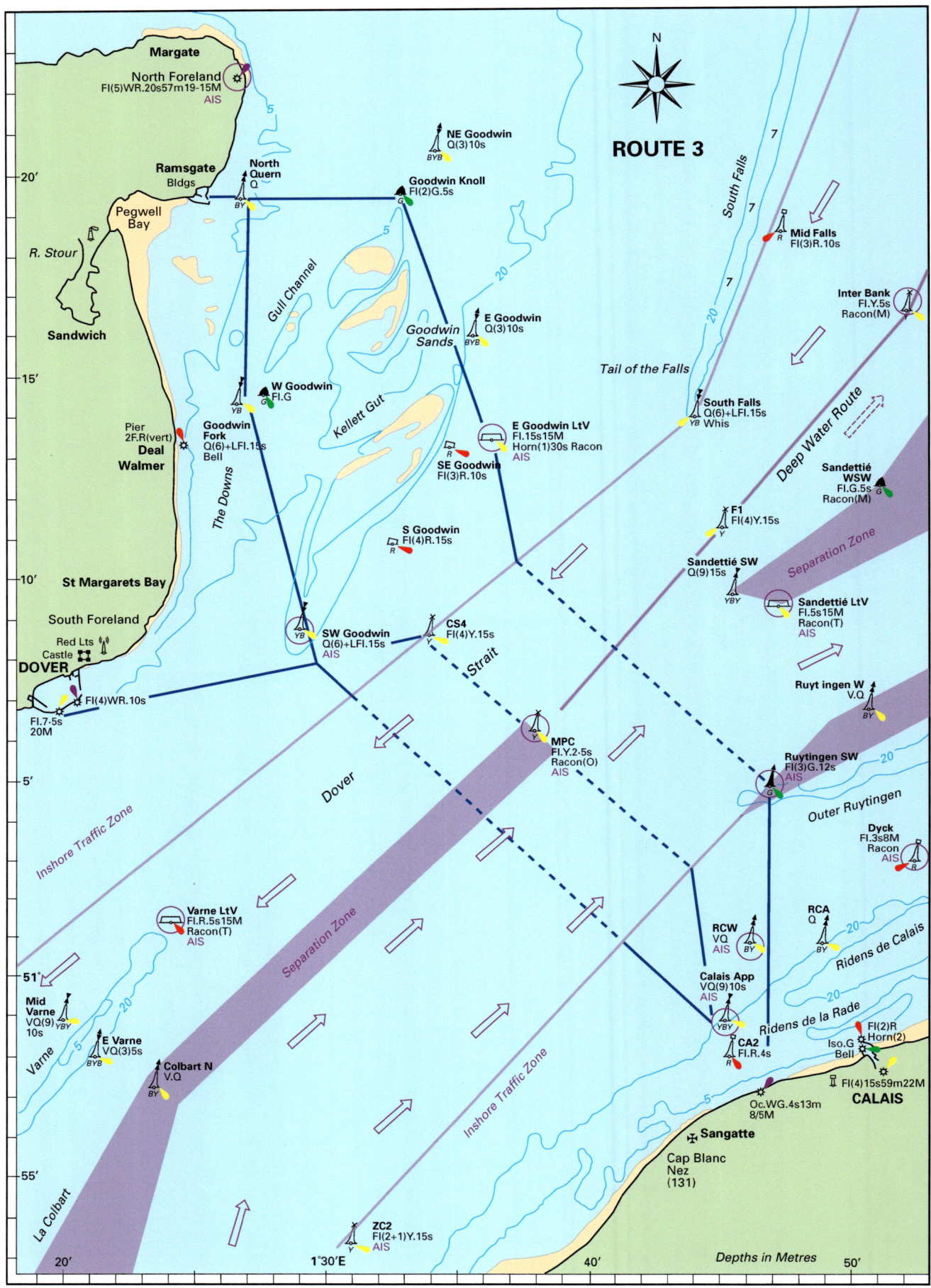

3. RAMSGATE OR DOVER TO CALAIS

Ramsgate to Calais

Distance
32M
Duration
5·5hrs, 1 tidal set
Charts
Imray C8, 2100 chart pack
Admiralty 323, 1351, 1827, 1828, 1892
Recommended start time outward HW
Dover +6,
Arrival time outward
HW Dover −0.5 HW Calais −1
Key tidal gate
Arrive Calais at Calais HW −1
Recommended start time return
HW Dover −1.5, HW Calais −2
Arrival time return
HW Dover +4, HW Ramsgate +3.5
Key tidal gate
Depart Calais at Calais HW −2
Tidal streams
Off Ramsgate N-going starts at HW Dover −1 and S-going at HW Dover +5, i.e. at about the same time as off Dover and Calais

There are two routes from Ramsgate to Calais, both of which will involve quite strong cross tides. Each aims to arrive at Calais at HW −1 to ensure entry through the bridge into the marina.

The first, going north and outside of the Goodwins (via **Goodwin Knoll** (G), **E Goodwin** (ECM), **E Goodwin** (Lt Flt) across the TSS to **Ruytingen SW** and then due S to **CA2**. At Ruytingen SW you can head up the coast to Dunkerque as well. In moderate to good weather conditions, you should be able to cross the banks on the second half of the rising tide to **CA2**. The tide will be slack, and it may be a race to enter the tidal lock in Calais.

The second route is south of the Goodwin banks via the Gull Channel to **Goodwin Fork** (SCM), **SW Goodwin** (SCM) and straight across the TSS to **CA2**. The tide in the Gull can be quite strong as the stream gets squeezed between the Goodwins and the shore. The first half of the outward passage can be done in most conditions, being well protected by the Goodwins as well as by the land, and in bad weather Dover is always an alternative refuge if the Strait looks rough.

Calais to Ramsgate

On the return trip it's vital to take the first bridge lift in Calais, 2 hrs before HW. Motor against the tide along the channel buoys to **CA2**, or in good weather cross the Ridens shoal. Alter course to cross the TSS at right angles and finally, when clear of the lanes, make a down-tide correction for the **E Goodwin** (ECM). Then head for the vicinity of **Goodwin Knoll** (G) and follow the southern edge of Ramsgate Channel into Ramsgate.

Looking across Ramsgate Harbour from the east pier. Entrance on left, with Outer Western Marina next
© *Beata Aldridge / Dreamstime*

II. SOUTHERN CROSSING ROUTES

Dover to Calais

Distance
25M
Duration
4–5 hrs, <1 tidal set
Charts
Imray C8, 2100 chart pack, 2110 chart pack
Admiralty 323, 1351, 1698, 1892
Recommended start time outward HW Dover −6hrs
Arrival time outward
HW Dover −0·5 HW Calais −1
Key tidal gate: Arrive Calais at Calais HW −1
Recommended start time return
HW Dover +5·5 HW Calais +5 (Hang on buoy in harbour)
Arrival time return
HW Dover −2 to −1
Key tidal gate
Depart Calais at Calais HW +5
Tidal streams
At both Dover and Calais NE-going starts at HW Dover −1 and SW-going at HW Dover +5

The route from Dover is probably the most difficult route to assess as strong cross tides will take you well up or down channel from your target route. You can't, however, make the usual course allowance for the tide because of the TSS. Times are therefore certainly going to be longer than that expected for the distance. The crunch point will be arrival at Calais (HW−1) in time to go through the bridge into the marina; otherwise, you hang on a white buoy in the inner harbour.

On leaving Dover head ENE towards **CS4** then head for **CA2** (R), to cross the traffic lanes at right angles you'll need to make a tidal correction for **CA2** when well clear of the lanes, then follow the channel buoys into port.

Approaching Calais, it's important to monitor Calais Port Radio on VHF 17. You must obey the International Port Traffic Signals (IPTS) and only enter when allowed to do so. If lights forbid entry, then clear the entrance channel and wait. The port is busy with a steady stream of ferries and not a great deal of space to circle around.

Calais to Dover

Coming back it's vital to take the first bridge lift in Calais, 2 hrs before local HW. You'll have to punch the tide along the approach channel. Immediately on rounding **CA2** alter course to cross the TSS at right angles, and finally make a down-tide correction for Dover when well clear of lanes.

Passing Dover cliffs

Looking ENE over Calais yacht harbour basin and the new harbour extension © *Inglebert Valery / Dreamstime.com*

4. RAMSGATE OR DOVER TO DUNKERQUE

See plan page 53

Ramsgate to Dunkerque

Distance
44M
Duration
7+hrs, 1.5+ tidal sets
Charts
Imray C30, 2100 chart pack, 2110 chart pack
Admiralty 323, 1350, 1827, 1828, 2449
Recommended start time outward
HW Dover −5
Arrival time outward
HW Dover +3, HW Dunkerque +2
Key tidal gate
Ruytingen SW Dover HW −1
Recommended start time return
HW Dover −5
Arrival time return
HW Dover +3, Ramsgate +2.5
Key tidal gate
Ruytingen SW Dover HW −1

A direct route out to the **NE Goodwin** (ECM) buoy and straight to Dunkerque Port Est is not recommended since it crosses the Sandettié, Ruytingen and Dyck banks, which are uncomfortable and dangerous in anything above Force 4. It also crosses a wide section of diverging TSS lanes causing complicated course changes. The route recommended below is a dogleg so in NE or SW weather there are easy and difficult stretches in each direction. All the traffic, weather hazards and other advice described for Route 3 apply.

The target crossing point to achieve a right angle crossing of the TSS from either port is **CS4** to **Ruytingen SW** (G). Alter course in the vicinity of **Ruytingen SW** towards **Dyck** (Fl.R.4s), on to **DW5** (Q.G.) and follow the buoyed Passe de l'Ouest and the Chenal Intermediaire and past the entrance to Dunkerque Port Ouest, and continue to Dunkerque, Port Est entrance, and the yacht basin within.

Dunkerque to Ramsgate

Coming back keep to the starboard side of the buoyed channel to **Haut-Fond de Graveline** (WCM). Again, a slack then NE-going tide from the vicinity of Ruytingen SW (G) buoy will give a good northerly tidal drift on the right-angled heading across the TSS, pushing the vessel towards the **E Goodwin LtV** and on to the **NE Goodwin** (ECM), then nearing the final cross-tide approach from **Goodwin Knoll** (G) buoy to the Ramsgate channel on a slackening tide. Follow the southern edge of the channel into the harbour.

Approaching Dunkerque at dawn from the north

II. SOUTHERN CROSSING ROUTES

Distance
40M

Duration
7 hrs, 1+ tidal sets

Charts
Imray C30, 2100 chart pack, 2110 chart pack
Admiralty 323, 1350, 1827, 1828, 2449

Recommended start time outward
HW Dover −1

Arrival time outward
HW Dover +6, HW Dunkerque +5

Key tidal gate
Depart Dover at Dover HW −1

Recommended start time return
HW Dover −5,
HW Dunkerque +4

Arrival time return
HW Dover -1

Key tidal gate
Arrive Dover at Dover HW −1

Tidal streams
As these routes are a dogleg via the Ruytingen SW buoy it is essential to catch the turn of tide N to NE in the vicinity of this mark on both outward and return routes. The stream turns NE-going at this point at HW Dover −1. At both Ramsgate and Dunkerque NE-going starts at approximately HW Dover −1 and SW-going at HW Dover +5.

Dover to Dunkerque

On leaving Dover head east-northeast towards **CS4** then aim for **Ruytingen SW** (G). Close to **Ruytingen SW** head for **Haut-Fond de Graveline** (WCM) and take the NE-going tide keeping well N of the buoyed channel to the entrance of Dunkerque Port Ouest and continue along the coast to Dunkerque Port Est entrance and the yacht basin inside.

Dunkerque to Dover

Coming back to Dover, follow the return route for Ramsgate. The NE-going tide will push the vessel out the far side of the TSS at a point, depending on strength of tide, in the vicinity of the **E Goodwin LtV**. At **E Goodwin LtV** turn southwest to the **S Goodwin** (R) and on to **SW Goodwin** (SCM) to Dover E entrance.

Chemical plant N bank Dunkerque

Entering Dover from E

Dunkerque entrance from E

Ramsgate or Dover to Dunkerque

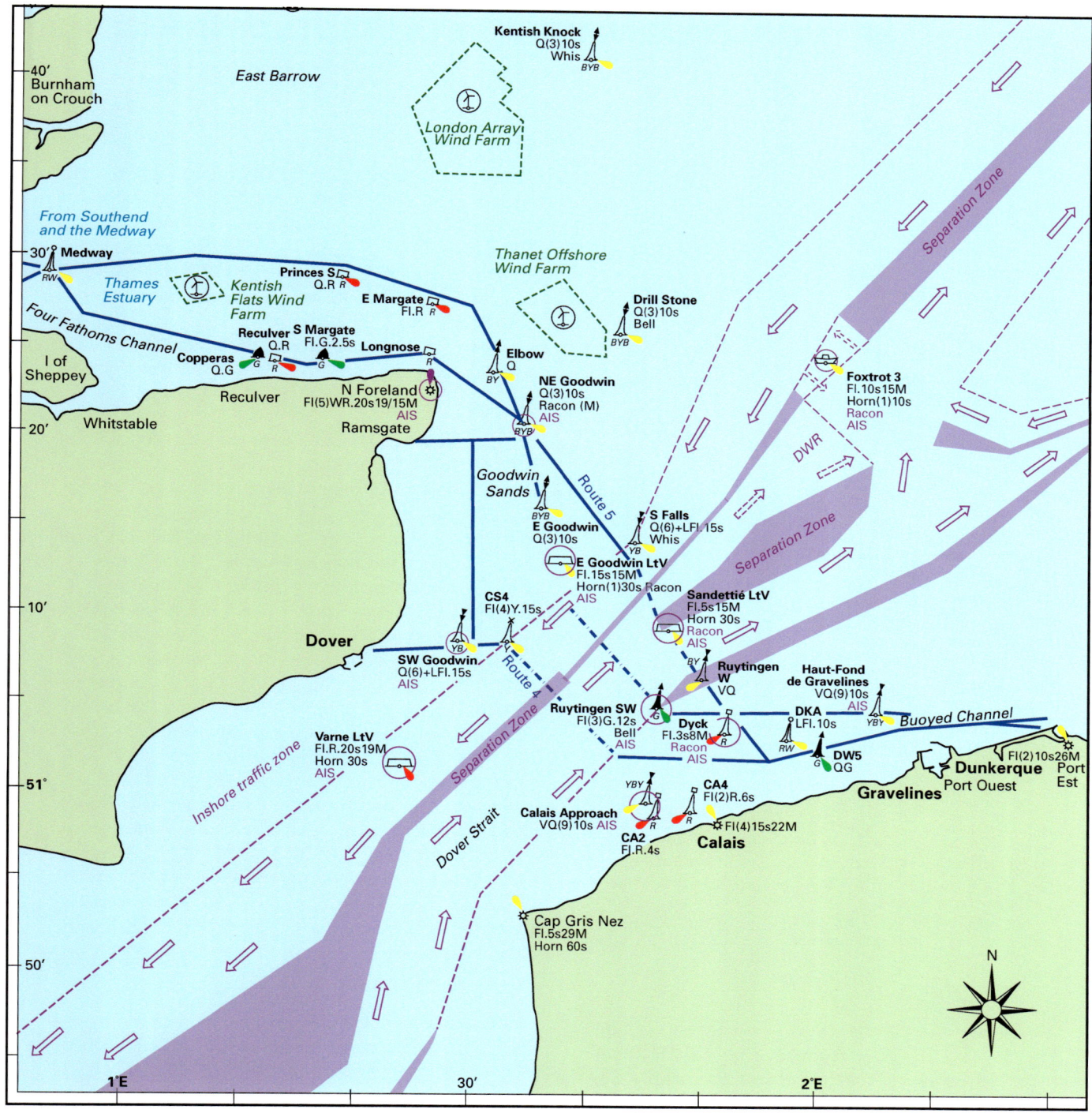

ROUTES 4 AND 5

II. SOUTHERN CROSSING ROUTES

5. THAMES AND MEDWAY TO CALAIS

See plan on page 53

Distance
67M
Duration
11+hrs, 2 tidal sets
Approach routes
See East Coast Pilot, Thames Estuary and North Kent Coast
Charts
Imray C1, C8, Y7, 2100 chart pack
Admiralty 323, 1185, 1351, 1607, 1892
Recommended start time outward
HW Dover, HW Sheerness −1·5
Arrival time outward
HW Dover −0·5, HW Calais −1
Key tidal gate
North Foreland HW Dover +5
Key tidal gate
Arrive Calais at HW Calais −1
Recommended start time return
HW Dover, HW Calais −0·5
Arrival time return
HW Dover −1, HW Sheerness −2·5
Key tidal gate
North Foreland HW Dover +5
Key tidal gate
Depart Calais at HW Calais −2
Tidal streams
From Sea Reach No 1 tides start flowing E out of the Estuary at HW Sheerness (HW Dover +1·5). North Foreland is the critical point, and at HW Dover +5 the tidal stream 'turns the corner' S towards Calais. At Calais NE-going (unfavourable) starts at HW Dover −1·5. Returning: NE-going (favourable) tide starts at HW Dover −1. At NE Spit, the tide turns ingoing/westwards into the Estuary at HW Dover −4, so it is impossible to avoid motoring hard to push some foul tide albeit a weakening to slack stream for 2hrs or so into the Princes Channel. Arriving at North Foreland by HW Dover +5 is critical; arrive any later and you'll have to stem a strong S-going stream.

Distances, times, tidal sets, and most of the directions are the same from Medway (SWM) buoy in the Medway approach as from the nearby Sea Reach No1 on the Thames. These are popular passages although the beginner tends to break the journey at Ramsgate, particularly on the return where the tides are more difficult. A third of each passage crosses the throat of the Dover Strait while the other two-thirds follows the Thames Estuary channels and sandflats. Again, winds tend to be SW or NE, into and out of the Estuary rather than across. The worst conditions are generated by E to N winds due to their much longer fetch. Since the passage is a dogleg, part of it is usually to windward and part freed off.

Several of the passages in the Estuary are out of sight of land but are well marked and in addition to the immense number of lit and unlit buoys you're never far from one of the towers, wrecks and beacons that litter the area. For those yachts with radar the marks (all lit) with Racons in this area are: **Sea Reach No.1** (Y), **Barrow No.3** (ECM), **NE Goodwin** (ECM), **E Goodwin LtV**, **Sandettié LtV** (see photo on page 59), **MPC** (Y), **Varne LtV**, **Dyck** (R).

Thames to Calais

Leaving from around **Sea Reach No.1** the first 1-2hrs will be against the stream. Follow the southern edge (R buoys) of the Princes Channel. This part of the route follows the extreme southern edge of the South Oaze Precautionary Area to **Red Sand Tower**, **E Red Sand** (R), and the **Princes Channel** (R) to **Princes S** (R). Then take the strong favourable stream to **E Margate** (R), **Elbow** (NCM) and the **NE Goodwin** (ECM) and correct your course across the tide towards **S Falls** (SCM). A right-angled course across the traffic lanes will take you to **CA4** (R) and then turn to follow the channel buoys into Calais. In moderate to good weather, you may be able to cross the banks on the second half of the rising tide. The same applies to the return passage from Calais.

Vessels transiting from the East Swale will almost certainly take the so called 'Overland Route' close inshore across the Kentish Flats, missing the Kentish Flats wind farm, and joining the Thames route at the **Elbow** (NCM). Details of this local route can be found in *East Coast Pilot*: Chapter 18, The North Kent Coast.

Calais to Thames

Coming back, lock out of Calais inner harbour as early as possible on the rising tide. It may be better to lie in the outer harbour to start promptly and avoid the possibility of missing the tide at North Foreland and having to stop at Ramsgate. Follow the channel buoys to **CA4**, rounding to cross the traffic lanes at a right angle. The NE-going tide will push the vessel out the far side of the TSS at a point, depending on strength of tide, in the vicinity of the **E Goodwin LtV**. Then take a tide-corrected course east of **E** and **NE Goodwin** (ECMs), **Elbow** (NCM) and **E Margate** (R), by which time some motoring will be required to catch a favourable tide back along the Princes Channel. As a sensible alternative, a night in Ramsgate to catch a favourable tide into the Thames is probably preferable.

6. ESSEX RIVERS TO CALAIS

See plan on page 56 / 57

Distance
85M
Duration
14hrs, 2 tidal sets
Charts
Imray C1, C30, 2000 chart pack, 2100 chart pack
Admiralty SC5607, SC5605
Recommended start time outward
HW Dover –3
Arrival time outward
HW Dover –0·5, HW Calais –1
Key tidal gate
Arrive Calais at Calais HW –1
Recommended start time return
HW Dover –1, HW Calais –1·5
Arrival time return
HW Dover –1, HW Burnham-on-Crouch and Bradwell (Blackwater) –2
Key tidal gate
Depart Calais at Calais HW –2

There are several routes out of the Essex rivers. The longer and perhaps safer one from the Crouch, certainly for the first timer, is up the Kings Channel and north of the **Sunk Head Tower**, while from the Blackwater and Colne it's up the Wallet to NE Gunfleet. Another is via an unmarked swatchway through the Sunk Sand a little up the Black Deep from Fisherman's Gat (see page 39 for Sunk Sand details.)

Distances, times, and tidal sets are the same from the Nass Beacon in the Blackwater as from the Inner Crouch buoy. You'll need to cross several Estuary swatchways and zigzag around the banks and wind farms and cross the shipping channels at right angles, so there are a number of course changes, some beating and use of engine. Estimating tidal depths is critical in crossing the banks and if in doubt do not hesitate to detour.

There are six wind farms in the area to be factored into route plans. The River Crouch to Calais, for example requires navigating past the Gunfleet and London Array farms via Fisherman's Gat Precautionary Area. Harwich-Calais route passes between the Gabbard and London Array, and E of the Thanet farms. The Southend-Calais routes pass the Kentish Flats and Thanet farms. This certainly means giving a wide berth to some of the major shoal areas in the Estuary.

Caution In addition to the hazard of skirting several windfarms, this passage also clips the edge of **Outer Tongue DW Anchorage** some 2–3M north of the **NE Spit** buoy, so watch out for large anchored ships.

Essex rivers to Calais

Targeting to arrive in Calais by local HW –1 means leaving the Essex rivers while they are still flooding. However, if you choose to use the Sunk Sand swatchway (see page 39 for details) the distance is reduced to 67M or a travelling time of 11hrs, so you won't need to leave so early, and you'll have less tide to punch. Punching a foul tide is inevitable. The fair tide starts at **NE Spit** buoy assisting the passage to Calais. Join Route 3 at **NE Goodwin**.

Working your tides is essential in the Thames Estuary, so it might pay you to break your crossing at Ramsgate (and follow Route 3 from there); this would give you an ebb up to **Sunk Head Tower** and a flood down Black Deep and beyond.

Calais to Essex rivers

This will be a difficult tidal route. If in any doubt it pays to break the journey at Ramsgate and cross the Thames Estuary the following day. The NE-going tide starts at Calais at HW Dover –1. The north going ebb tide will run out around **Outer Fisherman**, so you'll face some foul tide through Fisherman's Gat and up the Black Deep, but a fair tide will help the last stretch back into the Essex Rivers (20-25M).

Leave Calais at the first bridge lift, at HW –2hrs and motor against the tide along the channel buoys to **CA2**, or in good weather cross the Ridens shoal. Alter course to right angles to the TSS. The NE-going tide will push the vessel out the far side of the TSS at a point, depending on strength of tide, in the vicinity of the **E Goodwin LtV**. When clear of the lanes make a down-tide correction for the **E Goodwin** (ECM). From off N Foreland aim for **E Margate** (ECM), then to **NE Spit** (ECM) and to Fisherman's Gat. North Foreland should be rounded by about HW Dover +4-5 with some remaining fair or cross-tide to Fisherman's Gat.

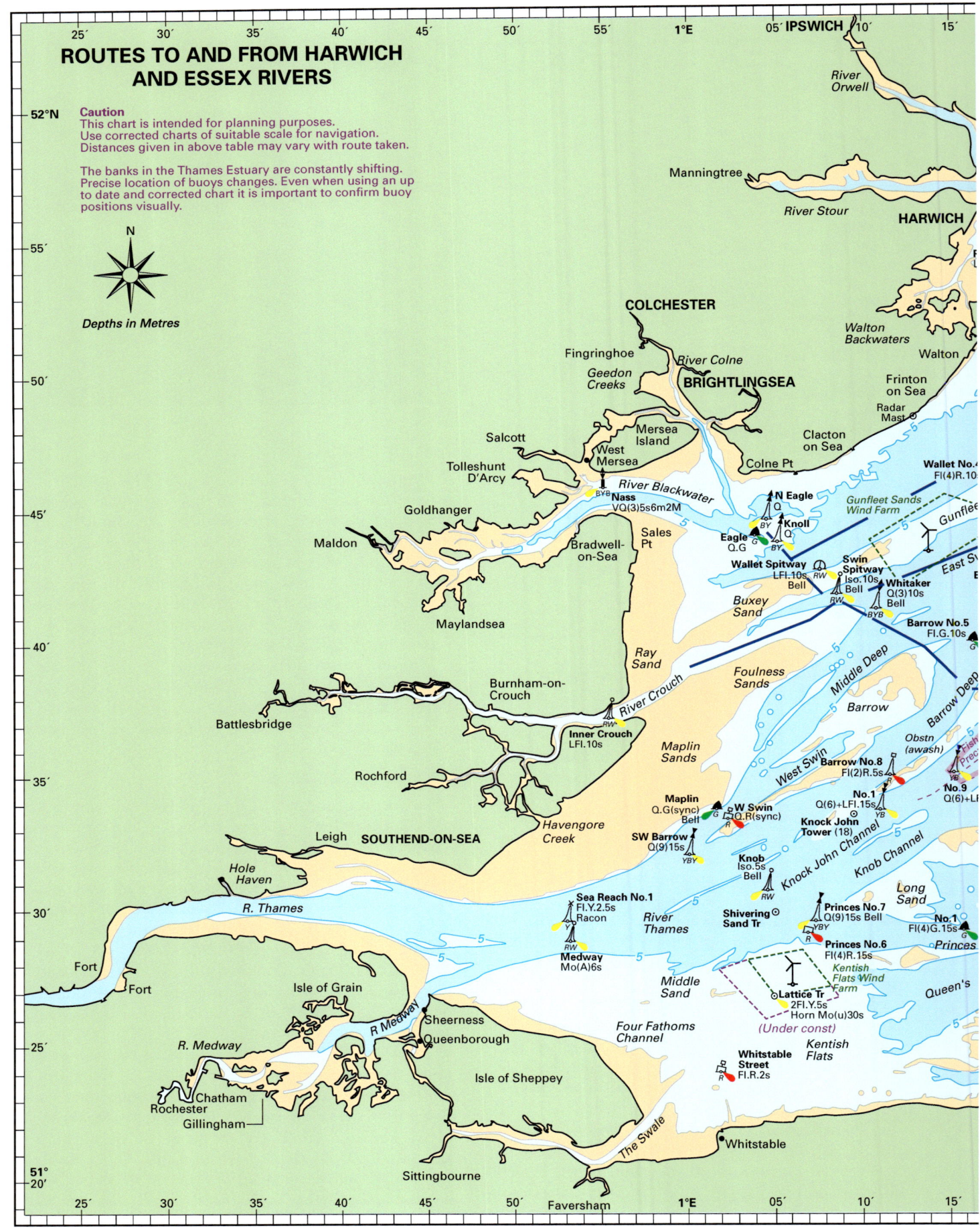

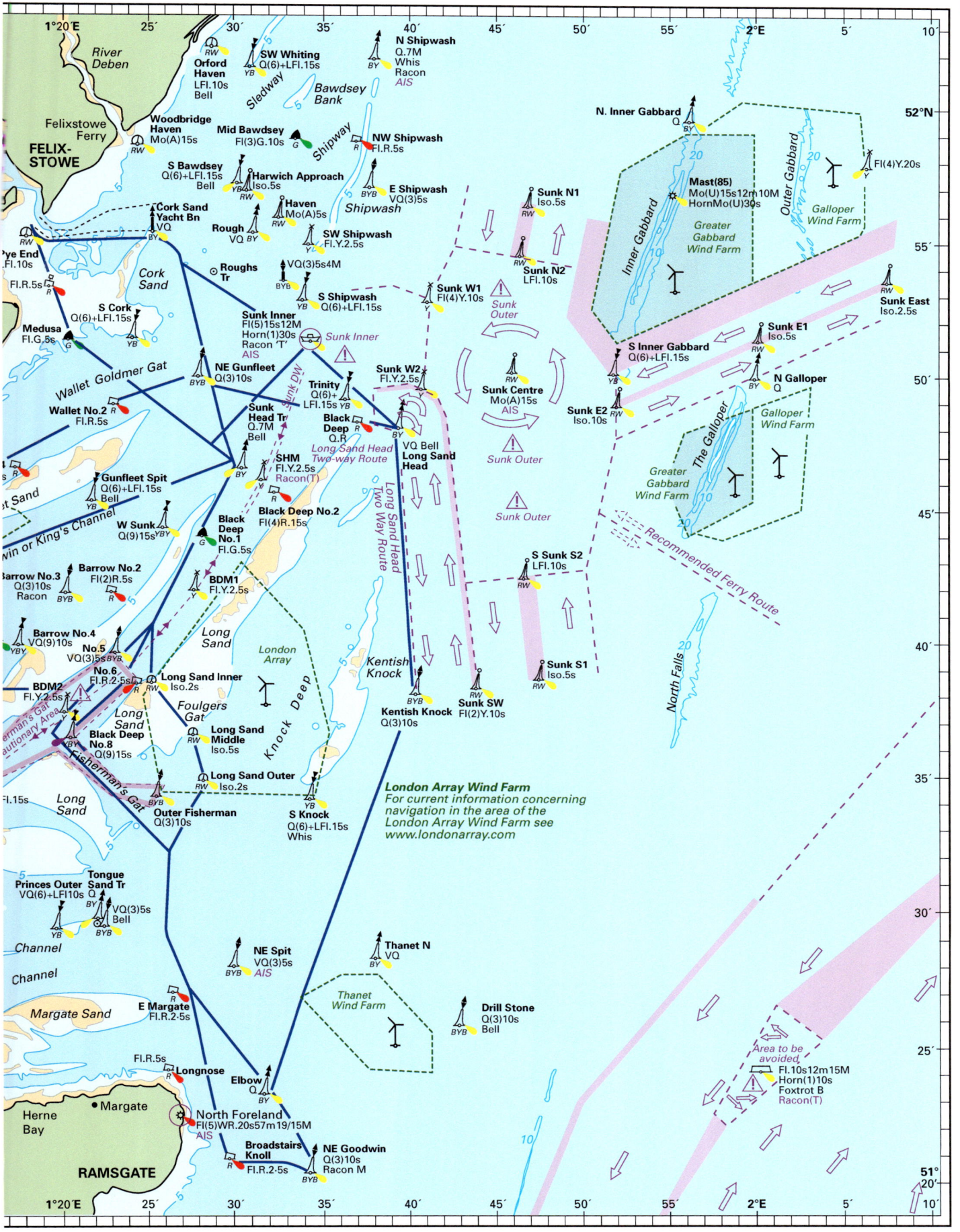

Routes to and from Harwich and Essex rivers

NORTH SEA PASSAGE PILOT 57

II. SOUTHERN CROSSING ROUTES

7. HARWICH TO CALAIS

See plan on pages 56 / 57

Distance
71M
Duration
12hrs, 2 tidal sets
Charts
Imray C1, C30, 2000 chart pack, 2100 chart pack
Admiralty SC5607, SC5605
Recommended start time outward
HW Dover −1, HW Harwich −2
Arrival time outward
HW Dover −0·5, HW Calais −1
Key tidal gate
Arrive Calais at Calais HW −1
Recommended start time return
HW Dover −1·5 HW Calais −2
Arrival time return
HW Dover −1·5, HW Harwich −2·5
Key tidal gate
Depart Calais at HW Calais −2
Tidal streams
Streams start running in the middle of the Estuary approaches between Long Sand Head and Kentish Knock, they turn S at HW Dover −6 (HW Harwich +6), and N at HW Dover (HW Harwich −1). At Calais NE- going starts at HW Dover −1·5 and SW-going at HW Dover +4·5.

Although there is not the complication of a zigzag course to avoid shoals, Harwich and Felixstowe are both extremely busy ferry and container ports with a major dredged channel approach and a major routeing system just offshore. There are several widely separated lit cardinal marks enroute but in daylight these are often difficult to see. On a first-time cruise the skipper may prefer to head inshore to sight North Foreland and **NE Goodwin** (ECM) before heading for **S Falls** (SCM) and the Dover Strait TSS.

The timings of leaving Harwich will depend on whether you are going the whole course or breaking the journey at Ramsgate (which would make sense for a family-crewed yacht). Leaving for Calais direct, and to meet the requirement to arrive an hour before HW, will mean leaving Harwich near local HW and pushing the ebb, particularly in the Black Deep. Leaving for Ramsgate you can leave three hours later and cross the ebb to **Sunk Head Tower** and pick up the flood going south down the Black Deep.

Looking SE over Felixstowe container port towards Landguard Point, the start of many a North Sea passage
© Graham Harris / Dreamstime.com

Harwich to Calais

The route from **Landguard** (NCM) or **Pye End** (RW) is to turn southeast down the Medusa Channel via **Stone Banks** (R) to **Medusa** (G) to **Sunk Head Tower**, then down the Black Deep and through Fisherman's Gat. This route keeps you clear of the Sunk Precautionary Area. You join Route 3 at NE Goodwin.

An alternative to the Black Deep/Fisherman's Gat route is to continue east from **Sunk Head Tower** to **Long Sand Head** and take the route south outside all of the sand banks via **Kentish Knock** (ECM). There is likely to be less tide running outside than down the Black Deep and it's a more direct course from **Long Sand Head**, without the dogleg of Fisherman's Gat. Aim for **NE Spit** (ECM) where the routes merge. (This alternative can also work for vessels leaving the Essex Rivers.)

Calais to Harwich

Leave Calais at HW–2 (the first bridge opening) and follow the channel buoys out to **CA4** and cross the TSS at right angles. The NE-going stream should start on the English side when outside the lanes, and deposit you somewhere near **NE Goodwin** (ECM). Past North Foreland you then continue with the N-going fair stream to the vicinity of **Kentish Knock** (ECM) when the tide turns SW into the Estuary and is against you for 1–2hrs while following the east side of the Two-Way Route to **Long Sand Head**. Leave **Trinity** (SCM) to starboard and head across the last four hours of flood tide to **NE Gunfleet**, **Medusa** and up the Medusa Channel to Harwich. If you are in luck you will carry the end of the flood into the River Orwell.

You could take the alternative route via Fisherman's Gat and travel up the Black Deep to **Sunk Head Tower** and from there take the Medusa Channel into Harwich (see Route 6).

Above: Sunk Head Tower (NCM) *Trinity House*

Below: Sandettié LtV

Calais Avant Port entrance

III. MIDDLE CROSSING ROUTES

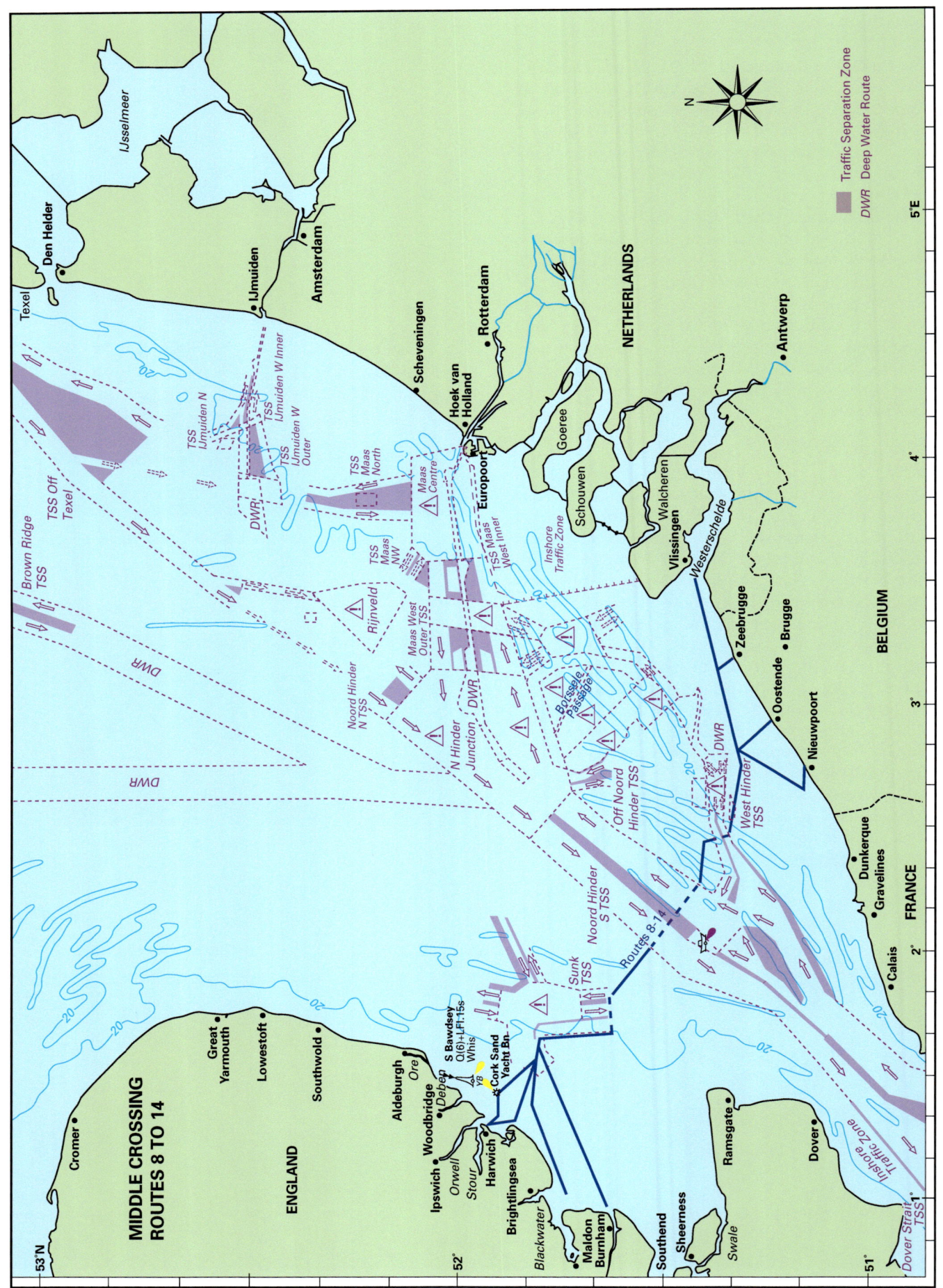

8. ESSEX RIVERS TO OOSTENDE

Distance
92M
Duration
15+hrs, 2.5 tidal sets
Charts
Imray C1, C30, 2000 chart pack, 2120 chart pack
Admiralty 183, 1406, 1610, 1872, 1873, 1975, 2449, 3741, 3750
Dutch small craft series 1801
Recommended start time outward
HW Dover, HW Burnham-on-Crouch and Bradwell (Blackwater) –1
Arrival time outward
HW Dover +5, HW Oostende +4
Key tidal gate
Long Sand Head HW Dover –6
Key tidal gate
West Hinder HW Dover to HW Dover +1
Recommended start time return
HW Dover –4, HW Oostende –5
Arrival time return
HW Dover, HW Burnham-on-Crouch and Bradwell –1
Key tidal gate
West Hinder HW Dover
Key tidal gate
Long Sand Head HW Dover –6
Tidal streams
On the Belgian coast the stream turns E-going at approximately HW Dover –1 and W-going at HW Dover +5, and the final approaches to Oostende are cross-tide.

Essex rivers to Oostende

From the Essex rivers head up the East Swin (Kings Channel) or Wallet to **Sunk Head Tower**, then east to **Long Sand Head** to turn and run down between the Long Sand and the Sunk S TSS. Cross the TSS at right angles at **Kentish Knock** to **Sunk SW** at the entrance to the TSS and when clear alter course for the **West Hinder** Lt.

Tidal streams turn at **Long Sand Head** (NCM) approximately 30M from the start point, i.e., roughly one tidal stream distant, going SW at HW Dover –5.5, and NE-going at HW Dover +1 (near to local HW). A useful objective, therefore, in either direction on this route is to reach **Long Sand Head** buoy at latest by HW Dover –5.5 (near to local LW), and thus have a favourable tide along King's Channel, and Whitaker Channel or Blackwater, then pick up the SW flood while doing the 40M to **W Hinder**. Arrive at **W Hinder** just after HW Dover.

Distances, times, tidal sets, and most of the notes are the same from the Nass Beacon on the Blackwater as from the Inner Crouch buoy. These are good routes for the prevailing SW or NE wind direction, which is beam on to the main course between **Long Sand Head** and **West Hinder**, but with some complications on the doglegs at both ends. Shipping is light in the Crouch and Blackwater approaches and along King's Channel, but near Harwich is heavy. Traffic is heavy in the TSS crossings and in the approaches to the Westerschelde.

The **West Hinder Lt** is a major mark on these routes, and although the bank to its north has 9m and can be crossed near to the light in most weather, in Force 5 and over it is advisable to pass south of the light, leaving a good clearance.

A heading from **Long Sand Head** to **W Hinder** will cross the Noord Hinder south TSS at right angles, with the SW-going stream pushing the vessel southwestwards. The stream turns NE-going just before arriving at **W Hinder**. However, with these tidal sets east of Sunk TSS the track crosses North Falls bank (north end of bank 9·5m minimum sounding), and beyond North Hinder TSS it crosses Fairy Bank (south end of bank 6·6m minimum sounding). In winds of Force 5 and over, therefore, it is safer to divert south of North Falls bank then head for **Garden City** (WCM) then keep north of Fairy Bank towards the **W Hinder Lt**.

From the **West Hinder Lt**, the next course is across the West Hinder TSS at right angles. Then follow the buoyed southern edge of the TSS to the **KB Kwintebank** (NCM) with a continuing NE-going fair stream helping you eastwards. At **MBN** (NCM) head to **Oostendebank E** (G) and enter the buoyed channel into the port. The near approaches to Oostende are a maze of banks with many buoys, not to be taken lightly in rough weather.

Oostende to Essex rivers

Leave Oostende at HW Dover –4 and aim to be in the vicinity of **W Hinder** around HW Dover (22M or 4hrs). Then take full advantage of the ebb to **Long Sand Head** (40M), to catch the flood home.

III. MIDDLE CROSSING ROUTES

9. ESSEX RIVERS TO NIEUWPOORT

See plan on page 60

Distance
87M
Duration
14 +hrs, 2·5 tidal sets
Charts
Imray C30, 2000 chart pack, 2120 chart pack
Admiralty 1183, 1406, 1610, 1872, 1873, 1975, 3741, 3750
Dutch small craft series 1801
Recommended start time outward
HW Dover, HW Burnham-on-Crouch and Bradwell (Blackwater) −1
Arrival time outward
HW Dover +3 to 4, HW Nieuwpoort +2 to +3
Key tidal gate
Long Sand Head Dover HW−6
Key tidal gate
West Hinder HW Dover to HW Dover +1
Recommended start time return
HW Dover −3, HW Nieuwpoort −4
Arrival time return
HW Dover, HW Burnham-on-Crouch and Bradwell −1
Key tidal gate
West Hinder HW Dover
Key tidal gate
Long Sand Head HW Dover −6
Tidal streams
On the Belgian coast the stream turns E-going at approximately HW Dover −1 and W-going at HW Dover +5. The suggested timing gives a favourable tide for Nieuwpoort outwards from KB (Kwintebank) buoy and a slack stream to Kwintebank on the return.

Essex to Nieuwpoort and return

This voyage follows Route 8 to **KB** (NCM), turn south to **Middelkerk** BK, then southwest to **D1** (WCM), then to **Nieuwpoortbank** (ECM), turning east to pass N of **Whitley** (NCM) into the port entrance. Be careful to avoid the marine farm in the Westdiep, approximately 2M east of the **Nieuwpoortbank** buoy. Start times are the same as Route 8. The return is the same.

10. HARWICH TO NIEUWPOORT

See plan on page 60

Distance
75M
Duration
12·5 hrs, 2+ tidal sets
Charts
Imray C30, 2000 chart pack, 2120 chart pack
Admiralty 1183, 1406, 1491, 1610, 1872, 1873, 2052, 2693
Dutch small craft series 1801
Recommended start time outward
HW Dover +3, HW Harwich +2
Arrival time outward
HW Dover +3 to +4, HW Nieuwpoort +2 to +3
Key tidal gate
Long Sand Head Dover HW −6
Key tidal gate
West Hinder HW Dover to HW Dover +1
Recommended start time return
HW Dover −3, HW Nieuwpoort −4
Arrival time return
HW Dover −3, HW Harwich −4
Key tidal gate
West Hinder HW Dover
Key tidal gate
Long Sand Head HW Dover −6
Tidal streams
Tides start out of and into Harwich at HW Dover +1 and −5·5. On the Belgian coast the stream turns E-going at approximately HW Dover −1 and W-going HW Dover +5. The approach to Harwich is cross-tide so there is some flexibility with the start times, but to and from Nieuwpoort it helps to have a fair tide along the Negenvaam.

Harwich to Nieuwpoort

From Harwich take the alternative Route 7 to **Long Sand Head**, aiming to be there at local LW. Then follow the routeing instructions for Route 8 to be at **W Hinder** by HW Dover to take advantage of the NE-going ebb to help you east to **KB** (NCM). From there head south to Middelkerke Bank (G) to **DI** (ECM) to **Nieuwpoortbank** (ECM) then due east to the entrance, avoiding the marine farm in Westdiep. The near approaches to Nieuwpoort are a maze of banks with many buoys, not to be taken lightly in rough weather.

Nieuwpoort to Harwich

For the return journey, leave Nieuwpoort with the aim of following the return of Route 8, reaching **West Hinder** at HW Dover to take the ebb up to **Long Sand Head**. At **Long Sand Head** you join the return of Route 7.

The unmistakable lighthouse to the east of the port hand pier helps to identify the entrance into Nieuwpoort
© *aniad / Shutterstock*

62 NORTH SEA PASSAGE PILOT

11. HARWICH TO OOSTENDE

See plan on page 60

Distance
80M
Duration
14hrs, 2+ tidal sets
Charts
Imray C30, 2000 chart pack, 2120 chart pack
Admiralty 183, 1406, 1491, 1610, 1872, 1873, 2052, 2693
Recommended start time outward
HW Dover +3, HW Harwich +2
Arrival time outward
HW Dover +4, HW Oostende +3
Key tidal gate
Long Sand Head HW Dover –6
Key tidal gate
West Hinder HW Dover –1 to HW Dover +1
Recommended start time return
HW Dover –4, HW Oostende –5
Arrival time return
HW Dover –3, HW Harwich –4
Key tidal gate
West Hinder HW Dover
Key tidal gate
Long Sand Head HW Dover –6
Tidal streams
On the Belgian coast the stream turns E-going at approximately HW Dover –1 and W-going HW Dover +5. Both the approaches to Harwich and to Oostende are cross-tide, so the above start time is only one of several possibilities.

Harwich to Oostende

There are two local routes out of Harwich, both merge into Route 8 at **Long Sand Head**. The first route is via the Medusa Channel; **Stone Banks** (R), **Medusa** (G), **NE Gunfleet** (ECM), **Trinity** (SCM) and **Long Sand Head**. This is a straightforward cross tide passage detailed in Route 7.

The other involves leaving Harwich at half tide with 3hrs of NE and N-going ebb at the start. Following the southern edge of the Harwich Channel along the recommended yacht track until the **Cork Sand** (R) and **Cork Sand Yacht** (NCM) beacons are on either hand, then take a direct course south of the **Roughs Tower** and, with great caution, cross the Inner Precautionary Area to **Black Deep** (QR), near the end of the Long Sand shoal. This course enables an approach to **Long Sand Head** (NCM) on the correct side of the entrance to the Long Sand Head Two-Way Route. At **Long Sand Head** join Route 8.

Oostende to Harwich

Coming back from Oostende aim to be at **W Hinder** at HW Dover (22M or 4hrs travel) to take the ebb the 40NM to **Long Sand Head**. The reciprocal return routes from **Long Sand Head** into Harwich will take you across the flood but you should start to carry that as a favourable stream as you approach the harbour.

Oostende pier

Entering Oostende

III. MIDDLE CROSSING ROUTES

12. ESSEX RIVERS TO ZEEBRUGGE

See plan on page 60

Distance
99M
Duration
22hrs, 3·5 tidal sets
Charts
Imray C30, 2000 chart pack, 2120 chart pack
Admiralty 325, 1183, 1406, 1610, 1872, 1975, 3741, 3750,
Dutch small craft series 1801
Recommended start time outward
HW Dover, HW Burnham-on-Crouch and Bradwell (Blackwater) –1
Arrival time outward
HW Dover +5, HW Zeebrugge +3·5
Key tidal gate
Long Sand Head Dover HW –6
Key tidal gate
West Hinder HW Dover to HW Dover +1
Recommended start time return
HW Dover –5, HW Zeebrugge +6
Arrival time return
HW Dover, HW Burnham-on-Crouch and Bradwell –1
Key tidal gate
West Hinder HW Dover
Key tidal gate
Long Sand Head HW Dover –6
Tidal streams
On the Belgian coast the stream turns E-going at approximately HW Dover –1 and W-going at HW Dover +5. The suggested timing gives a slightly unfavourable tide to Zeebrugge outwards from KB (Kwintebank) buoy and a slack stream to Kwintebank on the return.

Essex to Zeebrugge

Going to Zeebrugge means following Route 8 all the way to **KB** (NCM), then go due east to **MBN** (NCM) and then **AW1** (G) to **Z** (G) at the approach entrance to the port. The adverse SW-going stream from the Schelde will have started when making the final approach. The approaches to Zeebrugge are not difficult.

Zeebrugge to Essex

Aim to be at the **KB** (NCM) buoy at slack water or at the beginning of the N-going ebb tide and return via Route 8.

13. HARWICH TO ZEEBRUGGE

See plan on page 60

Distance
90M
Duration
15 hrs, 3 tidal sets
Charts
Imray C30, 2000 chart pack, 2120 chart pack
Admiralty 325, 1183, 1406, 1491, 1610, 1872, 2052, 2693
Dutch small craft series 1801,
Recommended start time outward
HW Dover +3, HW Harwich +2
Arrival time outward
HW Dover +5, HW Zeebrugge +3·5
Key tidal gate
Long Sand Head HW Dover –6
Key tidal gate
West Hinder HW Dover to HW Dover +1
Recommended start time return
HW Dover –5, HW Zeebrugge +6
Arrival time return
HW Dover –3, HW Harwich –4
Key tidal gate
West Hinder HW Dover
Key tidal gate
Long Sand Head HW Dover –6
Tidal streams as Route 13

Harwich to Zeebrugge

Leaving Harwich and follow Routes 8 and 10 to the **KB** (NCM) buoy by when you should be well into a NE-going fair stream. The adverse SW-going stream will start as you make the final approach. The approaches to Zeebrugge are not difficult; from **KB** (NCM) go to **MBN1** (NCM) then to **Z** (G) and head E into the harbour entrance.

Return

Leaving Zeebrugge aim to be at **KB** (NCM) at slack water or at the beginning of the NE-going ebb and follow the return via Route 8.

The wind turbines on the eastern breakwater of Zeebrugge entrance are a useful aid to navigation
© Roger Utting / Dreamstime.com

14. ESSEX RIVERS AND HARWICH TO VLISSINGEN

See plan on page 60

Distance
115M
Duration
19 hrs, 3+ tidal sets
Charts
Imray C30, 2000 chart pack, 2120 chart pack
Admiralty 325, 1183, 1406, 1610, 1872, 1975, 3741, 3750
Dutch small craft series 1801
Recommended start time outward
HW Dover, HW Burnham-on-Crouch and Bradwell (Blackwater) −1
Arrival time outward
Depends on progress pushing against the Scheur Channel ebb
Key tidal gate
Long Sand Head HW Dover −6
Key tidal gate
West Hinder HW Dover to HW Dover −1
Recommended start time return
HW Dover +3, HW Vlissingen +1
Arrival time return
HW Dover +3·5, HW Burnham-on-Crouch and Bradwell −1
Tidal streams
Tides in the constricted Scheur/Westerschelde entrance are extremely fast and turn ingoing at HW Dover −3 (HW Vlissingen −5) and outgoing at HW Dover +3 (HW Vlissingen +1).

Outward

Going out, follow Route 8 to MBN (NCM) and on to **AW1** (G), take care crossing the entrance to Zeebrugge to **W** (G) just N of Zeebrugge entrance. Follow the starboard hand buoys up the Scheur. At **W3** (G) you can turn to starboard into Cadzand and at **Het Veer** (G) into Breskens. Cross the Schelde here to Vlissingen. Commercial traffic is heavy and fast. While it seems logical to go out following Route 8 and continue into the Westerschelde, the route puts you north of Oostende at around Dover HW +3, which is bad timing for continuing into the Westerschelde, as the outpouring from the Schelde will overpower the NE-going ebb. An ideal passage from this aspect would start at Dover HW −3 and finish at Vlissingen at Dover HW +2 (Vlissingen HW). To avoid pushing a strong foul tide for many hours at the end of a long passage, overnight in Oostende or Zeebrugge.

If you choose to split this voyage with a stopover either in Oostende or Zeebrugge, then from Oostende aim for **Oostende Bank E** (G). From here you can continue to follow the coast round and drop down to Zeebrugge or continue into the Scheur Channel and round into the Westerschelde. From Zeebrugge, once clear of the harbour entrance head for **W3** (G) and join the Scheur Channel.

A yacht leaving the entrance lock at Vlissingen
© *Hadot / Dreamstime.com*

Return

Returning from Vlissingen is a matter of getting the right tides out of the Scheur and down the Kings Channel on the UK side. Starting out at HW Dover +3, gives you 9hrs of fair stream from Vlissingen, which will take you to the **W Hinder Lt** by HW Dover (without the need to stop in Oostende). The route back is the same as Route 8, using the ebb to carry you up to **Long Sand Head**. The course follows the east side of the Two-Way Route round to **Trinity** (SCM). From **Long Sand Head**, the flood returns you to the Crouch or Blackwater, or cross the flood towards Harwich and pick up the last favourable stream as you enter the harbour.

Distance
33M
Duration
5·5 hrs, 1 tidal set
Charts
Admiralty 325, 1183, 1406, 1610, 1872, 1975, 3741, 3750
Imray C30, 2000.1, 2120 atlas
Dutch small craft series 1801
Recommended start time outward
HW Dover −4, HW Oostende −5
Arrival time outward
HW Dover +2, HW Vlissingen

IV. NORTHERN CROSSING ROUTES

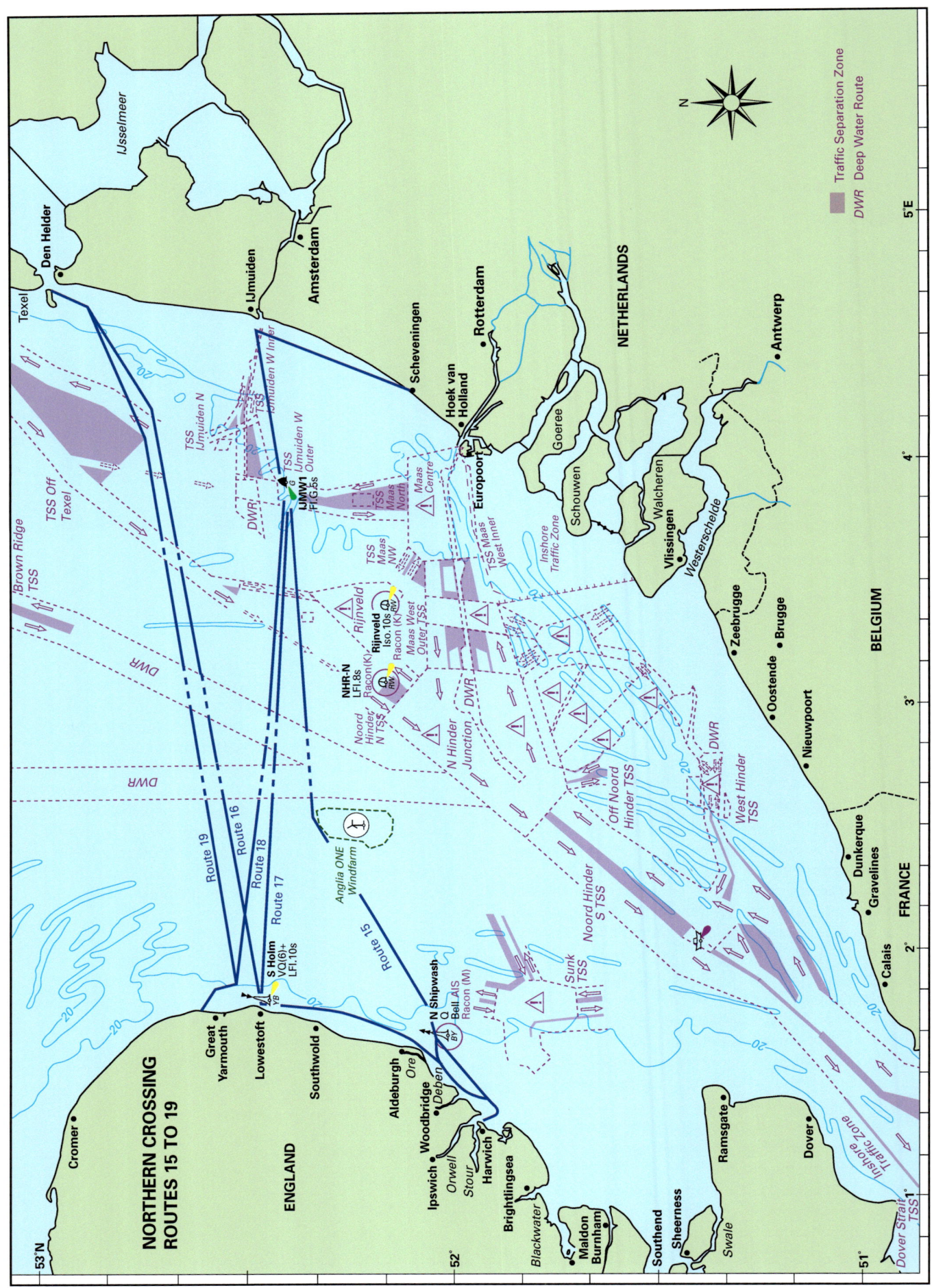

15. HARWICH TO IJMUIDEN

See plan opposite

Distance
126M
Duration
21 hrs, 3·5 tidal sets
Charts
Imray C25, 2000 chart pack, 2120 chart pack
Admiralty 124, 1408, 1491, 2052, 2322, 2693
Dutch small craft series 1801
Recommended start time outward
HW Dover, HW Harwich −1
Arrival time outward
HW Dover −3, HW IJmuiden +6
Key tidal gate
Depart Harwich at Dover HW
Recommended start time return
HW Dover +3, HW IJmuiden −1
Arrival time return
HW Dover, HW Harwich −1
Key tidal gate
Target N Shipwash for HW Dover −2
Tidal streams
Near Orfordness the stream starts NE-going at about HW Dover +0·5 (Harwich −0·5) and SW-going at HW Dover −6 (Harwich +6). In the area of the DWR the stream starts N-going at about HW Dover +0·5 and S- going at HW Dover −5·5hrs. Near IJmuiden N-going starts slightly later at HW Dover +1·5 and S-going also later at HW Dover −4·5.

Harwich to IJmuiden

Leave Harwich at local HW to take advantage of the ebb up to **N Shipwash** (NCM). Follow the recommended yacht route out of Harwich and cross the channel at right angles between **Rolling Ground** (G) and **Platters** (SCM). From the Platters buoy there are three possible routes:

1. Via the Sledway channel, passing to the east of **Cutler** (G) to Bawd Head, rounding **NE Bawdsey** (G), keeping north of **N Shipwash** (NCM).
2. Via the Shipway channel, passing close to **S Bawdsey** (SCM) then crossing the channel to the starboard side and following the port hand markers to **N Shipwash** (NCM). Keep a close eye out for commercial traffic in The Shipway.
3. Keeping approximately 1M offshore but closing in to about 0·5M near to Orfordness and heading offshore from between Orfordness and **NE Whiting** (ECM).

From either N Shipwash or inshore, set a course of approximately 55° for **EA1 NW** (NCM) on the northwest corner of the East Anglian One wind farm. From there, change course onto approximately 84° for **IJMW1** (G). This course should be adjusted at the appropriate time to cross the DWR as close to

EA1-NW buoy

Radio transmitter tower just off IJmuiden approach

a right angle as is practicable. This is not a large change of course since the DWR widens to fork into two branches at this point, but a good lookout must be kept, adjusting the vessel's heading slightly when necessary depending on the traffic, which can be travelling on any of four possible headings.

From **IJMW1** (G) change course slightly to run between the southern edge of the IJ Geul and the northern edge of the Lucterduinen wind farms to the **IJM C** (SWM). From there you can head to the entrance to IJmuiden ideally with a N-going tide. Keep a good look out approaching **IJ-Guel** as there is a busy ship anchorage to the south. Make sure you miss the large yellow tower (a radio transmitter) close to your track and just off the entrance.

NORTH SEA PASSAGE PILOT

IV. NORTHERN CROSSING ROUTES

Steelworks to N of IJmuiden entrance

The IJmuiden steelworks chimneys (166m) and factory buildings can be seen well offshore, as can the 29M range light at night.

IJmuiden to Harwich

The reciprocal route from IJmuiden clears **IJ-Geul** on a course to pass north of the EA1 wind farm. The aim is to arrive at N Shipwash with 2–3hrs of flood tide to carry you to Harwich and into the Orwell and Stour. **N Shipwash** (NCM) is a good landfall by night or day, and then the reciprocal of one of the three routes described above for the outward journey can be followed to Harwich entrance.

Harwich to Scheveningen

The route is somewhat complicated by the need to miss a windfarm, the Noord Hinder TSS N, the Maas Outer and the notorious Maas Central traffic management systems. A much easier way is to go to IJmuiden and stop over, then take the flood tide down the coast to Scheveningen. At 27M it's a relaxed day sail.

IJmuiden harbour

16. HARWICH / LOWESTOFT TO DEN HELDER

See plan on page 66

Caution: TSSs
This passage crosses the southern approaches to the **Off Texel TSS** and passes the corner of the N–going lane of the TSS close N of **TX1** buoy, requiring care and the appropriate course adjustments.

It is important to plan this passage around arrival at **TX1** (G) at the bottom of the Off Texel TSS, about 20M southwest of **SG** (RW), an hour or so before local low water. **SG** marks the entrance to the Schulpengat, the channel leading to Den Helder and the Waddenzee. This will mean you will face an adverse tide for maybe an hour or so. Tidal streams in the Schulpengat can be more than 2·5kts (mid-tide on springs) so it is worth getting the timing right to ride the flood in. The flood tide goes south in the North Sea outside Den Helder but turns in and NE-going in the Schulpengat. The distance from **TX1** to Den Helder is 28M, say 5 hrs. So, the trick would be to be past **TX1** before the North Sea ebb turns to the flood (thereby not encountering too much adverse tide) and then ride the flood to Den Helder to arrive before, and certainly not long after, HW.

Harwich to Lowestoft

Distance
48M
Duration
6 – 6·5hrs, 1 tidal set
Charts
Imray C25, 2000 chart pack
Admiralty 1408
Recommended start time outward
HW Harwich
Tidal streams
Near Orfordness the stream starts NE-going at about HW Dover +0·5 (Harwich –0·5) and SW-going at HW Dover –6 (Harwich +6).

From Harwich it makes sense to coast up to Lowestoft and kick off from there. This minimises the need to factor in punching a foul tide at the beginning or end of the journey.

Lowestoft to Den Helder

Distance
120M
Duration
20 hrs, 3 tidal sets
Charts
Imray C25, 2000 chart pack
Admiralty 1408, 1491, 1546, 2052, 2322, 2693
Dutch small craft series 1801
Recommended start time outward
HW Dover –1, HW Lowestoft +0·5
Arrival time outward
HW Dover –5, HW Den Helder –0·5
Key tidal gate
TX1 by HW Dover +2 to +3, HW Den Helder –6
Recommended start time return
HW Dover –4·5, HW Den Helder
Arrival time return
HW Dover +5, HW Lowestoft –6
Key tidal gate
Depart Den Helder HW Dover –4·5, HW Den Helder
Tidal streams
Outside Lowestoft entrance the S-going stream begins at about HW Dover –6 (HW Lowestoft –4) and N-going at HW Dover (HW Lowestoft +2). In the area of the DWRs the stream starts N-going at about HW Dover +0.5, and S-going at HW Dover –5·5hrs. Near Scheveningen N-going starts slightly later at HW Dover +1·5 and S-going also later at HW Dover –4·5.

From **S Holm** (SCM) lay a course direct to **TX1** (G) and on to **SG** (RW) some 20M to the northeast. Leave **S Holm** about 1hr after local HW with the ebb beginning to push north. While you are crossing the wide DWR junction the tide will turn. You should be clear of the DWR around 8 – 9hrs into the passage. During the following 6hrs, the tide will initially set you south and then slacken as you approach the Off Texel TSS and TX1. You should reach **TX1** approximately 15hrs into the passage, at around HW Dover +2 or 3. The tide will then be fair to enter the Schulpengat and arrive at Den Helder at HW.

It is essential to keep a good day and night lookout for the oil and gas platforms and yellow well-head buoys which are scattered around this course. Petten Nuclear Power Station, a square building with two 44m chimneys, 6M south-southeast of the **SG** buoy, is a good daylight landfall, whilst the 55m pencil-like Kijkduin Lt tower (30M range) (see photo on page 30) in the narrows opposite Noorderhaaks Island is also visible well out

IV. NORTHERN CROSSING ROUTES

Huisduinen lighthouse in the approach to Den Helder © *TasfotoNL / Shutterstock*

to sea. The Schulpengat channel is particularly well marked with port and starboard hand buoys. There are also leading lights on Texel Island, the rear being a church spire, with 10M range daylight-intensity (18M at night). From Kaap Hoofd at the end of the Schulpengat/Breewijd channel the final approach route to Den Helder is east along the Marsdiep. This is a steep-sided channel with several lit buoys near the harbour entrance, which itself has two further sets of leading lights. Keep a sharp lookout for ferries coming out of the Veerhaven and heading for 't Horntje on Texel, and especially for naval shipping.

Den Helder to Lowestoft

Returning to Lowestoft, leave Den Helder at local HW and take the ebb down the Schulpengat to **SG** (RW). Then set a direct course to **TX1** (G) and then on toward **S Holm** (SCM). Again, you should keep a good lookout for oil and gas platforms and well heads. A change of course should be made to cross the DWR as close to a right angle as practicable, as in the outward passage, and on estimating the departure point from the DWR a tide-corrected course should be set for **S Holm** (SCM). You will arrive at **S Holm** just before local LW with an easy final leg up the Stanford Channel into port before the S-going flood tide sets in.

Den Helder port

70   NORTH SEA PASSAGE PILOT

17. LOWESTOFT TO IJMUIDEN (SCHEVENINGEN COASTING)

See plan on page 66

Distance
103M
Duration
17+hrs, 3 tidal sets
Charts
Imray C28, C25, 2120 chart pack
Admiralty 122, 1408, 1536, 1543, 2322
Dutch small craft series 1801
Recommended start time outward
HW Dover −4, HW Lowestoft −2·5
Arrival time outward
HW Dover +2, HW IJmuiden −2
Key tidal gate North going ebb starts before EA1 wind farm (HW Dover to HW Dover +1)
Recommended start time return
HW Dover +4, HW IJmuiden
Arrival time return
HW Dover −2, HW Lowestoft −0·5
Key tidal gate
N-going ebb starts before DWR at HW Dover to HW Dover +1
Tidal streams
Outside Lowestoft entrance the S-going stream begins at about HW Dover −6 (HW Lowestoft −4) and N-going at HW Dover (HW Lowestoft +2). In the area of the DWRs the stream starts N-going at about HW Dover +0.5, and S-going at HW Dover −5.5hrs. Near Scheveningen N-going starts slightly later at HW Dover +1·5 and S-going also later at HW Dover −4·5.

While a direct course from Lowestoft to Scheveningen is feasible, you've got to fiddle round a couple of wind farms, a TSS and the huge Mass traffic system. Therefore, it's recommended to cross to IJmuiden for a short break and then carry the tide down the coast for the 36M to Scheveningen next day.

Lowestoft to IJmuiden

Leaving Lowestoft set a course from **S Holm** (SCM) to **IJMW1** (SHM) and join Route 15.

This route is cross tide all the way. On the way you have the S-going flood, with the N-going ebb starting before you get to **EA1** (30M) and the DWR junction. You should arrive off IJmuiden at slack water.

IJmuiden to Lowestoft

On the return set off back from IJmuiden aiming for **EA1 NE** (NCM) and change course to **S Holm** (SCM) aiming to arrive with about an hour of ebb to take you up the Stanford Channel into harbour. You should come out of IJmuiden to **IJM1**, on a N-going tide, which will go slack and turn south at Dover HW −4 (4·5hrs or about 27M down track). It switches to N-going again at HW Dover +1 (9 hrs, 54M), just before you reach the DWR. You'll have a NE-going ebb crossing the DWR and going over the top of **EA1**. You might have to push some flood for about 2M in Stanford Channel approach to Lowestoft.

Gas rig IJmuiden approach

Scheveningen from S

IV. NORTHERN CROSSING ROUTES

18. GREAT YARMOUTH TO IJMUIDEN

See plan on page 66

Distance
105M
Duration
18 hrs, 3 tidal sets
Charts
Imray C28, C25, 2120 chart pack
Admiralty 124, 1408, 1536, 1543, 2322
Dutch small craft series 1801
Recommended start time outward
HW Dover −1, HW Gt Yarmouth +1
Arrival time outward
HW Dover +5, HW IJmuiden +1
Recommended start time return
HW Dover +2, HW IJmuiden −2
Arrival time return
HW Dover −6, HW Gt Yarmouth (Gorleston) −4
Tidal streams
Streams off Great Yarmouth start N-going at HW Dover +6 (HW Gt Yarmouth −4·5) and S-going at HW Dover − 0·5 (HW Gt Yarmouth +1·5). In the area of the DWRs the stream starts N-going at about HW Dover, and S-going at HW Dover −5·5. Streams in the Schulpengat (approach to Den Helder) flood NE at HW Dover +3 (HW Den Helder −5), and ebb SW at HW Dover −4 (HW Den Helder +0·5).

Great Yarmouth to IJmuiden

This is a straightforward route, leave Great Yarmouth harbour and head to **S Corton** (SCM) from where you set a course direct to **IJMW1** (G). From here you alter course slightly to pass to the south of the traffic lanes and N of Luchterduinen wind farm to the entrance. You'll have to cross two DWRs requiring small changes of heading to cross at right angles. Follow the directions for Route 17.

IJmuiden to Great Yarmouth

Coming back from IJmuiden aim for **EA1 NE** (NCM) and change course to S Holm (SCM) aiming to arrive with enough ebb to take you up the 10 mile inshore channel to Great Yarmouth entrance. You should come out of IJmuiden to **IJM1** on a N–going tide, which will go slack and turn south at Dover HW−4 (4·5hrs or about 27M down track). It switches to N-going again at HW Dover +1 (9 hrs, 54M), just before you reach the DWR. You'll have a NE-going ebb crossing the DWR and going over the top of **EA1**.

19. GREAT YARMOUTH TO DEN HELDER

See plan on page 66

Distance
120M
Duration
20hrs, 3.5 tidal sets
Charts
Imray C28, C25, 2120 chart pack
Admiralty 1408, 1536, 1543, 1546, 2322
Dutch small craft series 1801
Recommended start time outward
HW Dover −1, HW Gt Yarmouth +1
Arrival time outward
HW Dover −5, HW Den Helder −0·5
Key tidal gate
TX1 by HW Dover +2 to +3, HW Den Helder −6
Recommended start time return
HW Dover −4·5, HW Den Helder
Arrival time return
HW Dover +4, HW Gt Yarmouth +6
Key tidal gate Depart Den Helder HW Dover −4·5, HW Den Helder
Tidal streams
Streams off Great Yarmouth start N-going at HW Dover +6 (HW Gt Yarmouth −4·5) and S-going at HW Dover −0·5 (HW Gt Yarmouth +1·5). In the area of the DWRs the stream starts N-going at about HW Dover, and S- going at HW Dover −5·5. Streams in the Schulpengat (approach to Den Helder) flood NE at HW Dover +3 (HW Den Helder −5), and ebb SW at HW Dover −4 (HW Den Helder +0·5).

Great Yarmouth to Den Helder

On leaving Great Yarmouth aim for the Holm Channel to arrive at **S Corton** (SCM) at around 1hr after local HW. Set a course for **TX1** (G) 86M away on a course of 84°. From there set a course of 61° for 20M to **SG** (RW), marking the entrance of the Schulpengat. The final approach to Den Helder will be timed to coincide with the flood tide up the Schulpengat. You will need to cross the DWR at right angles. From **TX1**, follow Route 16.

Den Helder to Great Yarmouth

Coming back leave the area of Den Helder at the top of the tide to take advantage of a full 6hrs of ebb to help push you well southwest beyond **TX1** (G). Follow the Marsdiep and then the Schulpengat with the ebb to **SG** (RW). From **SG** aim for **TX1** (G), and then alter course direct for **S Corton** (SCM), continuing onwards to the boundary of the first DWR, where your heading should be altered to starboard to cross at right angles and a further change of heading made if necessary, to cross the second DWR. A further change of course may be necessary to home in on **S Corton**.

EUROPEAN MAINLAND PILOTAGE

CALAIS

Port contacts
Calais Port VHF Ch 17 (24hrs), HM ☎ +33 321 96 31 20
Calais Marina and lock VHF Ch 09 ☎ +33 321 34 55 23
www.calais-marina.fr
Calais Ecluse Carnot (lock) VHF Ch 17
Entry signals
Contact Calais harbour by VHF in English
International Port Traffic Signals are displayed from:
Jetée Est head, the N side of entrance to Bassin Est, the W side of entrance to Arrière-port and for small craft on Quai de la Colonne. Small craft may only use the entrance channel when vertical 2G over W, two-way traffic is displayed.
Lock/road bridge into Bassin de l'Ouest, Y Lt – standby for lock/bridge opening; G or R Lt – pass through or passage prohibited respectively.
Note Dock gates open HW –1·5hrs to HW+½hr. Bridge opening varies.
Customs
Rue Mollien ☎ +33 9 70 27 08 54
Tide
HW Dover –0·5

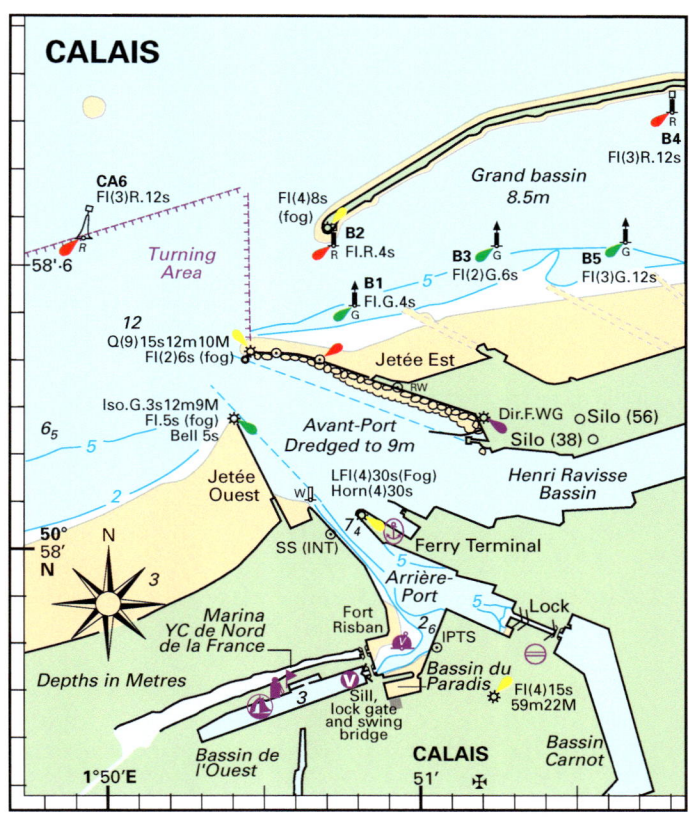

Approach and entrance

From the east, Calais is normally approached on a rising tide near HW. In good weather you can cross the corner of the Ridens banks direct to the Calais breakwaters. This timing is also convenient for going through the lock and bridge into Port de Plaisance. If you approach from the west, the buoyed ferry channel is a straightforward passage to CA2 from where you follow the buoyed channel to the breakwaters. Arriving in this direction at the end of a passage from the west, it is often close to low water, requiring a long wait to go through the lock. You must contact Calais Port on VHF 17 for permission to enter to make sure you do not impede a ferry.

Approach or departure northwards can often be timed at or near high water, convenient for the lock and, if the weather is suitable, for crossing the Ridens banks, which screen both the entrance and the western approach channel to just over 1M west of the entrance. If you have any doubt at all about the weather, then you should approach from the west along the buoyed channel.

Entry is between the outer breakwaters along the west side of the Avant Port, keeping away from the ferry traffic on the eastern side, then through the inner entrance into the Arrière Port.

The Bassin de l'Ouest has a sill at the entrance with a maximum of 3m clearance at HW and with access continuing to be limited by a bascule road bridge which opens at the following times: HW Calais –3hr, –2hr, –1hr at HW and again at HW + 1hr 15min and 2hr 30min. A fixed orange warning light is shown from 15 minutes before opening. There are depth gauges showing the water level both downstream and upstream of the sill, as well as lit signs on each side of the entrance when the sill depth exceeds 2m.

Since the establishment of the sill, mooring depths within Bassin de l'Ouest are reported to vary, with boats drying out in places, particularly in the busy season during rallies. A call to Calais Marina on VHF 17 or ☎ +33 (from UK) 21 34 55 23) is necessary for entry instructions. Up-to-date opening hours for Calais Marina's entrance bridge are available on their website *www.calais-marina.fr*.

V. EUROPEAN MAINLAND PILOTAGE

Heading SE across Calais Avant-Port towards the Arrière-Port © *Chon Kit Leong / Dreamstime.com*

Mooring and facilities

In the tidal Arrière Port there are several white mooring buoys on which to hang temporarily. However, during busy periods (such as the rallies held frequently by British clubs) you will often have to raft up on these buoys, with the rafts swinging around in the uncomfortable scend set up in this basin by weather and ferries.

Inside the yacht harbour, the finger pontoons are mainly occupied so you will probably have to lie or raft up alongside the long pontoon on the north wall. This is convenient for clubhouse and showers.

Alternatively, there is plenty of room on the south wall, but you need to be near a ladder to climb ashore, or provide your own. There is a scrubbing grid and repair facilities nearby.

You should contact Calais port authorities and the marina if you require up-to-date information about this access route to the French canals.

For French inland waters see:

Map of the Inland Waterways of France and
Inland Waterways of France Volumes I, II & III
David Edwards May

www.imray.com

Calais yacht harbour is entered through a lock and swing bridge

DUNKERQUE

Port contacts
Dunkerque VTS, VHF Ch 73, HM ☏ +33 328 28 75 96 / 328 28 78 78
Locks VTS, VHF Ch 73, Marinas VHF Ch 09
Port du Grand Large ☏ +33 328 63 23 00, www.dunkerque-marina.com
YC de la Mer du Nord Marina ☏+33 328 667 9 90, www.ycmn.com
Basins through the locks ☏ +33 328 24 58 80

Entry signals
Contact harbour control by VHF
Main Lt Ho on W jetty shows full international port traffic signals.
Ecluse Tristram (lock in Port d'Echouage for small craft).
Signals: G fixed light – enter lock and secure on side indicated by G flashing light; 2 R lights – entry prohibited, and when permission is about to be given the R light on the side of the lock, to which the vessel should secure, starts flashing. Sound signal requesting entry: 2 long blasts.
4 blasts – request Bridge Mole No. 2 open; 2 long 1 short blasts – request Bridge Darse No.1 open.

Customs
Rue l'Hermite ☏ +33 328 29 25 20 or 97 02 70 794

Tide
HW Dover –1

Entrance

This is France's industrial back yard. The entrance is at the western end of the large coastal industrial complex, with blast furnaces, chimneys, cooling towers, and numerous oil refinery tanks, usually topped with a cloud of orange-coloured smoke.

Entrance is just beyond the two Rade de Dunkerque channel buoys, **DW30** (R) and **DW29** (G). In the entrance the shoal at the end of Jetée Ouest should be given a wide berth. There are leading lights to help at night. Then follow Jetée Est and either peel off to starboard to go through Trystram lock and two opening bridges (synchronised with lock-opening) to the Bassin du Commerce, or continue ahead to the Port d'Echouage and the tidal Yacht Club de la Mer du Nord Marina. Trystram lock opens at any time between 0800 and 1930 daily for boats coming in or out. You should turn in circles before the lock gates to be seen from the control tower, or call them on VHF 73. Then continue slightly to port through Mole No.2 swing bridge (video camera control from the tower), then make a dogleg southward and the Pertuis Amont swing bridge will open. You should tie up at No.4 pontoon at the YC de Dunkerque marina.

Mooring and facilities

The tidal **Port du Grand Large** marina www.dunkerque-marina.com ☏ +33 328 632 300 has 250 berths and hoist and repair facilities. It is situated on the east side of the Port d'Echouage just before reaching the older **YC de la Mer du Nord Marina** www.ycmn.com ☏ +33 328 667 990 on the opposite side of the channel. There is another 250-berth non-tidal marina in the Bassin de la Marine at the southern end of the non-tidal harbour complex, accessed through Trystram lock.

YC de la Mer du Nord Marina is a tidal pontoon marina in the Port d'Echouage. It has toilets, showers, scrubbing grid and crane, repair, and chandlery facilities nearby, and is a 10–minute walk to town. The two smaller marinas further down the Port d'Echouage have no facilities for visitors.

Entrance to Dunkerque habour *Patrick Roach*

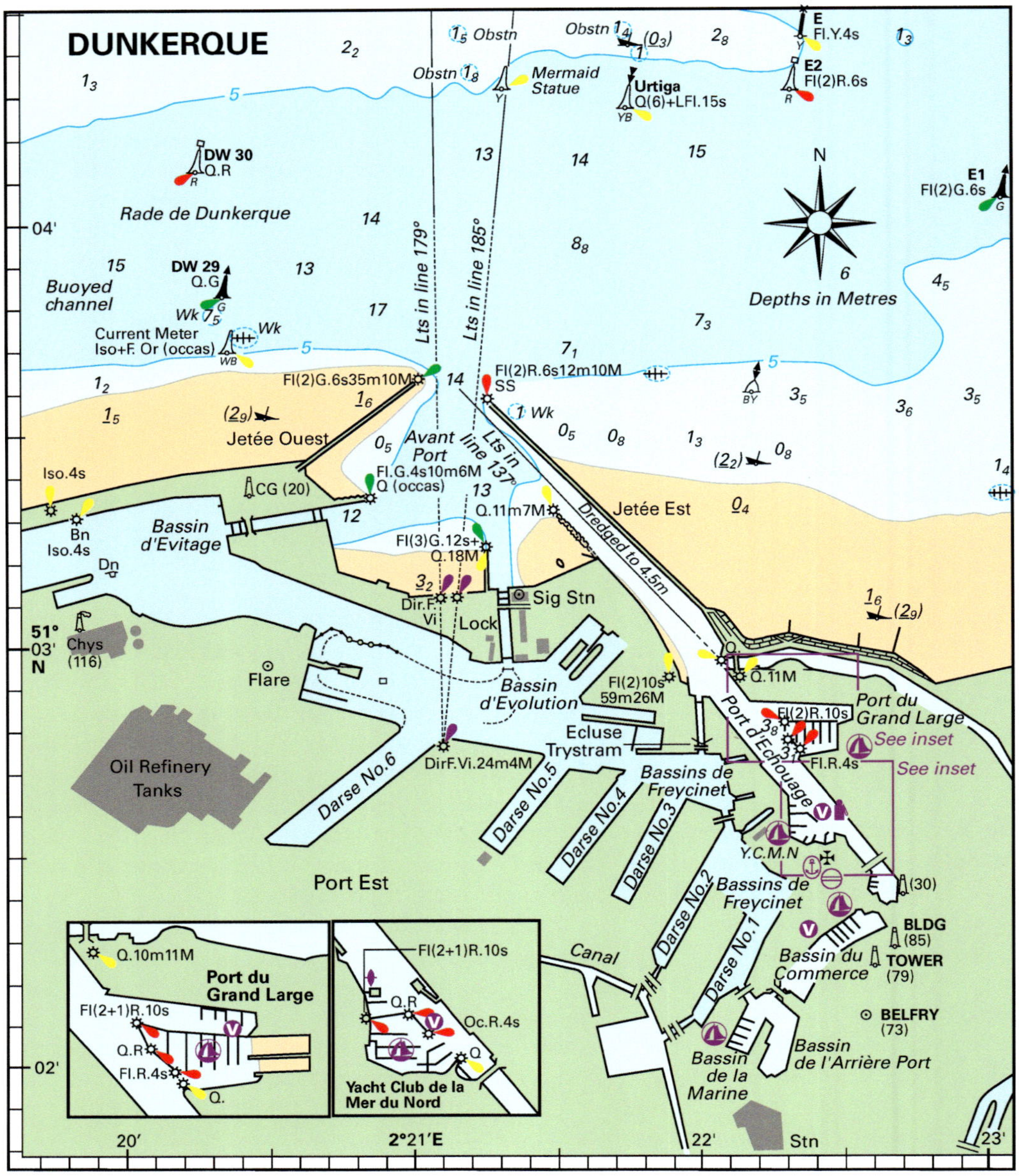

V. EUROPEAN MAINLAND PILOTAGE

The municipal marina with 120 berths in the Bassin du Commerce is entered through Trystram lock and the two swing bridges. It has showers and toilet facilities and a new clubhouse and is convenient for the town.

The town is largely modern, but still has some historic churches and buildings, bistros, restaurants, a good shopping area and market, a hypermarket, a museum of the Second World War British evacuation of Dunkerque and Malo-les-Bains seaside resort next door.

Entrance to the French / Belgian inland waterway system is through locks at Darses Nos 1 and 2, but advance contact with and information from the harbour authority is essential. Masts need to be lowered. See *Inland Waterways of France Vols 1-3* David Edwards-May (Imray).

To port is the Port du Grand Large marina while ahead to starboard is the YC de la Mare du Nord marina

NIEUWPOORT

Port contacts
Nieuwpoort VHF Ch 09, 16 (24hrs) ☎ +32 58 23 30 00
KYCN Ch 23, ☎ +32 58 23 44 13 www.kycn.be
WSKLuM Ch 23 ☎ +32 58 23 36 41 www.wsklum.be
VVW-N Ch 08 ☎ +32 58 23 52 32 www.vynieuwpoort.be

Entry signals
Contact port control by VHF 09
2 cones points together or Fl.Bu Lt – craft of 6m or less not to leave harbour (onshore wind Force 3 or over, offshore Force 4 or over)

Tide HW Dover –1

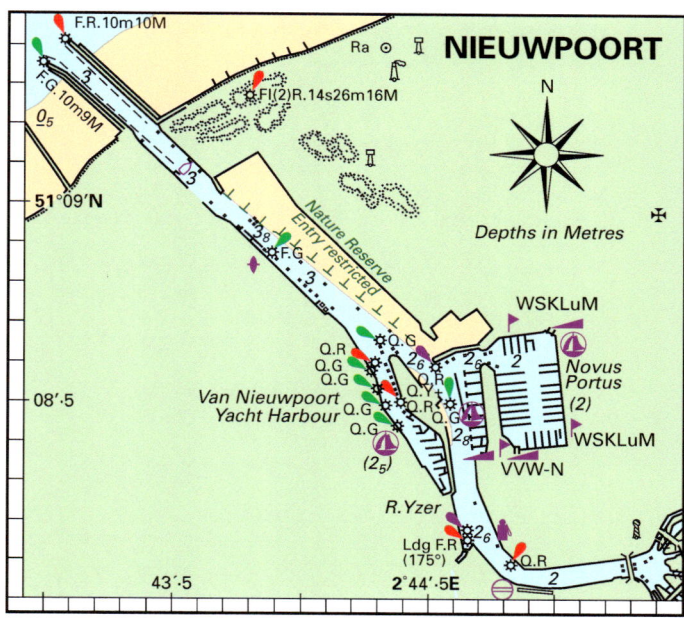

Entrance

There are no major problems with entry, as the minimum depth is 3·2m, however, things can be tricky around LW in onshore winds over Force 4/5. The lighthouse to the east of the entrance is unmistakable. From **Nieuwpoortbank** (SCM) turn east and pass north of **Whitley** (NCM). Enter directly between the two white entrance towers (lit) at the ends of the piers.

There are black and white dolphins along the sides of the channel and at the junction. At the junction turn to starboard for the South Basin or round another black and white dolphin with a wide turn to port for Vlaamse Vereniging voor Watersport and the Yacht Harbour.

Mooring and facilities

The marina to the east off the River Yzer has pontoon moorings in both an inner and outer basin with all the usual facilities. It is run by VVW (Vlaamse Vereniging voor Watersport), www.vynieuwpoort.be ☎ +32 58 23 52 32, VHF 08, with extensive repair and yard facilities nearby. In the South Basin another excellent marina is run by **Koninklijke Jachtclub Nieuwpoort**, www.kycn.be ☎ +32 58 23 44 13, VHF 23 and close south of this **WSKLuM Marina,** ☎ +32 58 23 36 41, VHF 72.

All these facilities are within a mile's walk from the shopping area. Yachts are not allowed to moor in the harbour 'canal' proper nor further down near the town in the fishing harbour. Not many historic buildings remain but the town has been rebuilt very well.

Nieuwpoort

V. EUROPEAN MAINLAND PILOTAGE

OOSTENDE

Port contacts
Oostende VHF Ch 09 (24h), HM ☎ +32 59 340 711
Mercator Marina VHF Ch 14 (24hrs) ☎ + 32 59 70 57 62, www.mercatormarina.be
Royal North Sea Yacht Club ☎ +32 59 43 06 94, www.rnsyc.be
Royal Yacht Club of Oostende ☎ +32 59 42 71 04, www.ryco.be
Entry signals Contact in advance with harbour control on VHF. Most significant signal is that for Cross Channel Ferries entering or leaving, all other traffic to keep clear:
Q.Y Lt from E pier – keep clear of harbour entrance and channel, to De Mey lock;
Q.Y from Pilot Station on Montgomerydok – keep clear of channel from Montgomerydok and from tidal harbour.
Three R stop lights are shown at the entrance to Montgomerydok and vessels leaving must wait until they go green.
Montgomerydok Pilot Station: 2 B cones points together or Fl.Bu Lt – craft of 6m or less not to leave harbour (onshore wind Force 3 or over, offshore Force 4 or over).
Customs
☎ +32 2 577 79 70
Tide
HW Dover –1

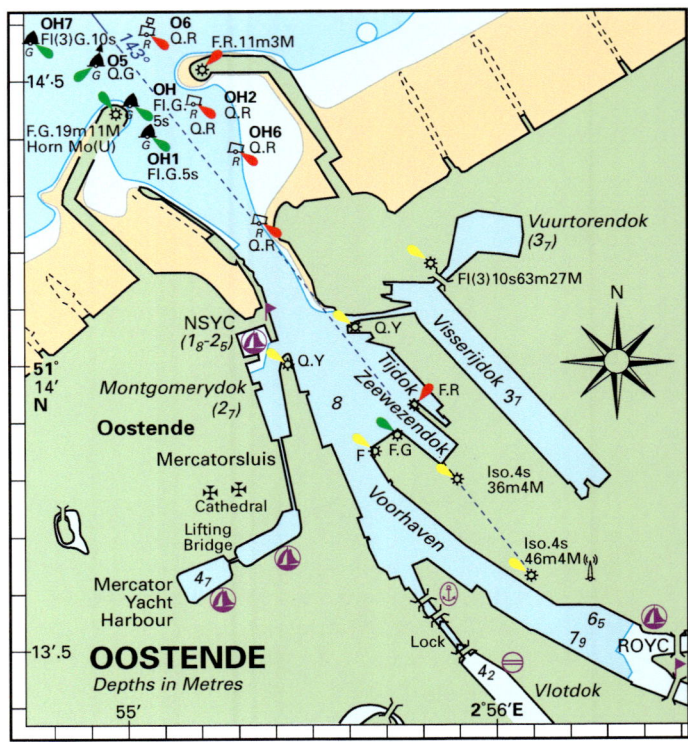

Entrance

Entry is through the outer piers into a large outer harbour. The western pier of the older harbour entrance remains, the eastern pier has been removed and the navigation channel is through a series of lateral lit buoys also marked by leading lights on 143°. Depths of 8m between the two outer walls and next to the old western pier.

The entrance can be uncomfortable in onshore winds over F5, especially when combined with the wash from ferries. From close to **Binnenstroombank** (ECM) head straight for the entrance and along the line of the leading lights.

Four cables in, turn to starboard into Montgomerydok. To starboard again takes you into the North Sea Yacht Club basin. Turn to port for the lock and two opening bridges into Handels Dokken and Mercator Jachthaven. Contact on VHF 14 to arrange the most convenient bridge and lock openings.

On past the Montgomerydok entrance, take the port fork of the Voorhaven where the Royal Yacht Club of Oostende is on the peninsula at the eastern end near the bridge into the Achterhaven.

Mooring and facilities

Royal North Sea Yacht Club, www.rnsyc.be, ☎ +32 59 70 27 54, runs a pontoon marina in Montgomerydok, which gets crowded. Visiting yachts raft up on the main central pontoon. There are toilets, showers, restaurant and drying and scrubbing facilities. It can sometimes get 'rolly' in here from the wash from commercial traffic entering and leaving the dock.

Mercator Marina, www.mercatormarina.be, ☎ +32 59 70 57 62, in the Handels Dokken is a large pontoon marina in the busy part of town next to the station, with toilet and shower facilities.

Royal Yacht Club of Oostende, www.ryco.be, ☎ +32 59 42 71 04, is a friendly pontoon marina, and has good club facilities including drying out, crane and slipway, and can certainly direct vessels to good repair facilities if not available on the spot. The town is well over a mile away and the bus (or a folding bicycle) helps.

Entrance to the Belgian inland waterways, which involves dropping the mast, is via the bridge into the Achterhaven and through the locks into the Oostende-Brugge canal.

Montgomerydok, looking south over the RNSYC towards the locks through to Mercator Marina

BLANKENBERGE

Port contacts
Oostende Radio VHF Ch16 (24hrs), all marinas VHF 23
VVW ☎ +32 50 41 75 36, www.vvwblankenberg.be
SYCB ☎ +32 50 41 14 20, www.scarphout.be
VNZ ☎ +32 50 42 52 92, www.vnzblankenberge.be

Entry signals
Storm and traffic signals are shown from a semaphore mast near the LtHo: 2 B cones points together or Fl.Vi Lt – no vessel under 5m may leave harbour.

Customs
☎ +32 2 577 79 70

Tide
HW Dover –1

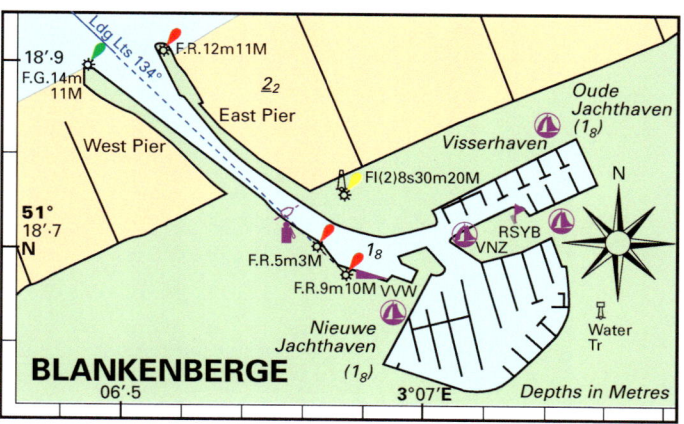

Entrance

The entrance is shallow, varying in depth following southwesterly gales or occasional dredging operations, but normally has at least 1m at MLWS. However, to be on the safe side entrance is not advisable in onshore winds of over Force 5, nor about 1·5hrs either side of LW. Entrance is preferable on the flood.

A black panel on the NE harbour light (with lit figures at night) shows the depth in decimetres at LWS (note, you need to correct for height of tide to find out actual depth on approach).

There are large square building blocks to the east of the entrance slightly higher than the lighthouse. Enter between the white round towers, port and starboard lit, at the ends of the piers. At night leading lights help to guide you in.

Fork to port for the town's old north harbour, the Oude Jachthaven, and starboard for VVW Yacht Harbour.

Mooring and facilities

Both harbours have pontoon moorings, and the minimum depth in both is claimed to be 1·5–2m, but the commodious **VVW Marina** tends to be a little shallow at LW and deeper draught vessels may touch.

There are all facilities, slipping, lifting, repair and chandlery, particularly near the south side of the entrance east of the leading lights.

There are three clubs, **VVW**, www.vvwblankenberg.be, ☎ +32 50 41 75 36 and **Royal Scarphout YC Blankenberge**, www.scarphout.be ☎ +32 50 41 14 20 on the peninsula between the two harbours which is usually open for long periods, and **VNZ** (Vrije Noordzeezeilers) in the Oude Jachthaven, www.vnzblankenberge.be ☎ +32 50 42 52 92.

A picturesque town with a market, interesting shopping streets, and a superb beach and promenade.

Looking NW over the VVW and out along the entrance channel

Oude Jachthaven, left, and VVW marina, right

V. EUROPEAN MAINLAND PILOTAGE

ZEEBRUGGE

Port contacts
Port Control VHF 71 (24hrs) ☎ +32 50 54 68 67
HM ☎ +32 50 54 32 41 / 50
Lock and Inner Hbr VHF 68 ☎ +32 50 54 32 31 (Lock)
RBSC (VZW) ☎ +32 50 54 49 03 www.rbsc.be

Entry signals
It is compulsory to contact Port Control on VHF.
Inner Mole head. Full International Port Traffic Signals. Pilot Station W entrance near lock: 2 B cones points together or Fl.Bu Lt – craft of 6m or less not to leave harbour (onshore wind Force 3 or over, offshore Force 4 or over).

Customs
☎ +32 2 577 79 70

Tide
HW Dover −1

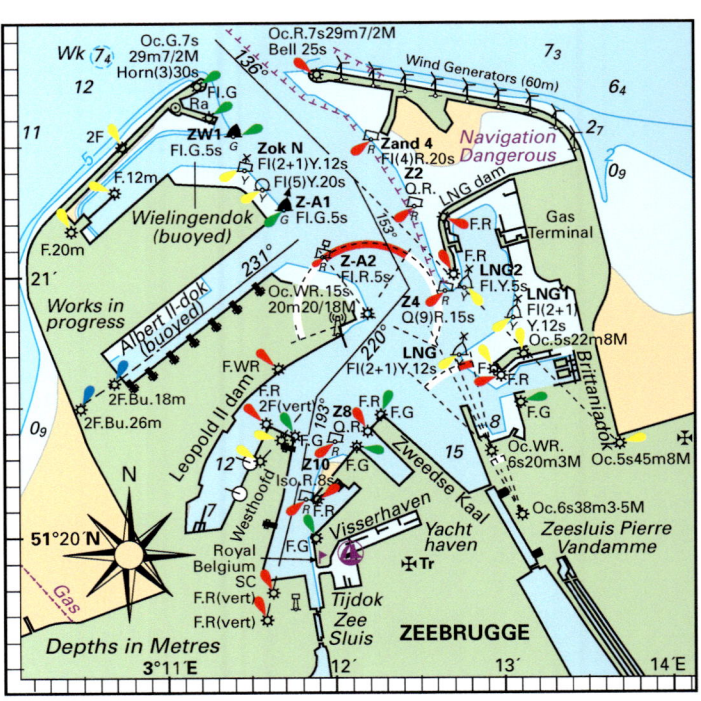

Entrance

There's plenty of water and although rough when strong winds blow directly into the harbour, this is one of the easiest to enter on this coast. The harbour has an encircling outer breakwater of concrete rubble blocks protruding over 1·5M offshore, with a central northern entrance. The main light and traffic signal station is on the end of the old curved Inner Mole.

Zeebrugge entrance

80 NORTH SEA PASSAGE PILOT

Zeebrugge

The outer entrance is between the breakwaters (lit), then directly across to the second, inner entrance between the older west mole head and **Z4** (R) which is just south of the head of the eastern wall, LNG dam. Take care not to stray out of the charted 2 to 3-cable-wide channel. From abeam **Z4**, head to starboard on 220°, keeping northwest of the red channel buoys through the third inner entrance on 193° between **Westhoofd** and **Z10** (R). Then head down the inner harbour channel, giving a wide berth to the drying area on the east side, south of **Z10** buoy. At the southern end of the basin turn hard to port and then port again into the Vissershaven and the pontoons of the Royal Belgian Sailing Club. These are on the curved wall at the west end of the Visserhaven.

There are four sets of leading lights for following the above approach at night. Do not stray out of the initial approach channel across the outer harbour, watch out for buoys (Y) (lit) being moved, and for some buoys used for current measurement.

Mooring and facilities

The south and east end of the Visserhaven is what it says – a fish dock, so keep to the pontoons of the **Royal Belgian Sailing Club** (250 berths), www.rbsc.be ☏ +32 50 54 49 03. This is a very friendly club with good facilities, some room for visitors, and boatyard, scrubbing, and chandlery nearby, as well as several restaurants. There is very little else worth seeing in Zeebrugge itself, but it is another convenient spot for taking a train into Belgium proper, or making a short pilgrimage to Brugge. By boat this is possible via a lock south of the Visserhaven entrance (VHF 68) into the Boudewijnkannal to Brugge. As all the bridges on this canal open you can leave your mast up.

Zeebrugge Visserhaven

V. EUROPEAN MAINLAND PILOTAGE

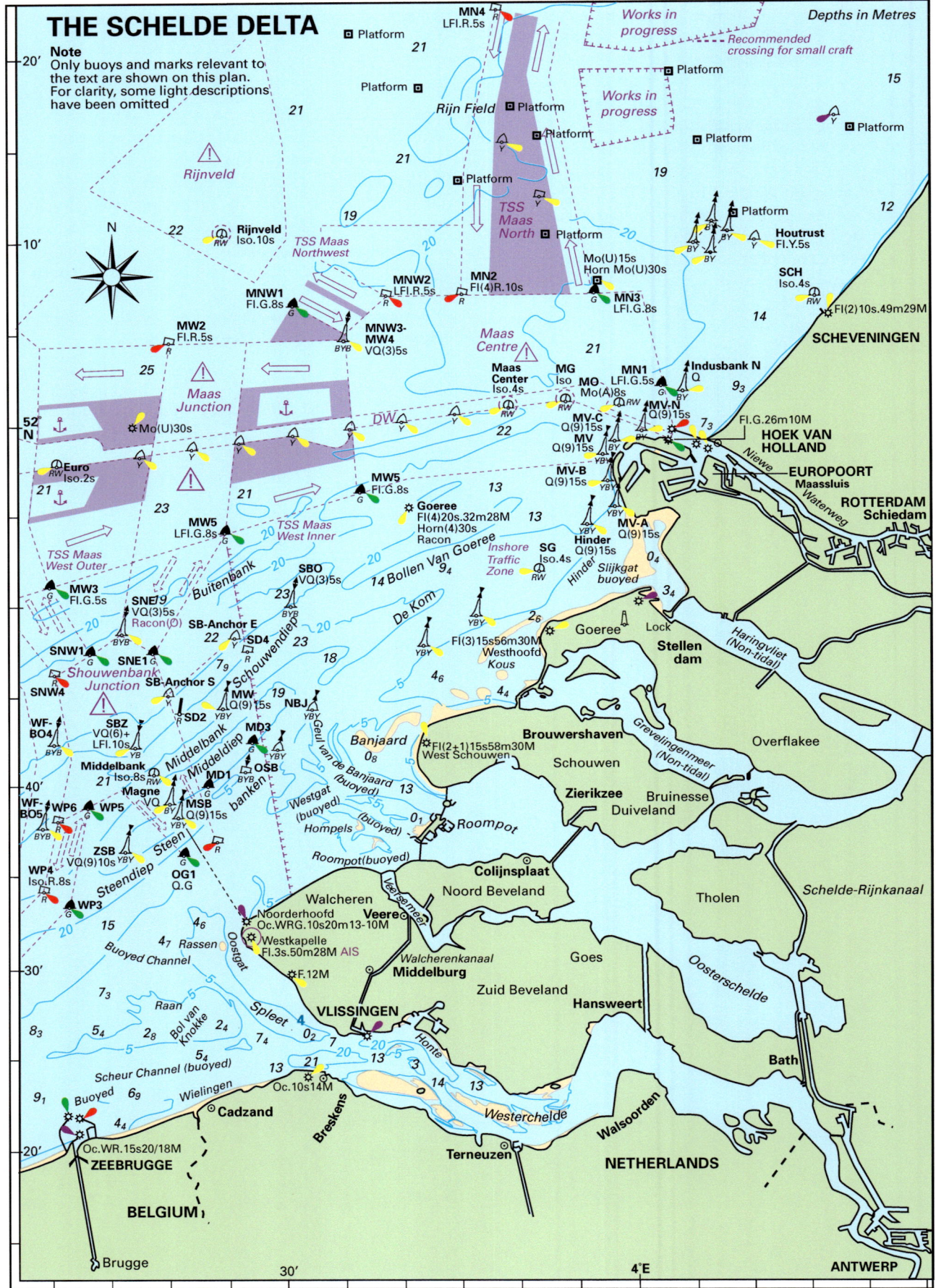

THE SCHELDE DELTA

Sailors making a determined passage to Den Helder and perhaps beyond, are likely to remain on Coastal Route 2, perhaps to Schevingen or IJmuiden, and bypass the Delta altogether. If the weather isn't pleasant, the crew doesn't fancy a long sea trip, or you're not in a hurry and exploring the inland routes attracts, then into the Delta could be the answer.

Navigationally the area is the best provided in the world. Offshore from the Delta the two major precautionary areas at Noord Hinder Junction and round Maas Centre guide traffic to and past Europoort. Maas Centre is covered with a radar surveillance area stretching for a 6–7M radius from the Hoek. It is easy to navigate outside these areas since the whole offshore and inshore region is profusely buoyed and lit, with offshore lights and long-distance onshore lights on the point of each island. Also, Netherlands Coastguard is one of NAVAREA I's special transmitting stations, feeding frequent weather, hazard, and other navigational information in English into the NAVTEX network.

Complicated tidal streams

Tidal streams north of the Westerschelde are straightforward offshore but complicated inshore, even without the distorting effects of the Delta Scheme:

Offshore in the 2hr period between 3·5 and 1·5hrs before HW Hoek van Holland there is a large area of slack water moving north after which the NE-going stream sets in for about 4hrs. From 2·5–4hrs after HW Hoek the stream first turns and runs outwards into the North Sea from the Delta channels and then turns and runs SW for another 5hrs.

At Hoek van Holland this results in a prolonged double LW and a 4·5hr rise of tide, with nearly 7·5 hrs ebb stream from Rotterdam. At the Maasmond entrance of the Nieuwe Waterweg near the Hoek the ingoing tide does not start until 5hrs after the first LW and 2·5 hrs before HW Hoek. At this point the tide is slack off the Delta and about to turn NE. Similarly, the outgoing tide at Maasmond is delayed until 2·5hrs after HW Hoek at the beginning of the second period, when the offshore stream turns outwards into the North Sea before running SW.

The timings of streams in the Brouwershavensche Gat off the Grevelingen Dam and the Slijkgat from the Haringvlietdam are the same as Maasmond, ingoing starting 3–3·5hrs before HW Hoek and outgoing 2–3hrs after HW Hoek.

The net effect of all these tidal timings is that it is easier to travel from north to south across the Delta entrances than in the opposite direction.

Inshore, in the channels north of the Oosterschelde, the NE and SW offshore streams tend to dam up the streams inside the Delta inlets for 4–5hr periods, delaying the times of the turns of tide and giving considerable periods of slack water in these channels.

Areas of less than 5m soundings and drying shallows stretch west and south from the point of each of the main islands: Voorne (near Europoort, the Bollen), Goeree (the Ooster), Schouwen (the Banjaard), and Walcheren (the Rassen and Raan).

Offshore banks lend some protection

Offshore the Delta is screened by three broken longitudinal banks generally with 7–8m depths and of danger to yachts in winds over Force 4. The outer and northernmost is the Schouwenbank; SE of that is a string of banks, Middelbank, Rabsbank and Thorntonbank, stretching from Schouwen to the Westerschelde approaches. The Steenbanken off the Roompot has some patches of less than 4m, to be avoided.

Yacht harbours

There are three ports of call at the mouth of the Westerschelde: Cadzand, a new yacht haven just inside the Dutch/Belgian border, Breskens, on the south side of the Delta and Vlissingen on the north side and giving access to the inland Mast Up Route to Amsterdam. All are a day sail from Oostende, with the tide. Because of the offshore sand banks, wind farms, traffic separation zones and precautionary areas that virtually block this coast, passages direct from the UK are not advised. A course from the UK east coast will require a loop south to enter the Schelde on the coastal running ebb tide (flood into the Schelde itself).

Details of local pilotage in the Schelde area can be found in *Cruising Guide to The Netherlands* (Imray).

V. EUROPEAN MAINLAND PILOTAGE

SCHELDE DELTA TIDAL STREAMS

Westerschelde approaches
(based on HW Vlissingen and HW Dover)

Position	Start times			
	VLISSINGEN		DOVER	
	East	West	East	West
4M NE Kwintebank (KB) buoy	−0230	+0330	−0030	+0530
Neths/Belg. frontier[1]	−0400	+0215	−0200	+0415
Westerschelde ent. (Nieuwe Sluis)	−0500	+0115	−0300	+0315
Oostgat (N end)	+0540	−0130	−0445	+0030

1. NE and SW-going

Westerschelde River
(based on HW Vlissingen and HW Antwerp)

Position	Start times			
	VLISSINGEN		ANTWERP	
	In	Out	In	Out
Vlissingen Road	−0515	+0100		
Terneuzen	−0430	+0130		
Ellewoutsdijk	−0500	+0130		
Hansweert	−0400	+0200	−0610	−0010
Bath	−0310	+0230	−0540	+0020
Lillo	−0315	+0230	−0525	+0020
Antwerp	−0230	+0300	−0440	+0050

Oosterschelde
(based on HW Vlissingen and HW Dover)

Position	Start times			
	VLISSINGEN		DOVER	
	In	Out	In	Out
Westgat approach to Oosterschelde[1]	−0400	+0200	−0200	+0400
Roompot	−0500	+0115		
Zierikzee	−0430	+0125		
Wemeldinge	−0450	+0135		
Zijpe	−0410	+0205		

1. Strong SW-going (in) and NE-going (out) offshore

North of Oosterschelde
(based on HW Hoek van Holland and HW Dover)

Position	Start times			
	H. VAN HOLLAND		DOVER	
	NE	SW	NE	SW
Offshore N of Oosterschelde to close S of Europoort	−0305	+0310	HW	−0530
	In	Out	In	Out
Mid Brouwershavensche Gat	−0305	+0255	HW	+0600
SW point of Goeree[1]	−0550	+0115	−0245	+0320
In Slijkgat	−0330	+0330	−0025	−0550
Off Maasmond entrance	−0200	+0430	+0105	−0450

1. Flood SSE, ebb NNW

Nieuwe Waterweg, Hoek van Holland to Rotterdam
(based on HW Hoek van Holland and HW Dover)

Position	Start times			
	H. VAN HOLLAND		DOVER	
	In	Out	In	Out
In Maasmond entrance	−0230	+0215	+0035	+0520
Maassluis	−0215	+0230	+0050	+0535
Rotterdam	−0145	+0300		

TIDAL DIFFERENCES AND RANGES (based on HW Dover)

Place	HW (time)	Springs/Neaps (range in metres)
Vlissingen	+0212	4·4/3·0
Terneuzen	+0236	4·7/3·2
Hansweert	+0314	
Antwerp	+0342	5·4/4·0
Zierikzee	+0322	3·3/2·4
Wemeldinge	+0347	3·9/2·7
Hoek van Holland	+0251	1·9/1·5
Rotterdam	+0414	1·8/1·6

MAJOR LIGHTS

Offshore
Goeree Mo(U)15s Horn(4)30s 51°55'·5N 3°40'·2E RW chequered tower on platform on piles, Racon, helicopter platform

Onshore
Hoek van Holland
Maasmond Ldg Lts 112° Front Iso.4s29m21M By day 11M 51°58'·9N 4°04'·9E Wh concrete tower, B bands, 101°-vis-123°
Rear Iso.4s47m21M 51°58'·7N 4°05'·8E 101°-vis-123°
Maasmond Ldg Lts 107° Front Iso.R.6s29m18M 51°58'·6N 4°07'·6E R tower, Wh bands, 099·5°-vis-114·5°
Rear Iso.R.6s43m18M 51°58'·5N 4°08'·0E 099·5°-vis-114·5°
Europoort Calandkanaal Ldg Lts 116° Front Oc.G.6s29m16M By day 7M 51°57'·6N 4°08'·8E W concrete tower, R bands, 108·5°-vis-123·5°
Rear Oc.G.6s43m16M By day 7M 108·5°-vis-123·5°
Westhoofd Fl(3)15s56m30M 51°48'·8N 3°51'·9E R sq stone tower
West Schouwen Fl(2+1)15s58m30M 51°42'·5N 3°41'·5E Grey round stone tower, R and W diagonal stripes on upper part
Westkapelle Fl.3s50m28M 51°31'·8N 3°26'·9E Sq stone tower, R metal superstructure
Nieuwe Sluis Oc.10s28m14M 51°24'·4N 3°31'·3E Tower 22m

MAJOR FIXED DAYLIGHT MARKS

Belgian frontier to Breskens
Isolated hotel (conspic) at Wielingen close E of the frontier
Nieuwe Sluis Lt (22m, B octagonal tower, Wh bands)
Breskens grain silo between Westhaven and Oosthaven

N bank of Westerschelde – Vlissingen to Noorderhoofd
Vlissingen: A windmill, St James Church spire, and Vlissingen main Lt (10m, brown metal framework tower at entrance to Koopmanshaven)
Kaapduinen: radio mast and two Ldg Lt towers (14 & 13m, yellow square stone, R bands)
Westkapelle Lt (52m, square stone tower, R metal superstructure)

Walcheren coast – Noorderhoofd to Roompot
Noorderhoofd Lt (16m, R round metal tower, Wh band)
Domburg church spire and nearby water tower
Veere church tower (square with dome) and town hall spire

Schouwen and Goeree coast (S to N)
Concrete lookout tower
West Schouwen Lt (50m, grey round stone tower, R diagonal stripes on upper part)
Westhoofd Lt (52m, R square stone tower)
Goedereede church tower

Voorne coast (S to N)
Brielle church tower
Oostvoorne church tower

Maasvlakte and Hoek van Holland
2 chimneys (175m, R Lts)
Wind generators
Maasvlakte Lt (62m, B octagonal tower, orange bands)
Europoort entrance Lts
Nieuwe Zuiderdam & Nieuwe Noorderdam entrance towers to Maasmond (31m, green and red towers, W bands, helicopter landing platforms on top)
Church towers of 's-Gravenzande, Monster and Ter Heijde
Caution Buoyage changes
There are constant modifications being made to the buoyage of the Schelde Delta and its major tributaries, so make sure you have up-to-date corrected charts.

WIND TURBINES AND WIND FARMS
Consult and update your charts frequently for these highly conspicuous objects which are increasing in number in this area.

NOORD AND ZUID HOLLAND

The British have erroneously named the whole of the Netherlands, 'Holland', after the two provinces of Noord and Zuid Holland, and to most foreign visitors this is probably all they will have time to see, since it includes the seat of government and the royal family in The Hague (Den Haag), the historic water-city of Amsterdam, and, above all, the bulb fields. But as a yachtsman you will have to work hard to see all of this from the limited coastal bases without cycling or using the comprehensive road and rail system.

Of the three harbours, only Scheveningen is worth a long visit, since as well as having its own seaside resort it is extremely convenient for Den Haag. IJmuiden is industrial, and Den Helder a somewhat stark naval harbour. There are, however, several other pleasant seaside resorts with first-class beaches and facilities which do not have harbours but can be reached by bus, tram, or train – Katwijk, Noordwijk, and Zandvoort in the flower-growing district between Scheveningen and IJmuiden, and Egmond and Bergen north of IJmuiden. Lisse and the nearby world-famous Keukenhof Gardens are about halfway between Scheveningen and Amsterdam, not far from Noordwijk, and are best seen early in the yachting season between end-March and mid-May.

Finally, a major attraction of this area is the ease of getting right into the centre of Amsterdam via the Noordzeekanaal (see p.90).

TIDAL STREAMS (based on HW Hoek van Holland, HW Helgoland and HW Dover)

Position	\multicolumn{4}{c}{Start times}			
	H. VAN HOLLAND		DOVER	
	North	South	North	South
Off Maasmond ent.	–0200	+0430	+0105	–0450
3M W of IJmuiden	–0120	+0430	+0145	–0420
Off IJmuiden ent.	–0210	+0350	+0055	–0530
	In[1]	Out	In[1]	Out
In IJmuiden ent.	–0110	+0250	+0155	+0555

[1] Runs clockwise round Buitenhaven

	HELGOLAND		DOVER	
Schulpengat	+0325	–0330	+0305	–0350

TIDAL DIFFERENCES AND RANGES (based on HW Dover)

Place	HW (time)	Springs/Neaps (range in metres)
Scheveningen	+0321	1·9/1·5
IJmuiden	+0401	1·8/1·6
Den Helder	–0438	1·5/1·1

MAJOR LIGHTS
Onshore
Scheveningen Ldg Lts 156° Front Iso.4s14M By day 6·5M 52°05'·8N 4°15'·7E White metal mast
Rear Iso.4s14M By day 6·5M White mast
Scheveningen Fl(2)10s49m29M 52°06'·3N 4°16'·2E Brown metal tower, 014°-vis-244°
Noordwijk aan Zee Oc(3)20s32m18M 52°14'·9N 4°26'·1E Wh square stone tower
IJmuiden Ldg Lts 100·5° Front F.WR.30m16/13M 050°-W-122°-R-145°-W-160° By day F.4·5M 090·5°-vis-110·5° 52°27'·8N 4°34'·5E Dark R round metal tower, RC
Rear Fl.5s52m29M By day F.4·5M 090·5°-vis-110·5° Dark R round metal tower
Egmond aan Zee Iso.WR.10s37m18/14M 010°-W-175°-R-188° 52°37'·2N 4°37'·6E Wh round stone tower
Grote Kaap Oc.WRG.10s31m8M 041°-G-088°-W-094°-R-131° 52°52'·9N 4°42'·9E Red tower 17m
Kijkduin Fl(4)20s56m30M 52°57'·4N 4°43'·7E Brown metal tower, rear Ldg Lt 253·5° with Den Helder Marinehaven Willemsoord, Harssens Island, W breakwater head
Schulpengat Ldg Lts 026·5° Dir.WRG.18m22-18M 53°01'·6N 4°45'·5E Church spire

Schilbolsnol F.WRG.27m8-3M 53°00'·6N 4°45'·8E Green tower, 333°-W-026°-G-033°-W-038° Ldg sector for Schulpengat 038°-R-070°
Den Helder Wierhoofd-haven, Ferry Ldg Lts 208° Front QBu16m 52°57'·8N 4°46'·8E Grey mast, 199°-vis-215°
Rear FBu17m Grey mast
Not visible when ferry is in port
Den Helder Ldg Lts 191° Front Oc.G.5s16m3M 161°-vis-221° 183°-vis-199° 52°57'·4N 4°47'·2E B triangle on building
Rear Oc.G.5s25m3M 161°-vis-247° 183°-vis-199° Grey post

MAJOR FIXED DAYLIGHT MARKS
Church towers of 's-Gravenzande, Monster and Ter Heijde S of Scheveningen
Kijkduin tower blocks
Radio masts (73m) close SW of Scheveningen
Scheveningen Lt (30m brown metal tower)
The Vredespaleis tower behind Scheveningen
Scheveningen pier N of the town and a water tower to its E
Katwijk aan Zee: 2 church towers
Noordwijk aan Zee: Main Lt (25m Wh square tower)
Zandvoort: water tower, 2 churches and tall buildings
IJmuiden: Main Lt (43m dark R tower), 2 steelworks chimneys N of entrance (138m and 158m, R Lts), 2 chimneys further inland (150m, 150m, R Lts), radio masts further N (76m)
Wijk aan Zee: 2 churches
Egmond aan Zee: Main Lt (28m Wh round tower), church spire
Bergen aan Zee: houses on dunes
Petten: nuclear power station with 2 chimneys (45m, R Lts)
Zanddijk: Grote Kaap Lt (17m, Lt 31m, brown round tower)
Huisduinen Lt (18m R square tower) and Kijkduin Lt (55m brown tower)
Texel: Schulpengat Ldg Lts can be seen by day, the rear being a church spire, Schilbolsnol Lt (21m G tower)
Den Helder: Town Hall midway between Kaap Hoofd and harbour entrance, a water tower inland behind it, and a church further E.

Caution buoyage: changes
There are occasional minor modifications being made to the buoyage of the offshore approaches to and in the vicinity of Den Helder and IJmuiden, so make sure you have up-to-date corrected charts.

V. EUROPEAN MAINLAND PILOTAGE

SCHEVENINGEN

Port contacts
Scheveningen VHF 21 (24hrs) Call Scheveningen Port
☏ +31 703 527 721
Traffic Centre Scheveningen VHF 21
YC Scheveningen VHF Ch 31 ☏ +31 (70) 352 00 17,
www.yachtclubscheveningen.com

Entry signals
Contact on VHF to obtain instructions for entering harbour. Traffic signals on mast on Coastguard VTS Centre on N side of entrance to Voorhaven: R Lt over Wh Lt means entry prohibited, Wh Lt over R Lt means departure prohibited. Y Fl Lt indicates that one or more large outward-bound vessels are leaving port and continues flashing until they are clear of moles. R light on inner end of passage into No.2 Haven (yacht marina) means vessels are prohibited from departing.

Customs
☏ +31 881 538 000

Tide
HW Dover –3

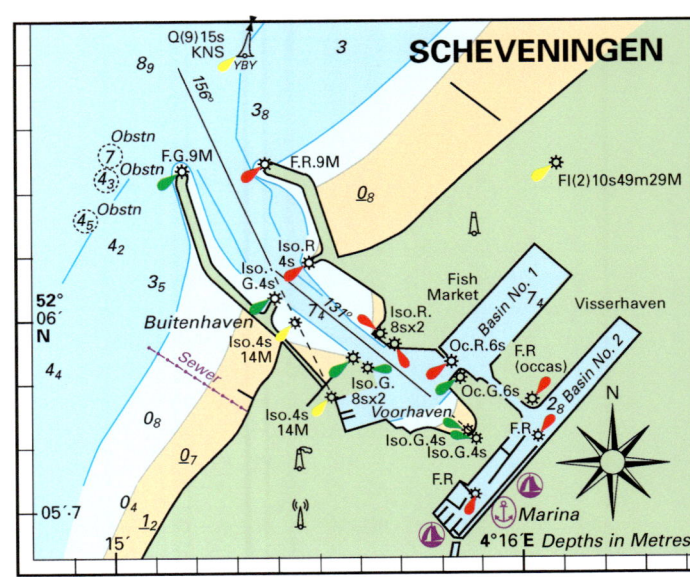

Approach and entrance

Approach is made easy by the 29M long-range light, as well as leading lights (daylight intensity 6M, night 14M) into the outer entrance and a second set into the Voorhaven (4M day, 11M night). There are several outstanding landmarks and there are no offshore hazards. The entrance faces north and is therefore uncomfortable in northerlies. Streams run extremely fast across the entrance at certain times, so it pays to consult *HP 33 Waterstanden en Stromen* (Dutch Hydrographic Office).

The entrance is a triple one, passing between three sets of port and starboard lights on the encircling walls and into the Voorhaven, then hard to port into the fish dock (Basin No.1, least depth 7m) or then hard to starboard along the short canal into the second Basin No.2 (least depth 3m). Turn to starboard again for the large pontoon marina at its southwestern end.

Scheveningen is a good bolthole in bad weather as well as being good for crew changes
© *Aerovista Luchtfotografie / Shutterstock*

Scheveningen

Scheveningen Yachtclub and Visserhaven

Mooring and facilities

The comfortable **Jachtclub Scheveningen** www.yachtclubscheveningen.com ☎ +31 703 520 017, VHF 31, has its own restaurant, as well as several others along the waterfront. There are repair, lifting and chandlery facilities nearby.

This is a good spot for tourism, a lively seaside resort with a Victorian casino, recreation centre, bathing beaches, and pier, as well as an interesting shopping street and historic fishing harbour. Den Haag, the Dutch seat of government and of the International Court of Justice, is only a short tram journey away along the delightful, tree fringed Scheveningseweg, with a plethora of museums, art galleries, royal palaces, and historic buildings. The Hoek ferries are only a short taxi or train journey away from Den Haag for meeting crew.

The marina pontoons in Basin No.2, Scheveningen
© *TasfotoNL / Shutterstock.com*

V. EUROPEAN MAINLAND PILOTAGE

IJMUIDEN

Port contacts
Call IJmuiden Traffic Centre (over 5M from harbour) VHF 07 (24hrs) ☎ +31 255 56 45 00
Call IJmuiden Port Control VHF Ch 61 (24hrs),
Seaport Marina VHF 74, ☎ +31 255 56 03 00,
www.marinaseaport.nl

Noordzeekanaal
IJmuiden Locks direct VHF 22 (24hrs); Nordzeekanal (inland) VHF 03 (24hrs)
Amsterdam (port basins) VHF 68 (24hrs) ☎ +31 205 234 500
Amsterdam (locks and inland waterways) VHF 22 (24hrs)
Oranjesluizen (locks) VHF 18
Broadcasts: When visibility is less than 1000m; Ch 12 H+00, Ch 11 H+30, Ch 14 H+00. Maintain continuous listening watch on the appropriate channel when in the Noordzeekanaal, mandatory during poor visibility.

Entry signals
It is important to make contact by VHF before entry, as the canal and lock entry signals are complicated and there are four locks. Yachts should use the smallest lock, the Kleinesluis. At night you may be directed through one of the other locks with a large ship, unless you decide to wait at the pilings near the smaller locks. Harbour Operations Centre (HOC) is located on the S side of the entrance to Zuider Buitenkanaal. Tidal signal lights (G over Wh rising tide, Wh over G falling tide) are displayed from a radar mast here and about 1 cable SSW of this, International Storm Signal lights are displayed.
Locks all have visual traffic signals with G (entry) or R (entry prohibited), while G and R together mean wait while lock is being prepared.

Tide
HW Dover –4hrs

Approach and entrance
The approach to IJmuiden is assisted by its 29M long-range light, and in daylight by the complex of chimneys as well as smoke rising from the steelworks north of the entrance, visible many miles out to sea. The IJmuiden-Geul approach area and channel has Y conical buoys (lit) on its south side as well as a RW offing buoy (lit) 5M from the entrance. It is easy for yachts to cross the channel at right angles and when approaching the harbour to keep out of the channel until the entrance. There are also leading lights with 4M daylight and 29/16M night range.

The entrance faces north so can be uncomfortable in strong winds from this direction. Tides also run fast across it, and it pays to consult *HP 33 Waterstanden en Stromen* (Dutch Hydrographic Office). Like Scheveningen, the entrance is a triple one, between an outer set, an inner set, and the Zuider Buitenkanaal entrance set of port and starboard lights. Between the inner set and the canal there is a channel with a buoy on the south side and one on the N side, off the end of the wall projecting from Forteiland. Then straight along the channel, past the fishing harbour entrance, to the locks.

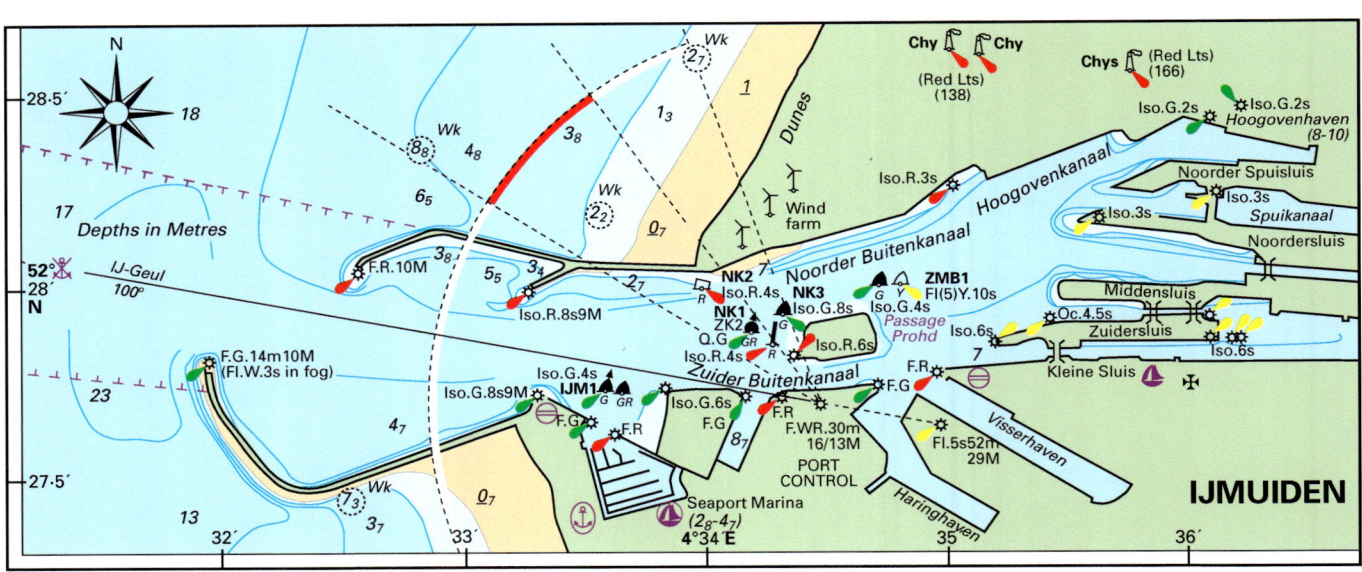

IJmuiden

Mooring and facilities

Prior to entering the Noordzeekanaal there is only one place to moor for any length of time and that is in the **Seaport Marina,** www.marinaseaport.nl ☏ +31 255 56 03 00, VHF 74, a large marina with depths of 3–4·2m, on the south side of IJmuiden's outer harbour close east of the starboard inner entrance light. The marina is entered southwards through two pairs of channel marking buoys and entrance lights and has a wide range of facilities.

Alternatively, once through the locks you can tie up temporarily on the starboard–side wall but beware the danger and discomfort of wash. The tidal Haringhaven and Vissershaven are extremely busy – this is the Netherlands' largest fishing port. Places of interest are the huge fish market, the beaches, and the Velserbeek Park.

Locking into the Noordzeekanaal at IJmuiden

Entrance to the Seaport Marina with fuel berth on right

Seaport Marina IJmuiden

V. EUROPEAN MAINLAND PILOTAGE

THE NOORDZEEKANAAL

The distance from the locks at IJmuiden to Amsterdam's **Sixhaven Marina** ✆ +31 206 329 429, www.sixhaven.nl, is 13·5M. Sheltered deep water (8m throughout) with no bridges, it is possible to sail in the initial country reaches, motoring in the later industrial built-up reaches where the wind is more erratic. Traffic is lighter than on the Nieuwe Waterweg or Westerschelde but still requires great caution, particularly nearer to Amsterdam with its many ferries.

Looking over Sixhaven Marina and the busy Noordzeekanaal   © *Marcel van den Bos / Shutterstock*

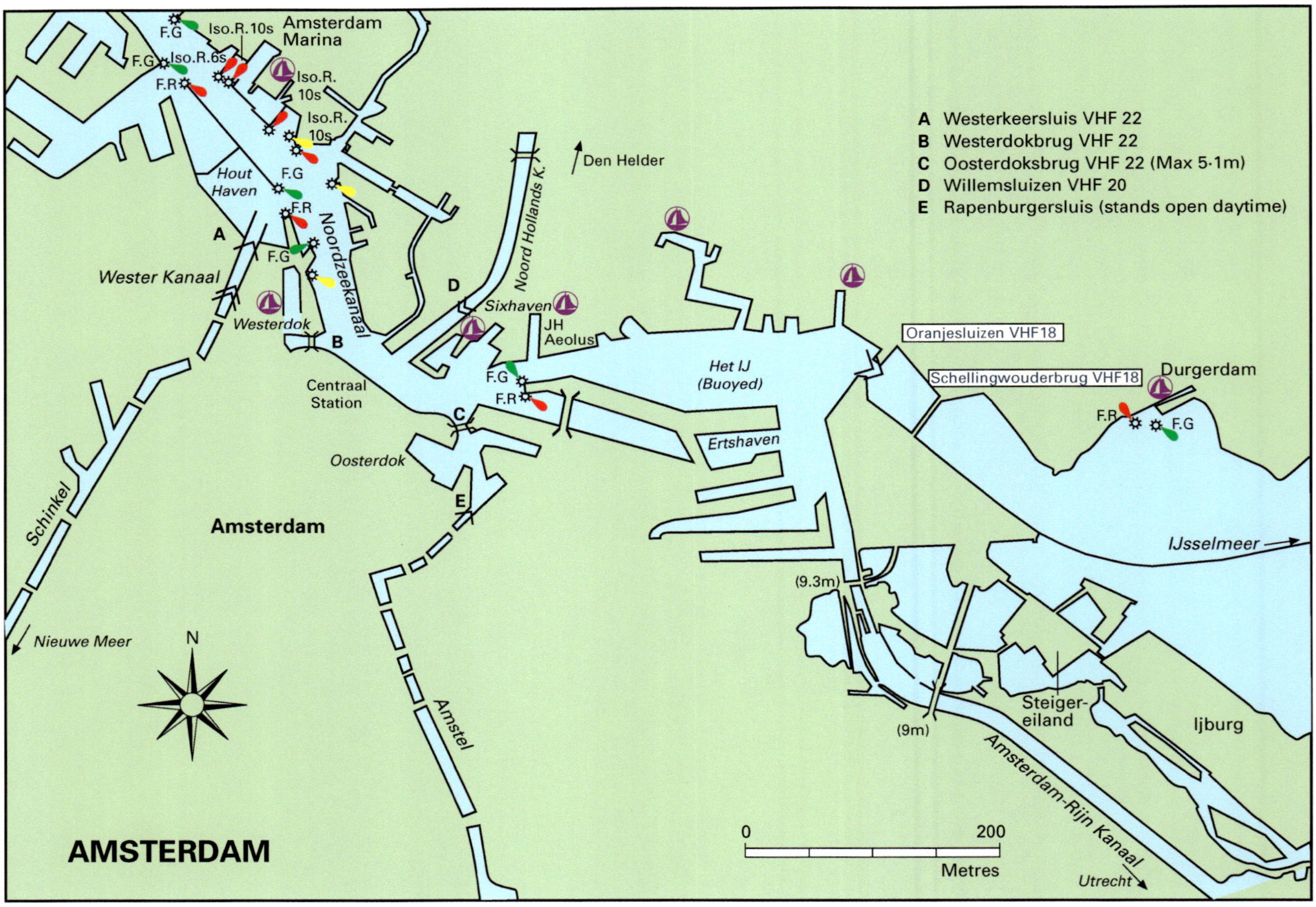

90   NORTH SEA PASSAGE PILOT

DEN HELDER

Port contacts
Traffic Centre Den Helder VHF 62 (24hrs) ☎ +31 652 55 38 15
Den Helder VHF 14 (24hrs) ☎ +31 223 61 39 55,
Moormanbrug VHF 18, Koopvaardersschutsluis VHF 22,
Den Oever lock VHF 20, Kornwerderzand locks VHF 18

Koninklijke Marine Jachtclub ☎ +31 223 65 26 45 (VHF 31)
www.kmjc.eu
WSOV Breewijd ☎ +31 223 61 55 00 www.wscbreewijd.nl
WV Helder-Willemsoord-Nieuwe Diep ☎ +31 223 62 44 22
www.wsvhwn.nl

Jachthaven Marine WV ☎ +31 223 65 21 73
Jachtwerf Den Helder ☎ +31 223 63 69 64
www.jachtwerfdenhelder.nl

Entry signals
Contact should be made first on VHF.
From the signal station on the root of the west pier (Harssens) a series of red and white lights dictate entry, exit and internal harbour movements.

Tide
HW Dover −4.5

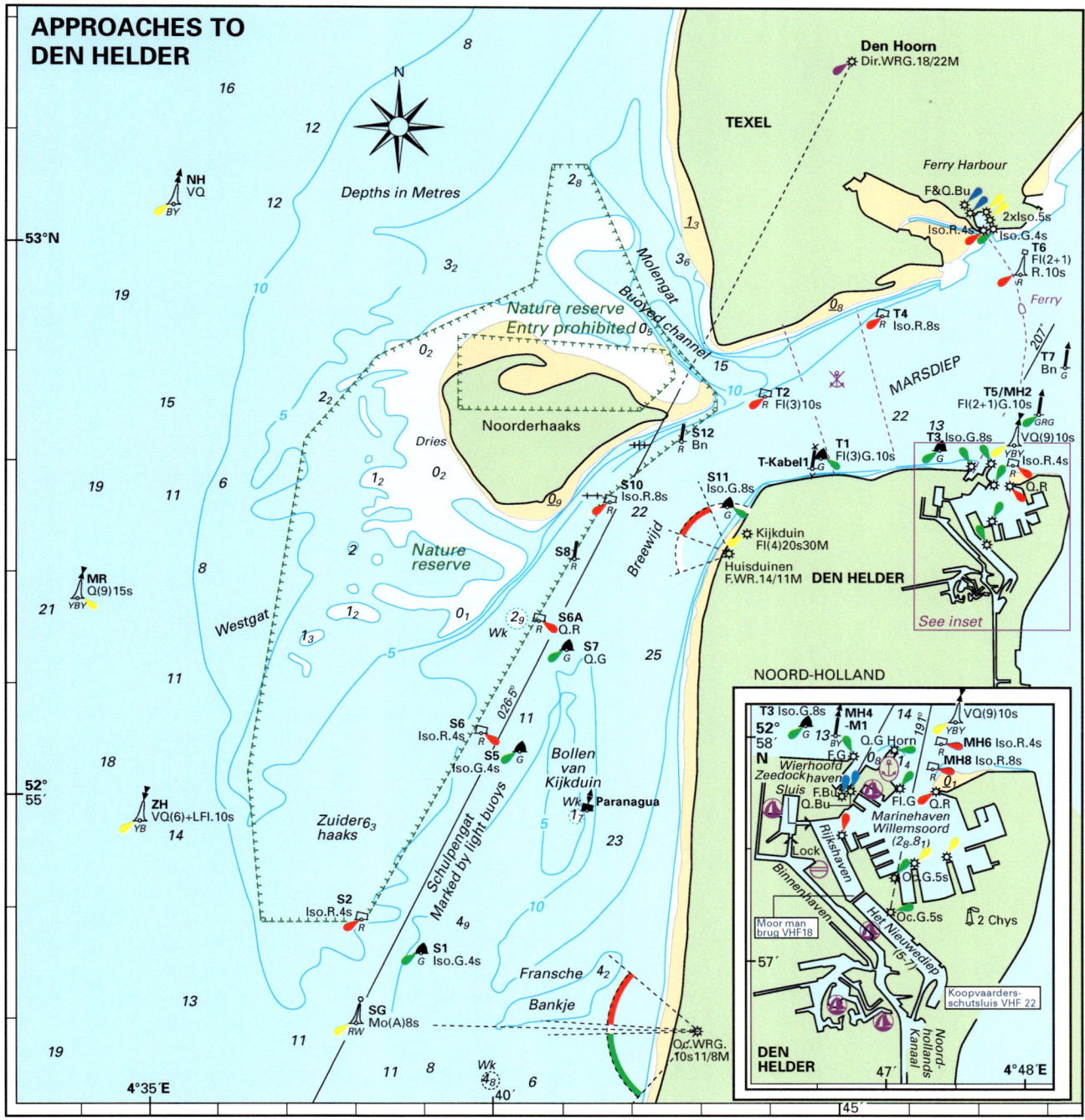

V. EUROPEAN MAINLAND PILOTAGE

The Koninklijke Marine Jachtclub close to the entrance to Den Helder

Approach and entrance

Approach to Den Helder is easy both in daylight and at night. Petten nuclear power station, a square building with two 45m chimneys, is 6M south-southeast of the Schulpengat offing buoy, **SG** (RW, Mo(A)8s). The 55m pencil-like Kijkduin light tower (see photo on page 30) in the narrows opposite Noorderhaaks island is also visible well out to sea. The Schulpengat channel is particularly well lit with R and G isophase buoys and 9M-range daylight (18M at night) leading lights on Texel island, the rear being a church spire. The Molengat approach from the north between Texel and Noorderhaaks is similarly well provided with isophase channel buoys, and a southerly cardinal buoy (lit) off the end of Noorderhaaks at the junction of the two channels with the Marsdiep. The Marsdiep leading to Den Helder is steep-sided and has several buoys (lit) near the harbour entrance which has two further sets of leading lights.

Tidal streams run fast across the entrance of Marinehaven Willemsoord (2·8–8·1m least depth), so once again it pays to use *HP Waterstanden en Stromen* on approach.

Nearing the entrance keep a sharp lookout for ferries coming out of the Veerhaven and heading for 't Horntje on Texel. The main harbour entrance has two successive sets of port and starboard entrance lights. The westernmost of the outer set of entrance lights is on the wall projecting out from Harssens island and the eastern one is a lit buoy **MH8** (R) on the north corner of a dangerous drying patch extending north from the east wall. Having passed between both sets of lights, the yacht harbour is hard to starboard into the first dock behind the island and signal station.

Mooring and facilities

Den Helder is the Netherlands' major naval port, used by merchant vessels only for shelter, repairs and provisions. Yachts and fishing vessels, however, have proved far more difficult customers to keep out, particularly as both pastimes have infiltrated the Navy itself.

Koninklijke Marine Jachtclub, www.kmjc.eu ⓘ +31 223 65 26 45 (VHF 31) is part of the Dutch Navy, and usually a few berths can be found at the pontoons. There is a small clubhouse with showers and toilets.

The town of Den Helder is a 15 to 30–minute walk west of the yacht harbour, and has a good modern shopping precinct, but little of historic interest is left, even though the place has been associated with the Dutch Navy since at least the 16th century. The main attraction is that it is a good stepping-stone to the Waddenzee and Frisian islands. Access to the IJsselmeer is via two deep-water channels to the two locks in its northern dam.

If you intend to take the inland route to Amsterdam and the Noordzeekanaal via the Noordhollands Kanaal, then you can continue down the Nieuwe Diep along the west side of the harbour, request an opening of the Vice-Admiral Moormanbrug (2·7m height unopened) and lock through the Koopvaardersschutsluis and a second opening bridge (both are in service throughout the

Den Helder

WV Helder-Willemsoord marina

day). Hard to starboard after the lock and 0·5M to the north in the Binnenhaven are three more marina clubs: **WSOV Breewijd**, www.wscbreewijd.nl ☏ +31 223 61 55 00, another naval club, **WV Helder-Willemsoord-Nieuwe Diep**, www.wsvhwn.nl ☏ +31 223 62 44 22 and **Jachthaven Marine WV**, ☏ +31 223 65 21 73, all with showers and toilets. There is a launderette nearby. At the southern, Westoever end of Industriehaven, is another marina with showers and toilets, **Jachtwerf Den Helder**, www.jachtwerfdenhelder.nl ☏ +31 223 63 69 64. This haven is entered through yet another opening bridge over an entrance through the west side of the Binnenhaven, south of the above two clubs. For details refer to *Cruising Guide to The Netherlands* (Imray).

Den Helder is a gateway into the canals © Traveller70 / Shutterstock.com

NORTH SEA PASSAGE PILOT   **93**

UK EAST COAST PILOTAGE

DOVER

Port contacts
Dover Port Control maintains a 24-hour listening watch on VHF Channels 74, 12 or 16. Call sign: Dover Port Control, ☎ +44 1304 240 400 ext. 5530 HM ext. 4522, mobile (0)7836 262 713. Automatic radar VHF/DF/AIS identification is also in constant operation. Dover Harbour Marina ☎ +44 1304 241 663, www.doverport.co.uk/marina/

Entry signals
Port traffic control signals are displayed at both entrances and control both entrance and exit. Three high-intensity lights are arranged vertically:
3 Fl.R vert: Emergency, entrance prohibited.
3 R vert fixed: Entry or exit prohibited from the direction indicated.
GWG: Ships may proceed to or from direction indicated

Customs
☎ 0300 123 2012 (National Yachtline)

Tide
HW Dover

Dover is the busiest ferry port in the UK, with up to 120 ferries going in or out every day.

Entering the port and marina

Dover has an Outer Harbour containing ferry and deep-water commercial berths and an Inner Harbour, where the Marina and Hoverport are located.

All small craft must call Dover Port Control on VHF 74 when two miles off to receive instructions for entering, you'll get permission to enter the Outer Harbour when 200 metres from either the Western or Eastern entrances.

Once inside the Outer Harbour proceed with caution to the Inner Harbour. As you approach the Wick Channel entrance call up for permission to enter, again on VHF 74. On passing the traffic lights switch to VHF 80 for marina instructions. At time of publication the new outer yacht harbour was not fully functional.

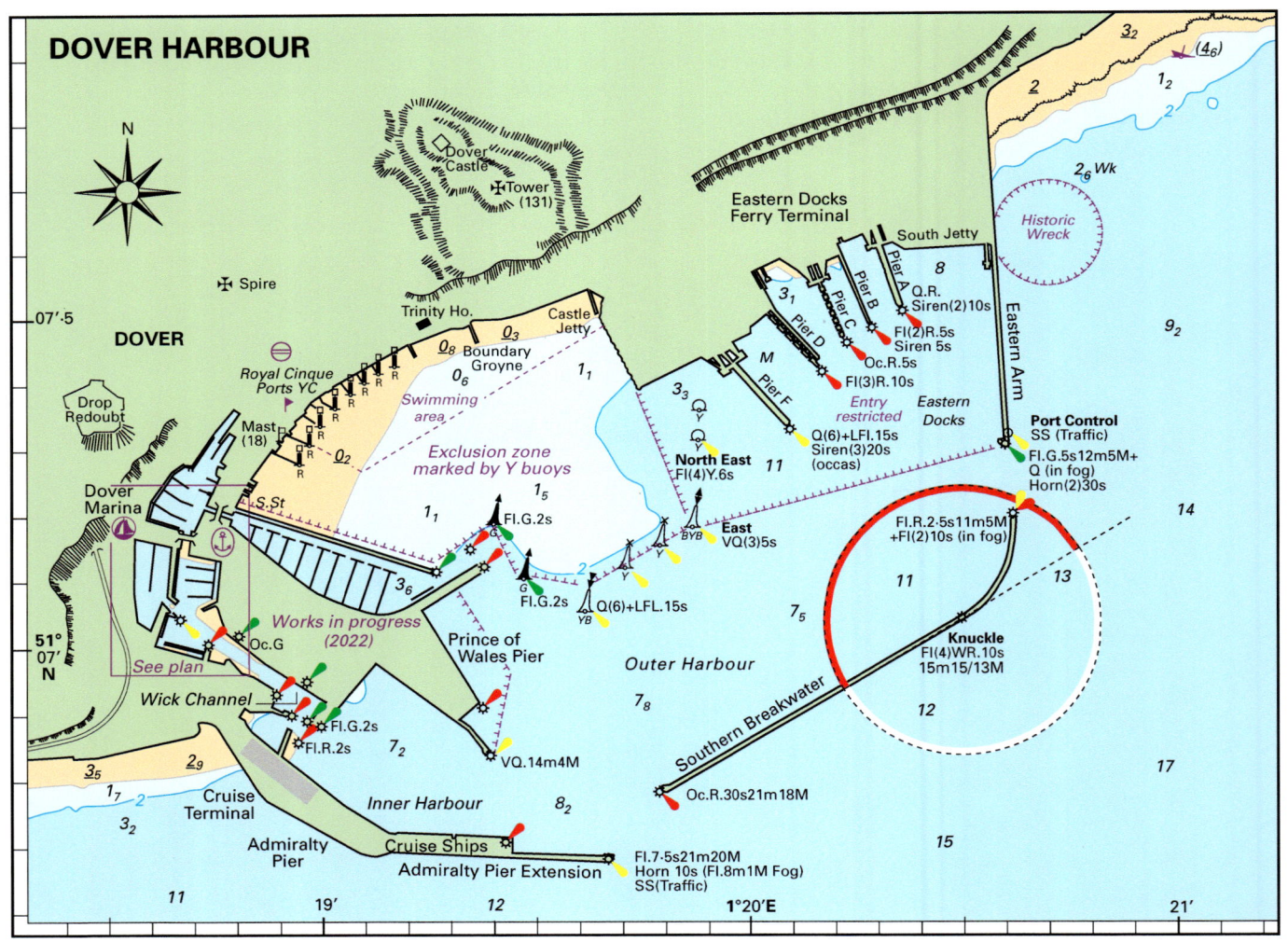

Dover

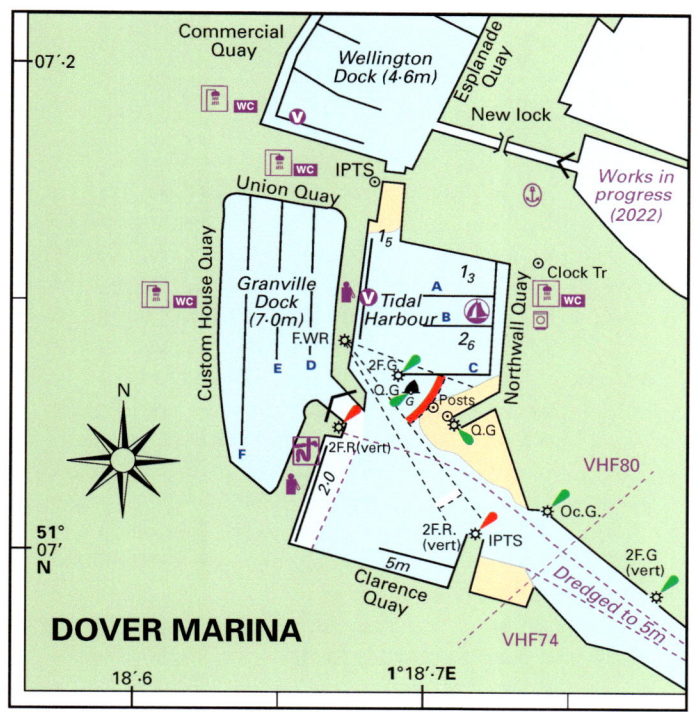

Entering the outer harbour from the East

Proceed along the Southern Breakwater towards the West Entrance. Once inside, cut across to the entrance of the new marina or turn to port into the Inner Harbour, located between the Admiralty and Prince of Wales piers. The entrance to the new marina is straightforward and you now pass through it to the lock into the Wellington Dock.

Dover Castle, sited on top of the cliffs behind the town, is a good landmark, as are the two entrances in the huge harbour wall. There are no hazards close to the harbour, but tides do run across the entrances quite strongly and seas can get quite rough, especially off the western entrance. Dover is a port of last resort.

Looking SW over Dover harbour from the castle. The new marina is at the far right
© Alberto Dubini / Dreamstime.com

Future development plans incorporate the filling in of the channel leading to the inner tidal harbour and Granville Dock to increase commercial dockside facilities

NORTH SEA PASSAGE PILOT 95

VI. UK EAST COAST PILOTAGE

RAMSGATE

Port contacts
Ramsgate Port Control VHF 14 (call from entry to recommended yacht track running parallel with the buoyed entrance channel)
☎ +44 1843 572 100, www.portoframsgate.co.uk

Entry signals
Displayed on the port Control building at the root of the N breakwater. 3 vert G, clear to enter, 3 vert R no entry. Fl.Or light on top of the building indicates a ship is manoeuvring within harbour and you can't enter or leave.
Landfall waypoint: 51°19'·53N, 1°30'·27E (immediately S of RA SCM)

Customs
☎ 0300 123 2012 (National Yachtline)

Tide
HW Dover +0030
Ramsgate is a port of last resort.

Approach and entrance

Although Ramsgate is no longer a ferry port, it is busy with wind farm, fishing, and pilot boat traffic. The Border Force bases two of its cutters in the harbour as well. The harbour entrance is shielded by two low lying rubble groynes, the northern one marked with a Q.G 5M beacon and the southern with a VQ.R 5M beacon. Tides run crosswise to the entrance channel at up to 2kn. Except in emergencies it is forbidden to enter with raised sails. From the **No.4** channel PHM and with permission, follow the charted Recommended Yacht Track. Pass close north of the **North Quern NCM** (Q) to clear shallows. Dead ahead on entering the outer basin is the **Western Marine Terminal**, keep an eye out for fast commercials running in and out. Aim for the **Harbour G** buoy and just beyond it the seasonal R buoy and turn to starboard between them towards the end of the West Pier.

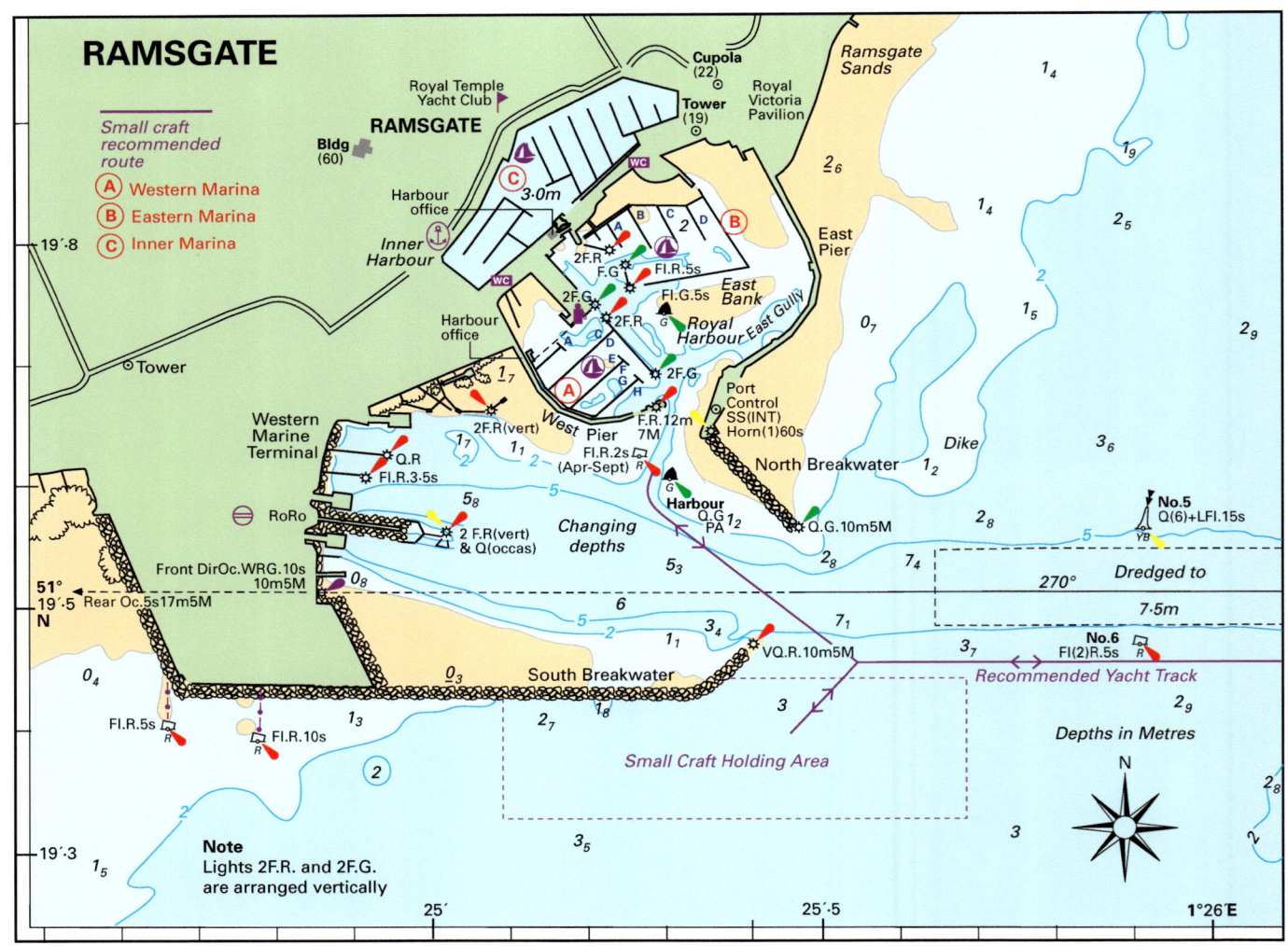

Ramsgate

Ramsgate's Royal Harbour *Patrick Roach*

Mooring and facilities

There are three parts to **Ramsgate Marina**. To port round the end of the West Pier lies the **Western Marina**, which is usually dredged to 2·5m and welcomes visitors. Commercial boats and small fishing craft are mainly in the **Eastern Marina** ahead to starboard. Beyond the tidal basin, and nestling close under the town cliff, is the **Inner Harbour**, entered through a lock. Marina facilities include water and electricity on the pontoons, showers and launderette.

To contact the marina call **Ramsgate Marina** on VHF 80. The fuelling station is the only one on the East Coast to offer white diesel at the pumps.

Ramsgate is not only a busy stopover for leisure craft, it has excellent eating, shopping and provisioning, an interesting maritime museum, and is a short bus ride away from historic Canterbury, Sandwich, and Broadstairs.

For detailed local pilotage see *East Coast Pilot* (Imray).

Ramsgate's historic Royal Harbour is a perfect place to prepare for a Channel or North Sea crossing
© *Beata Aldridge / Dreamstime.com*

NORTH SEA PASSAGE PILOT   **97**

VI. UK EAST COAST PILOTAGE

HARWICH

Port contacts
Port Radio: Harwich VTS on Ch 71 (you are required to monitor Ch 71 when entering and passing through the harbour, but only call in an emergency). HM ☎ +44 1255 243 030.
Shotley Marina ☎ +44 1255 788 982, www.shotleymarina.com

Entry signals
There are no traffic control signals, but yachts must follow the marked yacht channel through the harbour. You can enter at any state of the tide and all weather conditions day or night. Night entry is tricky as the powerful dock lights from the container port make spotting some of the buoys difficult.

Customs
☎ +44 300 123 2012 (National Yachtline)

Tide
HW Walton +0005

Landfall waypoint
51°55'.23N, 001°18'.39E (SW of the Landguard NCM (Q) on the recommended yacht track).

Harwich is a port of last resort.

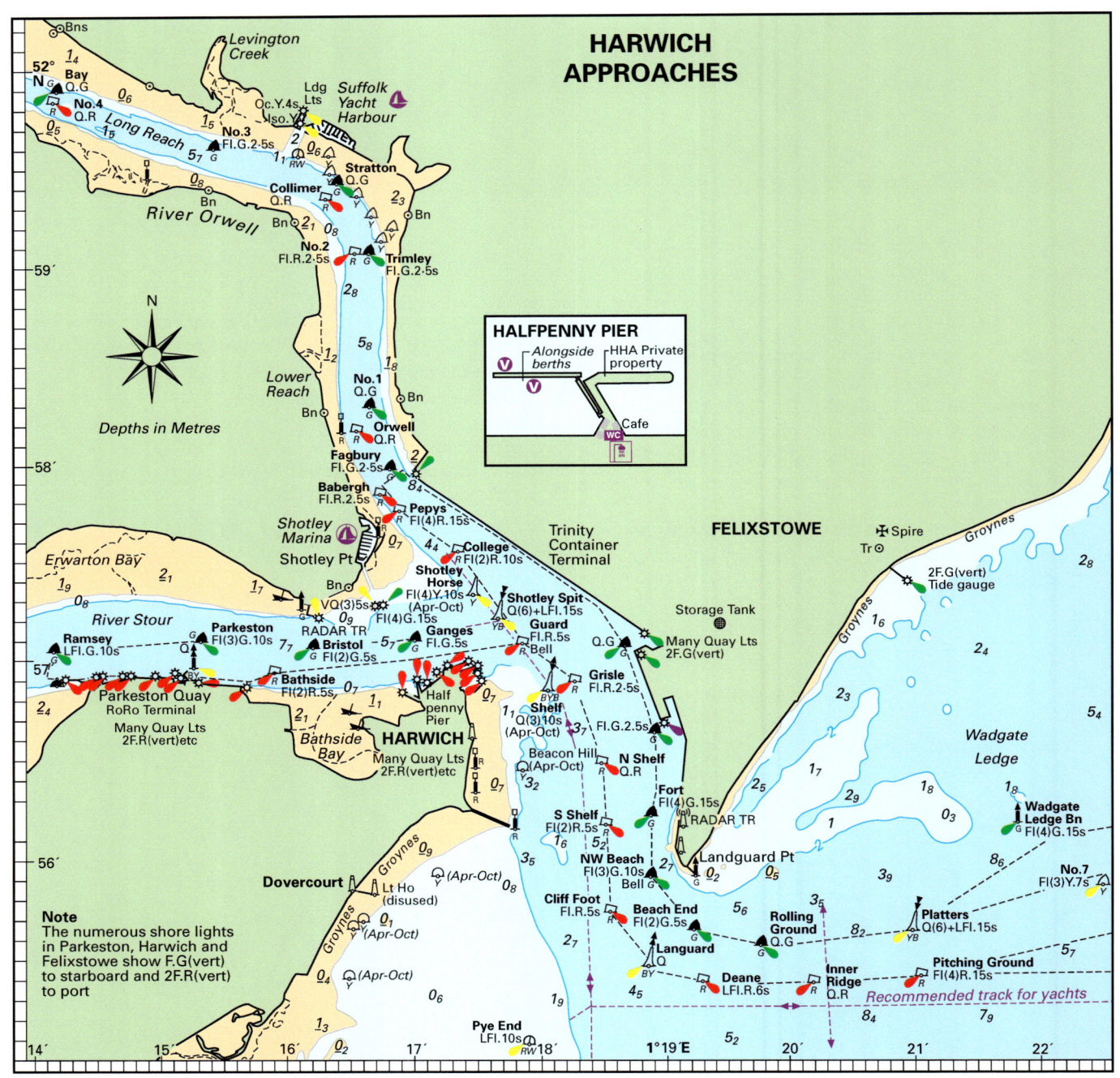

98 NORTH SEA PASSAGE PILOT

Harwich

Approach and entrance

Harwich Harbour is the largest port complex on the UK east coast and includes Felixstowe, the largest container port in Britain, the huge cranes of which can be seen from several miles at sea. The approaches are well marked. Great care must be taken to keep clear of the increasing number of ever larger container ships, dredgers, coasters, and work boats, including the fast pilot cutters taking pilots out to the Sunk pilot station. Follow the recommended yacht tracks. Keep a close eye on depths in the vicinity of **Shelf** (ECM) and the Shotley Spit shoal that extends south and east from Shotley Point.

Mooring and facilities

There are berths for visitors at **Ha'penny Pier**. First come, first served and no rafting. Beware of swells from passing ships while going alongside, the Pier is untenable in strong W or N winds. The gate at the top of the gangway between the leisure vessel pontoons and Ha'penny Pier itself is locked daily at 1730 for security reasons. Access between 1730 and 0900 is only possible using a code obtained from the PM. The office is located at the entrance to Ha'penny Pier. Water and electricity on the pier. There is a café at the root of the pier, with many more nearby in town.

Opposite Ha'penny Pier, on the north side of the River Stour is **Shotley Marina** ✆ +44 1255 788 982, www.shotleymarina.com; callsign Shotley Marina on VHF 80. Full service marina with lock entrance.

For detailed local pilotage see *East Coast Pilot* (Imray).

Harwich

View across Harwich Harbour from inside Ha'penny Pier

NORTH SEA PASSAGE PILOT

LOWESTOFT

Port contacts
Lowestoft Port Control, VHF Ch14, call up before entering.
HM ☎ +44 1502 572 286
RN&SYC ☎ +44 1502 566 726, www.rnsyc.net

Entry signals
On S Pier. 3 reds – no entry; Green-white-green enter on permission.

Customs
☎ +44 300 123 2012 (National Yachtline)

Tide
HW Lowestoft

Landfall waypoint
52°28'.18N, 001°46'.06E (1/2M E of entrance)

Lowestoft is a port of last resort.

Approach and entrance

Approaches to the harbour entrance by both day and night are easy if you follow the channels. Because of shifting sand banks and rough waters in certain weather conditions it is vital the first time visitor sticks closely to these channels.

There are some good landmarks to guide your approach. Close north of the entrance is Gulliver, the tallest and most easterly wind turbine in Britain and the rig and wind farm servicing yard. Often the top of a rig can be seen over the harbour wall. If coming from northeast, then the white-painted Lowestoft Lighthouse on the cliffs to the north of the harbour is a good aiming point. (It was the first lighthouse built under Samuel Pepys, the first Master of Trinity House). Once inside, the harbour opens out into a series of basins.

Opposite the Trawl dock, to port, is the yacht basin at the head of which stands the **Royal Norfolk and Suffolk YC (RN&SYC)**. Enter with care, because boats may be manoeuvring inside. Be aware too that there's a shallow sand bar on the corner of the starboard (W) entrance buttress, especially at lower stages of the tide.

Mooring and facilities

Berths can usually be found in the **Royal Norfolk and Suffolk YC** ☎ +44 1502 566 726, www.rnsyc.net. Contact on VHF 80 callsign Royal Norfolk Harbourmaster. Full service marina with shops and the Lowestoft Historic Ships Museum nearby.

For detailed local pilotage see *East Coast Pilot* (Imray).

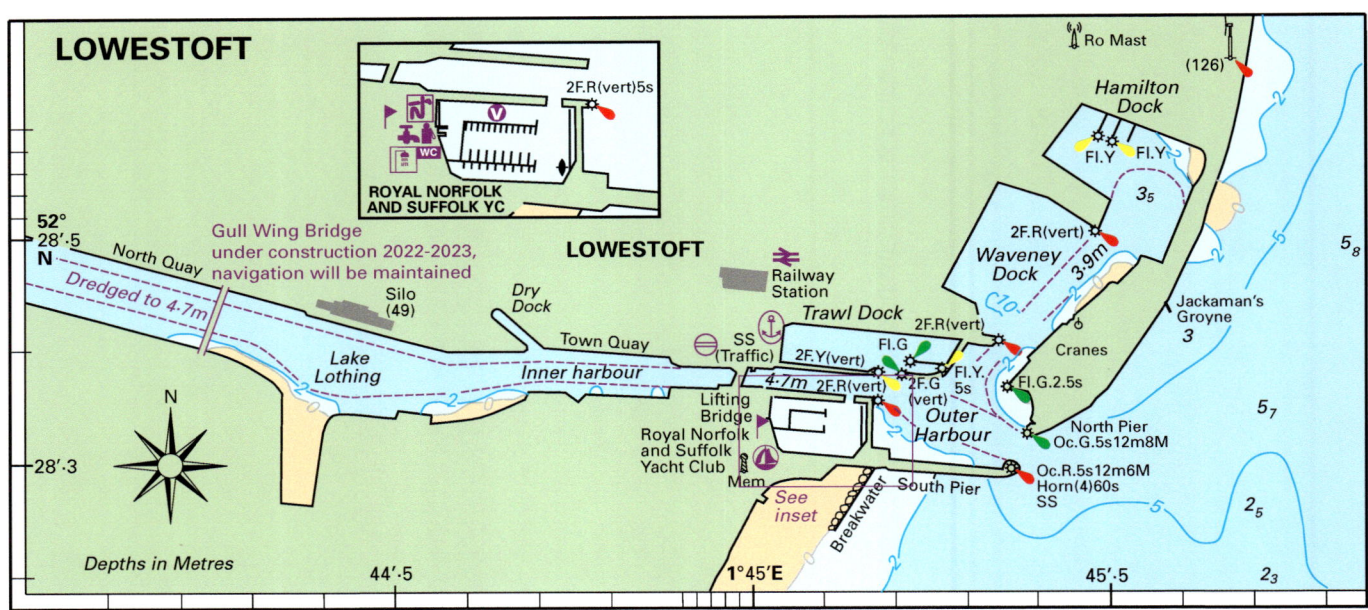

Lowestoft

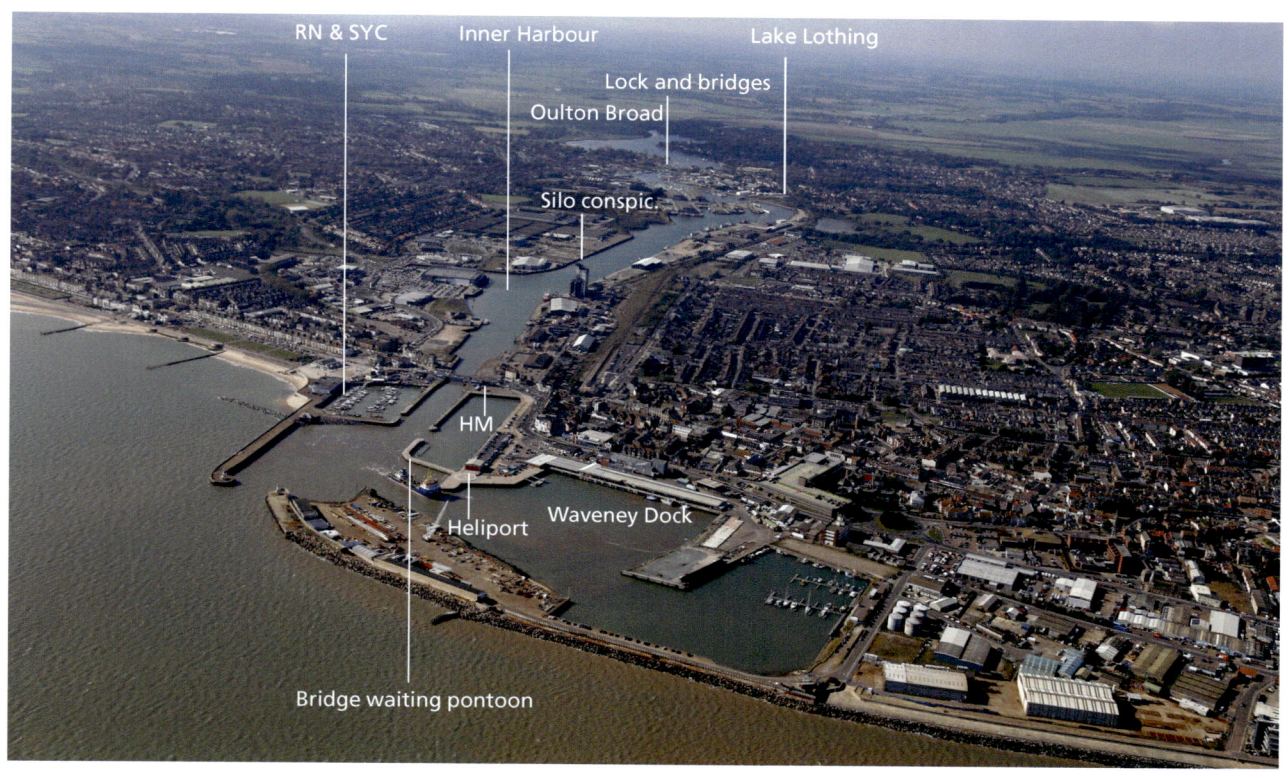

Looking west across the harbour and town of Lowestoft *Patrick Roach*

Royal Norfolk and Suffolk YC Marina

NORTH SEA PASSAGE PILOT   **101**

APPENDICES

i. RYA RECOMMENDATIONS FOR SAFETY EQUIPMENT FOR OFFSHORE CRUISERS (SAIL AND POWER)

UK Merchant Shipping Regulations

Private vessels of over 13·7m (45ft) in length are subject to the Merchant Shipping (Life Saving Appliances) Regulations, 1986, and the Merchant Shipping (Fire Appliances) Rule, 1984, Ships of Class XII.

RYA recommendations

The recommendations below published by the RYA apply to Category B yachts which cruise around the British Isles and NW Europe making offshore passages of between 50 and 500 miles. Yachts in this category are likely to be between 8m and 13·7m LOA.

1. **Means of propulsion**
   For sailing yachts only, a storm trysail or deep reef in the mainsail.
   For sailing yachts fitted with auxiliary engines: either a battery whose sole purpose is to start the engine, which is isolated from all other electrical systems, or a means of starting the auxiliary by hand.

2. **Anchors**
   Anchor(s) with length of warp and chain or chain only appropriate to the cruising area and a diameter appropriate to the size of the yacht. Anchoring fittings to include:
   a. A fairlead at the stem capable of being closed over the anchor warp or chain.
   b. A strong point, on the foredeck, either a mooring cleat, sampson post or anchor winch, securely fitted to the structure of the hull.

3. **Bailing and bilge pumping**
   - A hand bailer
   - Bucket(s) of not less than 9 litres (1·2 gallon) and not more than 14 litres (3 gallon) capacity fitted with a lanyard and a strongly secured handle
   - 2 Hand bilge pumps discharging overboard, and capable of operation with all hatches closed
     (An electric or engine driven bilge pump may be fitted in place of one hand-operated pump for category B or A yachts)
   - Softwood plugs attached adjacent to all through hull fittings
     All through hull fittings able to be closed.

4. **Detection equipment**
   - A radar reflector, properly mounted with as large a radar cross section as can reasonably be carried
   - Fixed navigation lights which comply with the International Regulations for Preventing Collisions at Sea, including motoring cone (sail only) anchor ball and light
   - A foghorn
   - Powerful torch ('steamer scarer').

5. **Pyrotechnics (in date)**
   - 4 hand-held red flares
   - 2 buoyant orange smoke signals
   - 4 red parachute rockets
   - 4 hand-held white flare – not available worldwide

6. **Firefighting equipment**
   - Fire blanket, for all yachts with cooking equipment (BS EN 1869).
   - For yachts either fitted with a galley and/or carrying fuel for an engine, 3 multi-purpose extinguishers of minimum fire rating 5A/34B (to BS EN 3).
   - For yachts with engines over 25hp a fixed automatic or semi-automatic fire fighting system installed to discharge into the engine space.

7. **Personal safety equipment for each member of the crew**
   - Warm clothing, oilskins, sea boots and hat
   - A lifejacket (BS EN 396) 150 Newtons
   - Lifejacket light
   - Face spray cover
   - A safety harness for each of the crew (BS EN 1095)
   - Immersion suit – per crew member
   - Jackstays and cockpit clip on points.

8. **Liferaft**
   - A liferaft designed for the sole purpose of saving life, of enough capacity to carry everyone on board
   - An emergency grab-bag.

9. **Man overboard recovery equipment**
   - Horseshoe lifebelts fitted with drogue and self-igniting light
   - Buoyant sling on floating line – may replace one horseshoe lifebelt if two are carried

- A buoyant heaving line, at least 30m in length, with quoit
- A boarding ladder capable of rapid and secure attachment
- A dan buoy with a large flag.

10. Radio
- A radio receiver, capable of receiving shipping forecasts on 198kHz and weather forecasts broadcast by local radio stations
- A VHF/DSC radio telephone
- 406MHz EPIRB – registered in the name of the vessel Navtex
- Radio transponder (SART)
- Emergency VHF radio aerial with a prepared deck mounting
- Waterproof VHF hand-held radio.

11. Navigational equipment
- Up-to-date charts of the local area and a local tide table
- Up-to-date charts, tide tables and navigational publications of the intended cruising area and adjacent areas into which the yacht may go under stress of weather
- Steering compass – able to be lit at night. Hand-bearing compass
- Navigational drawing instruments including parallel rulers, or a plotting instrument and dividers. Barometer
- Lead line and echo sounder. GPS. A watch or clock.
- Distance measuring log. Binoculars.

12. First aid kit
A first aid kit and manual.

13. General equipment
- Emergency tiller on all wheel steered vessels
- Towing warp (not required if anchor warp is carried). Mooring warps and fenders
- 2 waterproof torches
- A rigid or inflatable tender
- Tool kits for general, engine, electrical and sail repairs. Spares for engine and electrics, and bosun's bag of shackles and twine
- Emergency water supply, isolated from main tanks. Emergency repair materials
- Bosun's chair (sit harness BS EN 813 1997).

ii. RULE 10 'TRAFFIC SEPARATION SCHEMES'

1. This Rule applies to traffic separation schemes adopted by the IMO.
2. A vessel using a traffic separation scheme shall: proceed in the appropriate traffic lane in the general direction of traffic flow for that lane; and so far as practicable keep clear of a traffic separation line or separation zone; normally join or leave a traffic lane at the termination of the lane, but when joining or leaving from either side shall do so at as small an angle to the general direction of traffic flow as practicable.
3. A vessel shall so far as practicable avoid crossing traffic lanes, but if obliged to do so shall cross on a heading as nearly as practicable at right angles to the general direction of traffic flow.
4. A vessel shall not use an inshore traffic zone when she can safely use the appropriate traffic lane within the adjacent traffic separation scheme. However, vessels of less than 20 metres in length, sailing vessels and vessels engaged in fishing may use the inshore traffic zone. Notwithstanding sub-paragraph (d) (i) a vessel may use an inshore traffic zone when en route to or from a port, offshore installation or structure, pilot station or any other place situated within the inshore traffic zone, or to avoid immediate danger.
5. A vessel, other than a crossing vessel or a vessel joining or leaving a lane, shall not normally enter a separation zone or cross a separation line except in cases of emergency to avoid immediate danger; to engage in fishing within a separation zone.
6. A vessel navigating in areas near the terminations of traffic separation schemes shall do so with caution.
7. A vessel shall so far as practicable avoid anchoring in a traffic separation scheme or in areas near its terminations.
8. A vessel not using a traffic separation scheme shall avoid it by as wide a margin as is practicable.
9. A vessel engaged in fishing shall not impede the passage of any vessel following a traffic lane.
10. A vessel of less than 20m in length or a sailing vessel shall not impede the safe passage of a power-driven vessel following a traffic lane.
11. A vessel restricted in her ability to manoeuvre when engaged in an operation for the maintenance of safety of navigation in a traffic separation scheme is exempted from complying with this Rule to the extent necessary to carry out the operation.
12. A vessel restricted in her ability to manoeuvre when engaged in an operation for the laying, servicing, or picking up of a submarine cable, within a traffic separation scheme, is exempted from complying with this Rule to the extent necessary to carry out the operation.

APPENDICES

iii. COASTGUARD AND RESCUE FACILITIES IN THE SOUTHERN NORTH SEA

Access to all facilities via VHF 16.

British waters

Humber and Dover Coastguards keep watch on VHF 16 covering the whole east coast and Thames Estuary between the two centres. Call sign is UK Coastguard.

RNLI Offshore lifeboats

Wells-next-the-Sea, Cromer (independent), Gt Yarmouth, Lowestoft, Aldeburgh, Harwich, Walton-on-the-Naze, Sheerness, Ramsgate, Dover, Dungeness.

RNLI Inshore lifeboats

Wells-next-the-Sea, Cromer, Happisburgh, Great Yarmouth, Southwold, Aldeburgh, Harwich, Clacton-on-Sea, West Mersea, Burnham-on-Crouch, Southend-on-Sea, Sheerness, Whitstable, Margate, Ramsgate.

French waters

CROSS, the French rescue organisation for the English Channel and southern North Sea, keeps watch on VHF 16. Lifeboats and rescue tugs are stationed at Calais and Dunkerque.

Belgian waters

Offshore and inshore lifeboats are based at Nieuwpoort, Oostende and Zeebrugge. Call the nearest Coast Radio Station on VHF 16 or 2182kHz for assistance.

Netherlands waters

Life-saving service is supplied by the Koninklijke Nederlandse Redding Maatschappij (Royal Dutch Rescue Association), usually just called KNRM. Call on VHF 16 and the Dutch coastguard, which keeps 24 hours listening watch will answer.

KNRM Offshore lifeboats

Breskens, Noordland, Stellendam, Hoek van Holland, Scheveningen, IJmuiden, Den Helder.

KNRM Inshore lifeboats

Cadzand, Ouddorp, Ter Heijde, Katwijk aan Zee, Noordwijk aan Zee, Zandvoort, IJmuiden, Wijk aan Zee, Egmond aan Zee, Den Helder.

iv. CHARTS

IMRAY

Imray chart coverage for the North Sea can be found at **www.imray.com**

Imray Navigator app

Imray charts, as well as those from other official Hydrographic Offices, are available on the Imray Navigator app. Download the app for free on the App Store or Google Play for navigation software and demonstration charts. Subscribe to chart sets by area for updates throughout the year.

Imray 2000 series chart packs

2000 Suffolk and Essex Coast
Lowestoft to River Crouch

2100 Kent and Sussex coasts
Thames Estuary to the Solent

2120 Kent and Sussex coasts
Nieuwpoort to Den Helder (including North Sea Passage Planning sheet)

2110 North France
Hauts-de-France and Normandy Coasts

Passage charts

Chart	Title	Scale
C25	Harwich to the River Humber and Holland	239,300
C26	IJmuiden to Die Elbe	338,000
C30	Thames to Holland and Belgium. Harwich and North Foreland to Hoek van Holland and Calais	182,000

Coastal charts

Chart	Title	Scale
C1	Thames Estuary. Tilbury to North Foreland and Orfordness	122,000
C2	The River Thames. Teddington to Southend. Teddington to Vauxhall	17,000
	Vauxhall to Barking	14,000
	Barking to Southend	40,000
C28	The East Coast. Harwich to Wells	126,000
C29	East Coast of England. Orfordness to Blyth	261,000

Approach/harbour charts

Chart	Title	Scale
C8	North Foreland to Beachy Head and Boulogne	115,000

Small format charts

Chart	Title	Scale
Y2	Rivers Ore and Alde	35,000
Y6	Suffolk and Essex Coasts	120.000
Y7	Thames Estuary South	120,000
Y12	Rivers Stour and Orwell	35,000
Y14	The Swale	35,000
Y16	Walton Backwaters to Ipswich and Woodbridge	32,000
Y17	The Rivers Colne to Blackwater and Crouch	49,000
Y18	River Medway. Sheerness to Rochester with River Thames, Sea Reach	21,000

NETHERLANDS HYDROGRAPHIC OFFICE
(Small Craft Charts)

Chart	Title	Scale
1801	North Sea Coast	375,000
1803	Westerschelde	250,000
1805	Oosterschelde	50,000
1807	Zommer, Volkerak	50,000
1809	Nieuwe Waterweg	250,000
1810	IJsselmeer & Randmeren	210,000
1811	Waddenzee (West)	250,000
1812	Waddenzee (East)	200,000

Only 1801, 1811 and 1812 are now revised annually.

GLOSSARIES

This a summary of the *major*, not all, differences in pronunciation between Dutch and English.

Most of the single consonants have similar pronunciations, some a little more abrupt than English. The ones which are significantly different together with some multiple consonants are:

ch	similar to the 'ch' in the Scottish 'loch'
g	as for 'ch' above
j	similar to English 'y'
r	rolled like the Scottish or guttural like the French
sch	combined 's' and 'ch' (above) - the most difficult (e.g. Scheveningen)
sj	similar to 'sh' in English
tj	similar to 'ch' in cheese
v	closer to English 'f' than to 'v'
w	closer to English 'v' than to 'w'

Most of the single vowels also have similar pronunciations, again some a little more abrupt than English. The ones which are significantly different together with the multiple vowels/ consonants are:

e, ee	often (not always) pronounced as the *a* in 'above' e.g. (*de* (the), *een* (a), *snedig*/witty *vriendelijk*/friendly)
i, ij	
aa	as in (BBC) English 'bath'
au	as 'ow' in 'how' (e.g. *blauw*/blue)
aai	as for aa with 'ee' as in 'cheese' added (e.g. *saai*/slow)
ee	as in 'train'
eeuw	as for ee with 'oo' as in 'moo' at the end (e.g. *leeuw*/lion)
ei	as in 'mail'
eu	difficult. As for 'er' in 'her' but shorter e.g. *keus*/choice)
ie	as in 'fleet'
ieuw	combined *ie* as in 'fleet' (above) and *oe* (below) (e.g. *nieuw*/new)
oo	as in 'boat' (the Dutch spelling is *boot*, pronounced as for the English)
oe	'oo' as in 'cool'
ooi	combined *oo* and *ie* above (e.g. *mooi*/pretty)
oei	combined *oe* and *ei* above (e.g. *moeilijk*/difficult)
ou	(same as *au* above) as 'ow' in 'how' (*oud*/old)
uu/uw	difficult. As for 'ee' in 'been' but with rounded lips, like 'u' in French 'lune' (*buur*/neighbour, *ruw*/rough)
ij	not to be confused with the short *ij* at the end of some words (above). Same as *ei* above i.e. pronounced as in 'mail'. Sometimes spelt 'y', and always placed near 'y' in the alphabet. (e.g. IJmuiden, both letters are capitals at the beginning of a word)
ui	close to ou above, as 'ow' in 'how' (e.g. IJmuiden)

ENGLISH TO DUTCH AND FRENCH

English	Dutch	French
aft	achter	arrière
anchor	anker	ancre
anchorage	ankerplaats	mouillage
anchorage prohibited	verboden ankerplaats	défense de mouiller
attendance	bediening	présence
bacon	spek	lard
baker	bakker	boulanger
batten	zeillat	latte
beacon	baken	balise
beef	rundvlees	boeuf
bell	mistklok	cloche
binoculars	verrekijker	jumelles
black	zwart	noir
block	blok	poulie
blue	blauw	bleu
boat	boot	bateau
boom	giek	bome
bread	brood	pain
breadth (beam)	breedte	largeur
bridge	brug	pont
brown	bruin	brun
bulkhead	schot	cloison
bunk/berth	kooi	couchette
buoy	ton, boei	bouée
butcher	slager	boucher
butter	boter	beurre
cabin	kajuit	cabine
chain	ketting	chaîne
channel/fairway	geul	chenal
channel/waterway	vaarwater	chenal/canal
chart	zeekaart	carte maritime
cheese	kaas	fromage
chemist	apotheek	pharmacien
clew	schoothoek	point d'écoute
closed	gesloten	fermé
cockpit	kuip	cockpit
current	stroom	courant
customs	douane	douane
cutter	kotter	cotre
dentist	tandarts	dentiste
depth	diepte	profondeur
diesel engine	dieselmotor	moteur diesel
dinghy	bijboot	prame
dinghy	jol	youyou
draught	diepgang	tirant d'eau
east	oost	est
ebb	eb	marée descendante
echo sounder	echolood	echosondeur
eggs	eieren	oeufs
ferry	pont	bac
ferry	veer	bac
fish	vis	poisson
fishing harbour	vissershaven	port de pêche
fishmonger	vishandel	marchand de poisson
fixed bridge	vaste brug	pont fixé
flood	vloed	marée montante
fog	mist	brouillard
foghorn	misthoorn	corne de brume
foot	onderlijk	bordure
fore	voor	avant
forecastle	vooronder	gaillard d'avant
foresail	voorzeil	voile de misaine
gale	storm	coup de vent
genoa	genua	gênois
grease	vet	graisse
green	groen	vert
greengrocer	groenteboer	marchand de légumes
grocer	kruidenier	épicier
halyard	val	drisse
ham	ham	jambon
harbour	haven	bassin
harbour master	havenmeester	capitaine de port
hatch	luik	écoutille
head	tophoek	point de drisse
height (air draught)	doorvaarthoogte	tirant d'air
high water	hoogwater	pleine mer
horn	misthoorn	nautophone
hospital	ziekenhuis	hôpital
immigration	immigratie	immigration
inner	binnen	intérieur
insurance	verzekering	assurance
jam	jam	confiture
keel	kiel	quille
ketch	kits	ketch
leech	achterlijk	chute arrière
lifting bridge	hefbrug	pont basculant
light float	lightvlot	feu flottant
light vessel	lichtschip	bateau feu

Glossaries

DUTCH TO ENGLISH AND FRENCH

lighthouse	vuurtoren	feu
lights	lichten	feux
lock	sluis	écluse
locker	kastje / kist	coffre
low water	laagwater	basse mer
luff	voorlijk	guidant
mainsail	grootzeil	grande voile
mast	mast	mât
mean	gemiddeld	moyen
meat	vlees	viande
mist	nevel	brume légère
mooring buoy	meerboei	coffre d'amarrage
mooring place	aanlegplaats	point d'accostage
mooring prohibited	verboden aan te leggen	accostage interdit
motor sailer	motorzeiljacht	bateau mixte
movable bridge	beweegbare brug	pont mobile
mutton	schapenvlees	mouton
neap tide	doodtij	morte-eau
no	ne	non
no, none	geen	pas de
north	noord	nord
office	kantoor	bureau
officer	beamte	agent
oil	olie	huile
open	open	ouvert
outer	buiten	extérieur
petrol engine	benzinemotor	moteur à essence
pork	varkensvlees	porc
port	bakboord	bâbord
post office	postkantoor	bureau de poste
prohibited	verboden	interdit
propeller	schroef	hélice
pulpit	preekstoel	balcon avant
pump	pomp	pompe
pushpit	hekstoel	balcon arrière
radio telephone	marifoon	telephone marin
radiobeacon	radiobaken	radiophare
range	verval	amplitude
red	rood	rouge
reed	mistfluit	trompette
rope	touw	cordage
rudder	roer	gouvernail
sailmaker	zeilmaker	voilier
sausage	worstje	saucisse
schooner	schoener	goélette
sea level	waterstand	niveau
shackle	harp	manille
shop	winkel	magasin
shrouds	want	haubans
siren	mistsirène	sirène
sloop	sloep	sloop
south	zuid	sud
speed	snelheid	vitesse
spinnaker	spinnaker	spinnaker
spring tide	springtij	vive-eau
stand	stilstaand / stilstaand water	étale
starboard	stuurboord	tribord
stay	stag	étai
stem	voorsteven	étrave
stern	achtersteven	poupe
supermarket	supermarkt	supermarché
swing bridge	draaibrug	pont tournant
tack	halshoek	point d'amure
tiller	helmstok	barre
toilet	WC	toilette
tower	toren	tour
vegetables	groenten	légumes
water	water	eau
west	west	ouest
whistle	mistfluit	sifflet
white	wit	blanc
withies (bound - leave to starboard)	steekbaken (gebonden)	osiers (reliés-laissez à tribord)
withies (loose- leave to port)	steekbaken (los)	osiers (non-reliés-laissez à bâbord)
yacht	jacht	yacht
yachtchandler	scheepsleverancier	fournisseur de marine
yawl	jol	yawl
yellow	geel	jaune
yes	ja	oui

Dutch	English	French
aanlegplaats	mooring place	point d'accostage
achter	aft	arrière
achterlijk	leech	chute arrière
achtersteven	stern	poupe
anker	anchor	ancre
ankerplaats	anchorage	mouillage
apotheek	chemist	pharmacien
bakboord	port	bâbord
baken	beacon	balise
bakker	baker	boulanger
beamte	officer	agent
bediening	attendance	présence
benzinemotor	petrol engine	moteur à essence
beweegbare brug	movable bridge	pont mobile
bijboot	dinghy	prame
binnen	inner	intérieur
blauw	blue	bleu
blok	block	poulie
boot	boat	bateau
boter	butter	beurre
breedte	breadth (beam)	largeur
brood	bread	pain
brug	bridge	pont
bruin	brown	brun
buiten	outer	extérieur
diepgang	draught	tirant d'eau
diepte	depth	profondeur
dieselmotor	diesel engine	moteur diesel
doodtij	neap tide	morte-eau
doorvaarthoogte	height (air draught)	tirant d'air
douane	customs	douane
draaibrug	swing bridge	pont tournant
eb	ebb	marée descendante
echolood	echo sounder	echosondeur
eieren	eggs	oeufs
geel	yellow	jaune
geen	no, none	pas de
gemiddeld	mean	moyen
genua	genoa	gênois
gesloten	closed	fermé
geul	channel/fairway	chenal
giek	boom	bome
groen	green	vert
groenteboer	greengrocer	marchand de légumes
groenten	mainsail	grande voile
halshoek	tack	point d'amure
ham	ham	jambon
handelaar	vegetables	légumes
harp	shackle	manille
haven	harbour	bassin
havenmeester	harbour master	capitaine de port
hefbrug	lifting bridge	pont basculant
hekstoel	pushpit	balcon arrière
helmstok	tiller	barre
hoogwater	high water	pleine mer
immigratie	immigration	immigration
ja	yes	oui
jacht	yacht	yacht
jam	jam	confiture
jol	dinghy	youyou
jol	yawl	yawl
kaas	cheese	fromage
kajuit	cabin	cabine
kantoor	office	bureau
kastje / kist	locker	coffre
ketting	chain	chaîne
kiel	keel	quille
kits	ketch	ketch
kooi	bunk/berth	couchette
kotter	cutter	cotre
kruidenier	grocer	épicier
kuip	cockpit	cockpit
laagwater	low water	basse mer
lichten	lights	feux
lichtschip	light vessel	bateau feu
lightvlot	light float	feu flottant
luik	hatch	écoutille
marifoon	radio telephone	telephone marin
mast	mast	mât
meerboei	mooring buoy	coffre d'amarrage

GLOSSARIES

melk	milk	lait
mist	fog	brouillard
mistfluit	reed	trompette
mistfluit	whistle	sifflet
misthoorn	horn	corne de brume
mistklok	bell	cloche
mistsirène	siren	sirène
motorzeiljacht	motor sailer	bateau mixte
nautofoon	horn	nautophone
ne	no	non
nevel	mist	brume légère
noord	north	nord
olie	oil	huile
onderlijk	foot	bordure
oost	east	est
open	open	ouvert
pomp	pump	pompe
pont	ferry	bac
postkantoor	post office	bureau de poste
preekstoel	pulpit	balcon avant
radiobaken	radiobeacon	radiophare
roer	rudder	gouvernail
rood	red	rouge
rundvlees	beef	boeuf
schapenvlees	mutton	mouton
scheepsleverancier	yachtchandler	fournisseur de marine
schoener	schooner	goélette
schoothoek	clew	point d'écoute
schot	bulkhead	cloison
schroef	propeller	hélice
slager	butcher	boucher
sloep	sloop	sloop
sluis	lock	écluse
snelheid	speed	vitesse
spek	bacon	lard
spinnaker	spinnaker	spinnaker
springtil	spring tide	vive-eau
stag	stay	étai
steekbaken (gebonden)	withies (bound leave to starboard)	osiers (reliés-laissez à tribord)
steekbaken (los)	withies (loose leave to port)	osiers (non-reliés-laissez à bâbord)
stilstaand / stilstaand water	stand	étale
storm	gale	coup de vent
stroom	current	courant
stuurboord	starboard	tribord
supermarkt	supermarket	supermarché
tandarts	dentist	dentiste
ton, boei	buoy	bouée
tophoek	head	point de drisse
toren	tower	tour
touw	rope	cordage
vaarwater	channel/waterway	chenal/canal
val	halyard	drisse
varkensvlees	pork	porc
vaste brug	fixed bridge	pont fixé
veer	ferry	bac
verboden	prohibited	interdit
verboden aan te leggen	mooring prohibited	accostage interdit
verboden ankerplaats	anchorage prohibited	défense de mouiller
verrekijker	binoculars	jumelles
verval	range	amplitude
verzekering	insurance	assurance
vet	grease	graisse
vis	fish	poisson
vishandel	fishmonger	marchand de poisson
vissershaven	fishing harbour	port de pêche
vlees	meat	viande
vloed	flood	marée montante
voor	fore	avant
voorlijk	luff	guidant
vooronder	forecastle	gaillard d'avant
voorsteven	stem	étrave
voorzeil	foresail	voile de misaine
vuurtoren	lighthouse	feu
WC	toilet	toilette
want	shrouds	haubans
water	water	eau
waterstand	sea level	niveau
west	west	ouest
winkel	shop	magasin
wit	white	blanc
worstje	sausage	saucisse
zeekaart	chart	carte maritime
zeillat	batten	latte
zeilmaker	sailmaker	voilier
ziekenhuis	hospital	hôpital
zuid	south	sud
zwart	black	noir

FRENCH TO ENGLISH AND DUTCH

French	English	Dutch
accostage interdit	mooring prohibited	verboden aan te leggen
agent	officer	beamte
amplitude	range	verval
ancre	anchor	anker
arrière	aft	achter
assurance	insurance	verzekering
avant	fore	voor
bâbord	port	bakboord
bac	ferry	pont
bac	ferry	veer
balcon arrière	pushpit	hekstoel
balcon avant	pulpit	preekstoel
balise	beacon	baken
barre	tiller	helmstok
basse mer	low water	laagwater
bassin	harbour	haven
bateau	boat	boot
bateau feu	light vessel	lichtschip
bateau mixte	motor sailer	motorzeiljacht
beurre	butter	boter
blanc	white	wit
bleu	blue	blauw
boeuf	beef	rundvlees
bome	boom	giek
bordure	foot	onderlijk
boucher	butcher	slager
bouée	buoy	ton, boei
boulanger	baker	bakker
brouillard	fog	mist
broume légère	mist	nevel
brun	brown	bruin
bureau	office	kantoor
bureau de poste	post office	postkantoor
cabine	cabin	kajuit
capitaine de port	harbour master	havenmeester
carte maritime	chart	zeekaart
chaîne	chain	ketting
chenal	channel/fairway	geul
chenal/canal	channel/waterway	vaarwater
chute arrière	leech	achterlijk
cloche	bell	mistklok
cloison	bulkhead	schot
cockpit	cockpit	kuip
coffre	locker	kastje / kist
coffre d'amarrage	mooring buoy	meerboei
confiture	jam	jam
cordage	rope	touw
corne de brume	foghorn	misthoorn
cotre	cutter	kotter
couchette	bunk/berth	kooi
coup de vent	gale	storm
courant	current	stroom
défense de mouiller	anchorage prohibited	verboden ankerplaats
dentiste	dentist	tandarts
douane	customs	douane
drisse	halyard	val
eau	water	water
echosondeur	echo sounder	echolood
écluse	lock	sluis
écoutille	hatch	luik
épicier	grocer	kruidenier
est	east	oost
étai	stay	stag
étale	stand	stilstaand / stilstaand water
étrave	stem	voorsteven
extérieur	outer	buiten
fermé	closed	gesloten
feu	lighthouse	vuurtoren
feu flottant	light float	lightvlot
feux	lights	lichten
fournisseur de marine	yachtchandler	scheepsleverancier
fromage	cheese	kaas

Glossaries

gaillard d'avant	forecastle	vooronder
gênois	genoa	genua
goélette	schooner	schoener
gouvernail	rudder	roer
graisse	grease	vet
grande voile	mainsail	grootzeil
guidant	luff	voorlijk
haubans	shrouds	want
hélice	propeller	schroef
hôpital	hospital	ziekenhuis
huile	oil	olie
immigration	immigration	immigratie
interdit	prohibited	verboden
intérieur	inner	binnen
jambon	ham	ham
jaune	yellow	geel
jumelles	binoculars	verrekijker
ketch	ketch	kits
lait	milk	melk
lard	bacon	spek
largeur	breadth (beam)	breedte
latte	batten	zeillat
légumes	vegetables	groenten
magasin	shop	winkel
manille	shackle	harp
marchand de légumes	greengrocer	groenteboer
marchand de poisson	fishmonger	vishandel
marée montante	flood	vloed
marée descendante	ebb	eb
mât	mast	mast
morte-eau	neap tide	doodtij
moteur à essence	petrol engine	benzinemotor
moteur diesel	diesel engine	dieselmotor
mouillage	anchorage	ankerplaats
mouton	mutton	schapenvlees
moyen	mean	gemiddeld
nautophone	horn	misthoorn
niveau	sea level	waterstand
noir	black	zwart
non	no	ne
nord	north	noord
oeufs	eggs	eieren
ouest	west	west
oui	yes	ja
ouvert	open	open
pain	bread	brood
pas de	no, none	geen
pharmacien	chemist	apotheek
pleine mer	high water	hoogwater
point d'accostage	mooring place	aanlegplaats
point d'amure	tack	halshoek
point de drisse	head	tophoek
point d'écoute	clew	schoothoek
poisson	fish	vis
pompe	pump	pomp
pont	bridge	brug
pont basculant	lifting bridge	hefbrug
pont fixé	fixed bridge	vaste brug
pont mobile	movable bridge	beweegbare brug
pont tournant	swing bridge	draaibrug
porc	pork	varkensvlees
port de pêche	fishing harbour	vissershaven
poulie	block	blok
poupe	stern	achtersteven
prame	dinghy	bijboot
présence	attendance	bediening
profondeur	depth	diepte
quille	keel	kiel
radiophare	radiobeacon	radiobaken
rouge	red	rood
saucisse	sausage	worstje
sirène	siren	mistsirène
sifflet	whistle	mistfluit
sloop	sloop	sloep
spinnaker	spinnaker	spinnaker
osiers reliés - laissez à tribord)	withies (bound- leave to starboard)	steekbaken (gebonden)
osiers non-reliés- laissez à bâbord)	withies (loose- leave to port)	steekbaken (los)
sud	south	zuid
supermarché	supermarket	supermarkt
telephone marin	radio telephone	marifoon
tirant d'air	height (air draught)	doorvaarthoogte
tirant d'eau	draught	diepgang
toilette	toilet	WC
tour	tower	toren
tribord	starboard	stuurboord
trompette	reed	mistfluit
vert	green	groen
viande	meat	vlees
vitesse	speed	snelheid
vive-eau	spring tide	springtij
voile de misaine	foresail	voorzeil
voilier	sailmaker	zeilmaker
yacht	yacht	jacht
yawl	yawl	jol
youyou	dinghy	jol

INDEX

abbreviations 8
Admiralty publications 17, 108–9
AIS (Automatic Identification Scheme) 11, 30
Aldeburgh Ridge 41, 42
almanacs 1, 5
Amsterdam 34
    inland route to Den Helder 46
    Noordzeekanaal 86, 90, 92
    Sixhaven Marina 90
ANWB Wateralmanaks 1
apps, weather 16
ATIS-enabled VHF radio 23, 46
automatic steering 37
AW1 (G) 64, 65

Barrow Deep 42
Barrow Deep No.5 42
Barrow No. 3 (ECM) 38, 54
Bassin de Commerce (Dunkerque) 75, 76
BBC shipping forecasts 15
bearings and directions 1
Beaufort scale 8
Belgium
    ATIS-enabled radio 23
    documentation 34, 35
    passages to/from Essex Rivers/Harwich 61, 63, 64
    ports of entry 34
    red diesel fuel 35
    wind farms 23, 24, 38
Belwind-Bligh Bank Wind Farm 38
Bergen (IJmuiden) 86
Black Deep 42, 55, 58–9
Black Deep No.7 42
Black Deep No.8 (WCM) 42
Black Deep (QR) 63
black water 35
Blackwater, River
    coastal route, UK 42
    passage to/from Calais 55
    passage to/from Oostende 61
    passages to/from Vlissingen 65
Blankenberge 32, 79
boat equipment and safety 10–11, 20–1, 35, 102–3
Borssele Passage 26, 38
Boudewijnkannal 81
Boulogne 34
BR/S (RW) 39
Breewijd, WSOV 92
Breskens 32, 65, 83
Brouwershavensche Gat 83
Brugge 81
buoyed channels, clearance 37

CA2 (R) 45, 49, 50, 55
CA4 (R) 54, 59
Cadzand 32, 65, 83
Calais 34, 73–4
    Arrière Port 74
    Bassin de l'Ouest 73–4
    coastal route to Den Helder 43–6
    passage to/from Dover 50
    passage to/from Harwich 58–9
    passage to/from Thames Estuary 53–4
    passages to/from Essex Rivers 55
    passages to/from Ramsgate 48–9
    port authority website 6
Cap Gris Nez 26
Certificate of Competence 10, 34
chart datum 1
charts
    Admiralty 108–9
    Imray publications 105–7
    symbols 7
    see also start of each section
Chenal Intermediaire 45, 51
Clacton 23, 24
coast radio 21–3
coastal route, UK 40–2
coastguard stations 21–3, 83, 104
collision avoidance 29–30
Colne, River
    coastal route, UK 42
    passage to/from Calais 55
ColRegs *see* International Collision Regulations
communications, marine 20–3
Cork Sand Beacon (R) 42, 63
Cork Sand Yacht (NCM) 63
Corton channel 41
crew 10, 19–20, 34–5
Cross Sand (RW Pillar) 39
Crouch, River
    coastal route, UK 42
    passage to/from Calais 55
    passage to/from Oostende 61
    passage to/from Vlissingen 65
cruising areas 11–12
CS4 50, 51, 52
customs requirements 33
Cutler (G) 67

D1 (WCM) 62
Deben, River 31, 42
Deep Water Routes (DWR) 28, 30
Delfzijl 34
Den Haag (The Hague) 85, 87

Den Helder 91–3
    approaches 34, 44, 91
    coast route from/to Calais 43–6
    inland route from Amsterdam 46
    inland route from Vlissingen 46, 47
    Jachthaven Marine WV 92
    Jachtwerf Den Helder 92
    Koninklijke Marine Jachtclub 92
    passage to/from Great Yarmouth 72
    passage to/from Harwich/Lowestoft 69 70
    port authority website 6
    WSOV Breewijd 92
documentation 20–1, 33–4
Dover 94–5
    marina 95
    passage to/from Calais 50
    passage to/from Dunkerque 52–3
    port authority website 6
DSC (Digital Selective Calling) 11, 20–1, 23
Dunkerque 34, 75–6
    Bassin de Commerce 75, 76
    coast route, Calais 45, 46
    passage to/from Dover 52–3
    passage to/from Ramsgate 51, 53
    port authority website 6
    Port du Grand Large 75
    YC de la Mer du Nord Marina 75
DW5 (Q.G.) 51
DW5 (R) 45
DWRs (Deep Water Routes) 28, 30
Dyck (Fl.R.4s) 51
Dyck (R) 54

E Barnard (ECM) 41, 42
E Goodwin (ECM) 49, 54, 55
E Goodwin (Lt Flt) 49
E Goodwin (LtV) 51, 52, 54, 55
E Margate (ECM) 55
E Margate (PHM) 42
E Margate (R) 54
E Red Sand (R) 54
E Shipwash (ECM) 41, 42
E12 (SCM) 45, 46
EA1 NE (NCM) 71, 72
EA1 NW (NCM) 67
East Swale 42, 54
Eemshaven 34
Egmond aan Zee 85
    wind farm 23, 46

Elbow (NCM) 54
electronic navigation aids 11, 30, 37
email weather forecasts 16
Essex Rivers
    passage to/from Nieuwpoort 62
    passage to/from Oostende 61
    passage to/from Vlissingen 65
    passage to/from Zeebrugge 64
    passages to/from Calais 55
    passages to/from Harwich 56–7
Euroguel 29
Europoort, approaches 27, 29, 83
Eveline (WCM) 46

Felixstowe 26, 58, 99
Fisherman's Gat and Precautionary Area 25, 42, 55, 59
fog 13–14
France
    ATIS-enabled VHF radio 23
    documentation 10, 34
    inland waterways access 74, 76
    ports of entry 34
    red diesel fuel 35
Frisian Islands 92
fuel 35

Gabbard wind farms 25, 55
Garden City (WCM) 61
glossaries 110–13
GMDSS 16, 21
Goeree 83
Goeree light tower 30
Goodwin Fork (SCM) 49
Goodwin Knoll (G) 49, 51
Goodwin Sands 49, 51–5
GPS (Global Positioning System) 11
Gravelines 6, 31–2
Great Yarmouth
    coastal route, UK 41
    passage to/from Den Helder 72
    passage to/from IJmuiden 72
    port authority website 6
    wind farms 23
Grevelingen Dam 83
Grevelingenmeer 29
Gull Channel 49
Gunfleet Wind Farm 23, 24, 25, 55

Hague, The *see* Den Haag
harbour authorities 6
Haringvliet 29
Haringvlietdam 83

Index

Harwich 98–9
  approaches 98
  Deep Water Channel 27
  moorings 99
  passage to/from Calais 58–9
  passage to/from Den Helder 69–70
  passage to/from IJmuiden/Scheveningen 67–8
  passage to/from Nieuwpoort 62
  passage to/from Oostende 63
  passage to/from Vlissingen 65
  passage to/from Zeebrugge 64
  passages to/from Essex Rivers 56–7
  port authority website 6
  port traffic signals 31
  Ramsgate/Lowestoft route 41, 42
Harwich Deep Water Channel No.1 (YM) 38
  Haut-Fond de Graveline (WCM) 51, 52
health matters 10, 35
Het Veer (G) 65
Hoek van Holland
  passage to/from Den Helder 44–5
  port traffic signals 32
  Schelde Delta tidal streams 83
holding tanks 35
Holm Channel 72

IJ-Guel 67, 68
IJM C (SWM) 67
IJM1 71, 72
IJmuiden 34, 85, 88–9
  approaches 44, 45–6
  harbour authority website 6
  passage to Den Helder 45
  passage to/from Great Yarmouth 72
  passage to/from Harwich 67–8
  passage to/from Lowestoft 71
  port traffic signals 32
  Seaport Marina 89
IJMW1 (G) 67, 71, 72
IJsselmeer 46
Imray charts 105–7
Indusbank (NCM) 45, 46
inland waterways access
  Belgium 76, 78, 80
  France 74, 76
  Netherlands 44, 46, 47, 88–9
inshore traffic zones (ITZs) 30

insurance, travel/health 35
International Collision Regulations 10, 29–30, 34
International Port Traffic Signals (IPTS) 31–2, 50
internet-sourced weather 15–16

Jachtclub Scheveningen 87
Jachthaven Marine WV (Den Helder) 92
Jachtwerf Den Helder 92

Katwijk 86
Kentish Flats Wind Farm 23, 25, 54, 55
Kentish Knock (ECM) 41, 42, 59
Keukenhof Gardens 85
Kijkduin Lt tower 69, 91
Kings Channel 55, 61, 65
Koninklijke Marine Jachtclub (Den Helder) 92
Koninklijke Yachtclub Nieuwpoort 77
Kwintebank KB (NCM) 38, 61, 62, 64

Lake Lothing 42
Landguard (NCM) 41, 59
Landguard Point 29
life-saving signals 9
lifeboat services 21, 22, 104
lights, navigational aids 30, 31
Lisse 86
log keeping 18–19
London Array Wind Farm 23, 25, 38, 55
Long Sand Head (NCM) 41, 42, 59, 61, 62, 63, 65
Lowestoft 100–1
  coastal route, UK 41–2, 69
  passage to/from Den Helder 69–70
  passage to/from IJmuiden and Scheveningen 71
  Royal Norfolk and Suffolk YC 100–1

Maas Precautionary Area 27, 83
Maasmond entrance 83
Malo-les-Bains 76
Maritime and Coastguard Agency 15
Maritime Mobile Service Identity (MMSI) number 21
Maritime Safety Information (MSI) broadcasts 15
Marsdiep 70, 92
MAYDAY call 21, 23
MBN (NCM) 61, 64, 65
MBN1 (NCM) 64

Medusa Channel 42, 59, 63
Medusa (G) 41, 42, 59, 63
Medway, River
  coastal route, UK 42
  passage to/from Calais 53–4
Medway (SWM) 42
Mercator Marina (Oostende) 78
Middelbank 83
Middelkerk BK 62
Middle Deep 42
MMSI (Maritime Mobile Service Identity) number 21
MN1 (G), Maas 44, 45, 46
Molengat 91–2
MOW 3 (Y) Lt beacon 38
MOW.0 (Y) Lt beacon 38
MPC (Y) 54
MV C (WCM), Maas 45, 46
MV (WCM), Maas 44, 45

N Middle (NCM) 42
N Shipwash (NCM) 41, 42, 67, 68
Nass Beacon 55, 61
navigation 11
  electronic aids 11, 30, 37
  equipment 103
  lights (inshore/offshore) 30, 31
NAVTEX 16
NE Akkaert (ECM) 44
NE Bawdsey (G) 67
NE Goodwin (ECM) 51, 54, 55, 58, 59
NE Gunfleet (ECM) 41, 42, 55, 59, 63
NE Spit (ECM) 42, 55, 59
NE Whiting (ECM) 67
Netherlands
  ANWB Wateralmanaks 1
  black water discharge 35
  Certificate of Competence 34
  documentation 34–5
  Hydrographic Office publications 5, 17, 107
  inland waterways access 44, 46, 47, 88–9
  ports of entry 34
  red diesel fuel 35
  tidal stream atlases 17
  wind farms 23, 24
Nieuwe Diep 92
Nieuwe Waterweg (Rotterdam) 27, 83
Nieuwpoort 77
  marinas 77
  passage to/from Essex Rivers 62
  passage to/from Harwich 62
Nieuwpoortbank (ECM) 45, 46, 62, 77

Noord Hinder Junction Precautionary Area 26–7, 29, 83
Noord Holland 86
Noorderhaaks Island 69, 91–2
Noordsholland Kanaal 92
Noordwijk 86
Noordzeekanaal 85, 89–90, 92
North Foreland 42, 54, 55, 58
North Sea Canal *see* Noordzeekanaal

Off Texel TSS 27, 69
oil and gas platforms 24, 38, 69
Oost Dyck Radar Tower 38
Oostende 34, 65, 78
  Mercator Marina 78
  passage to/from Essex Rivers 61
  passage to/from Harwich 63
  port authority website 6
  Royal North Sea YC 78
  Royal YC of Oostende 78
Oostende-Brugge Canal 78
Oostendebank E (G) 45, 46, 61, 65
Oosterschelde 83
Ore, River 31, 42
Orfordness 41, 42, 67
Orwell, River 29, 59, 68
Oude Jachthaven (Blankenberge) 79
Outer Fisherman (ECM) 42, 55
Outer Tongue DW Anchorage 55

P9-6 Platform (WCM) 39
passage planning 12–13, 19
Passe de l'Ouest 45, 51
Passe de Zuydcoote 46
passports 33–4
pets 35
Petten Nuclear Power Station 69, 91
Petten (WCM) 44, 46
pilotage 39
Platters (ECM) 41, 67
port authority websites 6
Port du Grand Large (Dunkerque) 75
Port of London Authority (PLA) 6, 26
port radio stations 23; *see also start of pilotage sections*
precautionary areas 26–9, 42, 55, 59, 83
Princes Channel 42, 54
Princes S (R) 54
pumping out 102
Pye End (RW) 59

INDEX

Raan sandbank 44
Rabsbank 83
racons 30
radar 11, 37
radio equipment 103
radio licences 20-1, 23
radio stations, coastal 21-3
radio weather forecasts 15, 16
Ramsgate 96-7
  Lowestoft/Great Yarmouth route 41-2
  marina 97
  passage to/from Dunkerque 51, 53
  passages to/from Calais 48-9, 55
  port authority website 6
Rassen 83
red diesel fuel 35
Red Sand Tower 54
regulations and laws 10-11, 30, 33-5, 103
rescue services 21, 23, 104
Ridens de Calais 49, 55, 73
Rijn Field 45
Rolling Ground (G) 41, 67
Rotterdam
  inland route to Amsterdam 46
  port authority website 6
  port of entry 34
  Schelde Delta 83
Rough Towers 63
route distances 36
routes
  coastal, 1 and 2 38, 40-7
  middle crossings 38, 62-5
  northern crossings 38-9, 66-72
  southern crossings 38, 48-61
  summaries 37-9
Royal Belgium SC (Zeebrugge) 80
Royal Norfolk and Suffolk YC (Lowestoft) 100-1
Royal North Sea Yacht Club (Oostende) 78
Royal Scarphout YC Blankenberge 79
Royal Yacht Club of Oostende 78
Ruytingen Banks 51, 52
Ruytingen SW (G) 49, 51, 52

S Bawdsey (SCM) 41, 67
S Corton (SCM) 72
S Falls (ECM) 54, 58
S Galloper (SCM) 38
S Goodwin (R) 52
S Holm (SCM) 69, 70, 71, 72
safety, crew 20
safety equipment 10-11, 102-3
Sandettié LtV 54
Schelde Channel 65
Schelde Delta 82-5
Schengen Convention forms 33-4
Scheur Channel 45, 46, 65
Scheveningen 86-7
  approaches 44

Jachtclub 87
  passage to/from Den Helder 45
  passage to/from Harwich 67-8
  passage to/from Lowestoft 71
  port authority website 6
  port traffic signals 32
Schooneveld 45, 46
Schouwen 83
Schouwenbank 83
Schulpengat 39, 44, 45-6, 69, 70, 72, 91
Scroby Sands Wind Farm 23
Sea Reach No.1 (Y) 42, 54
Seaport Marina (IJmuiden) 89
search and rescue services 21, 23, 104
seasickness 10
SG (RW) 39, 45, 46, 69, 70, 72
SG (SWM) 44
shapes, navigational 31
shipping forecasts 15, 16
ship's stores, restrictions 35
Shipway Channel 41, 67
Shotley Marina (Harwich) 99
Shotley Point 99
Sixhaven Marina (Amsterdam) 90
Sizewell Nuclear Power Station 41, 42
skipper and crew, requirements 10, 19-20, 34
Sledway Channel 67
Slijkat 83
Smith's Knoll (SCM) 39
SOLAS (*Safety of Life at Sea*) signals 9
sound signals 30
Southend, passage to Calais 55
Southwold 6, 31
Stanford Channel 41, 42, 70, 71
Steenbanken 83
Steendiep 45, 46
Stone Banks (R) 59, 63
Storm (SCM) 41, 42
Stour, River 68, 99
Sunk Centre Lanby 38
Sunk Head Tower (NCM) 42, 55, 58, 59, 61
Sunk Sand Swatchway 39, 42, 55, 61
Sunk Traffic Scheme 27, 28
SW Goodwin (SCM) 49, 52
Swale, River 23
Swin Spitway 42
Swins Channel 61

Terneuzen 32, 34
Texel Island 91-2
Texel separation Scheme 26, 27, 39
Thames Estuary
  coastal route, UK 42
  passage to/from Calais 53-4, 55
  traffic separation schemes 25-6
  wind farms 23

Thanet Wind Farm 23, 25, 38, 41, 55
Thorntonbank 83
tides
  passage planning 12-13
  tidal diamonds and atlases 17
  tidal streams and differences 1, 2-6, 16-17, 37
  tidal surges 18
  tide times and depths 17-18
  see also start of each section
tourism websites 6
traffic separation schemes (TSS) 24-7, 38, 103
traffic signals, ports 31-2
Trinity (SCM) 59, 63, 65
'Two-Way Route' 27
TX1 (G) 69, 70, 72

UK coast route 40-2
UK Hydrographic Office 5

Varne LtV 54
Veerhaven 70, 92
VG5 (G) 45, 46
VG6 (R) 45, 46
VHF radio 23
  ATIS-enabled 23, 46
visas 34
Vlissingen 34
  inland route to Den Helder 46, 47
  passage to/from Essex Rivers/Harwich 65
  port authority website 6
  yacht harbour 83
VNZ marina (Blankenberge) 79
Voorne 83
VTS (*Vessel Traffic Services*) 23, 31
VVW marinas
  Blankenberge 79
  Nieuwpoort 77

W (G) 65
W Hinder 61, 62, 63
W Hinder Lt beacon 38, 61, 65
W3 (G) 65
Waddenzee 69, 92
Walcheren 83
Wallet Channel 42, 61
watchkeeping 19-20
waypoints 13
weather and forecasts 13-16
websites
  port and harbour authorities 6
  tourism 6
  weather and forecasts 15 16
West Hinder TSS 38, 61
Westerschelde
  coast route, Calais 45, 46
  passages from Essex Rivers/Harwich 61, 65
  tidal streams 44, 83
  yacht harbours 83
Westgat 45
Whitaker Channel 42, 61
Whitley (NCM) 62, 77

Willemsoord, Marinehaven 92
wind farms and support vessels 23-4, 25, 38, 46, 55
winds 13-14
World Geodetic System 1984 (WGS84) 11
WP1 (G) 45, 46
WSKLM Marina (Nieuwpoort) 77
WSOV Breewijd (Den Helder) 92
WV Helder-Willemsoord Nieuwe Diep 92

YC de la Mer du Nord Marina (Dunkerque) 75
Yzer, River 77

Z (G) 64
Zandvoort 86
Zeebrugge 34, 80-1
  coast route, Calais 45, 46
  passages to/from Essex Rivers/Harwich 64, 65
  port authority website 6
  Royal Belgium SC 80
Zuid Holland 86